Suburban Refugees

The publisher and the University of California Press Foundation gratefully acknowledge the generous support of the Lisa See Endowment Fund in Southern California History and Culture.

Suburban Refugees

CLASS AND RESISTANCE IN LITTLE SAIGON

Jennifer Huynh

UNIVERSITY OF CALIFORNIA PRESS

University of California Press
Oakland, California

Library of Congress Cataloging-in-Publication Data

Names: Huynh, Jennifer, author.
Title: Suburban refugees : class and resistance in little Saigon / Jennifer
    Huynh.
Description: Oakland : University of California Press, [2025] | Includes
    bibliographical references and index.
Identifiers: LCCN 2024032185 (print) | LCCN 2024032186 (ebook) |
    ISBN 9780520403895 (cloth) | ISBN 9780520403901 (paperback) |
    ISBN 9780520403918 (ebook)
Subjects: LCSH: Vietnamese Americans—California—Westminster. |
    Refugees—California—Westminster. | Suburbs—California—
    Westminster. | Social classes—California—Westminster. | Little Saigon
    (Westminster, Calif.)
Classification: LCC F870.V53 H89 2025 (print) | LCC F870.V53 (ebook) |
    DDC 305.8959/22079496—dc23/eng/20241203
LC record available at https://lccn.loc.gov/2024032185
LC ebook record available at https://lccn.loc.gov/2024032186

34 33 32 31 30 29 28 27 26 25
10 9 8 7 6 5 4 3 2 1

For Dad, Phong Chu Huỳnh

CONTENTS

ACKNOWLEDGMENTS

I am grateful to the people I met for sharing their stories and experiences over the past fifteen years. This book would not exist without your generosity and openness. Thank you for trusting me.

Many organizations and people shared their inspiring activism, and this book is a small reflection of the organizing action and power on the ground. I am grateful to Cát Bảo Lê and Tín Nguyễn for sharing their wisdom and to Cát for reading drafts of chapter 4 and pushing me to improve it. My deepest thanks to VietRISE and its organizers, Tracy La, Vincent Trần, and Indigo Vũ, for sharing their programs and work in Orange County—this book is their story. Sơn Đỗ and the residents of Green Lantern warmly welcomed me into their homes and continue to advocate for rent control in Westminster and other mobile home communities in California—they are the heroes of this story.

Gratitude goes to Naomi Schneider, Aline Dolinh, Jeff Anderson, and the University of California Press staff for their editorial wisdom and support of this book. The thoughtful comments and suggestions from the faculty board, C. N. Lê, and the other anonymous reviewer improved the manuscript. I am also indebted to the UC Press FirstGen Program for its resources.

Fieldwork for this book began when I was a graduate student in sociology at Princeton. There, I met wonderful people who helped me grow as a scholar. I am thankful to my committee, Alejandro Portes, Patricia Fernández-Kelly, and Min Zhou, for their support at the initial stages of this project. Before graduation, I spent one year as an instructor in the Asian American Studies program at Northwestern University. This experience shaped the book through the interdisciplinary scholarship and a new intellectual home I found in Asian American Studies. I am grateful to Shalini Shankar and

Nitasha Sharma, who continue to inspire me, for introducing me to AAAS and the field.

The book continued to evolve in the Department of American Studies at the University of Notre Dame as new ideas, sources, fields, and colleagues shaped the project. I am grateful to my generous colleagues, including my chair, Jason Ruiz, who provided encouragement and support throughout the years. I am forever thankful to my mentor, Tom Tweed, for hiring and supporting me and for his wisdom and care in reading drafts. I am also indebted to Erika Doss for her unwavering support as a mentor and friend and for her astute wisdom in writing and the book publication process. My wonderful comrades and colleagues at Notre Dame eased the stress of writing. They provided much-needed advice and support at all stages of the book-writing process: Korey Garibaldi, Perin Gürel, Annie Coleman, Pete Cajka, Kathy Cummings, Sophie White, Chante Mouton Kinyon, Anna Haskins, Emily Wang, Xian Wang, Tarryn Chun, Patrick Deegan, Sonja Stojanovic, Ashlee Bird, and Katie Walden, among many others. My students in my courses, Asian American Experience and Critical Refugee Studies, read drafts and provided feedback since the intended audience for the book is students; I especially want to thank Trâm Trịnh, Kat Lê, and Jake Harris. I am grateful for the wonderful research assistance of Jessica Bùi and Kevin Nguyễn. I wish to thank the yearlong mentorship program through the Association for Asian American Studies, including my mentor, Augusto Espiritu, and my fellow mentees, Chinbo Chong and Catherine Nguyễn, for providing their support.

Generous financial and fellowship assistance from the Liu Institute for Asia and Asian Studies at the University of Notre Dame enabled this project, as did the kind support of its director, Michel Hockx, and associate director, Chris Cox. The Notre Dame Institute for Scholarship in the Liberal Arts, the Notre Dame Department of American Studies, and the Notre Dame Initiative on Race and Resilience provided financial support for this project to see its completion.

I thank Dr. Ellen Pader for helping me with the manuscript's developmental editing. Dr. Pader wasn't only an editor; she became a mentor, friend, and confidant and helped me strengthen and clarify my writing. I am further grateful to Morgan Pulliam for helping me organize the endnotes and references and to Dr. D. Scott and Leah Caldwell for their astute and excellent copyediting assistance. Gratitude also to Joseph Nguyễn for reading the final draft before copyedits. I am deeply thankful for the friendship and advice of

Professor Sharon Yoon. This book would not exist without our online writing sessions, discussion of ideas, and your caring for Daniel so I could write. Thank you.

The support and encouragement of family and friendship, and faith, saw me through this long process of writing and rewriting. Thanks to my parents for their positivity, love, and encouragement over many years. Thank you to my dad, who inspires me daily with his work ethic and devotion to his family. Thank you for your sacrifices. Thank you to my childhood friends who kept me grounded before and during academia, especially to Paul Lam for being a sounding board for ideas, taking photos, and attending organizing meetings at home; Janaya Nichols, my Berkeley roommate, for talking through ideas long-distance and being a critical voice; Bill Trịnh, Manka Vagal, Sara Winterbottom, Michelle Teng, Amy Surma, Yanran Chen, and many others who fed my soul through their friendship. My husband Anthony and my son Daniel helped immensely through this process. Daniel, thank you for being so enthusiastic and encouraging of the book. When you finally read this, the book is done.

Suburban Refugees

On a hot Sunday afternoon, a crowd of nearly one hundred people staged a rally in suburban Southern California. Protesters of all ages, from mothers with children in strollers to senior citizens, marched up and down the busy boulevard outside a mobile home park, carrying bilingual signs in Vietnamese and English: "Housing is a Human Right," "Bảo Vệ Quyền Lợi Cho Những Người Cao Niên," "Right to Stay in our Homes," and "Protect Senior Citizens." Cars streaming down the thoroughfare honked in solidarity to the sirens of chants. One resident, age eighty, explained why she was marching: "I thought I would stay the rest of my years in one last place. Now I [will] start over.... To even think of a place to move to ... how do you begin? We were refugees. We will be adrift again."[1]

A seventy-year-old man named Sơn Đỗ led the rally. Sơn is president and founder of the Orange County Mobile Home Resident Coalition. In 2016, a Southern California coalition of residents fighting to protect their communities against gentrification was formed, and the rally was one of their many actions.

Sơn began organizing the coalition after learning that the mobile home park he had called home since 2011 was being sold to a developer who planned to build luxury condominiums. He started by rallying local residents, more than 80 percent of whom were Vietnamese, into a homeowners' association. This quickly grew into a countywide activist coalition of over forty mobile home parks. After reading about their protests on the front page of the *Los Angeles Times*, I contacted Sơn and asked if I could interview him. I was curious to know more about the coalition's goals for this suburban Southern California homespace, a place I knew well. I grew up in a mixed-race Vietnamese refugee family in Little Saigon, and my uncles and friends lived in those parks.

FIGURE 1. VietRISE rally in Westminster, California (photo by Gaston Castellanos).

Suburban mobile home parks, like those dotting Little Saigon, represent America's largest source of unsubsidized affordable housing, sheltering working-class households, the aging, and disabled persons who are frequently priced out of traditional rental housing. As real estate prices skyrocket across the country, developers have started buying up mom-and-pop mobile home parks to convert into commercial or high-end developments. State codes offer only minimal protection to residents from eviction or rent hikes by new ownership or foreclosures.

In 2021, Sơn was the only resident chosen to present testimony before the California State Senate in favor of AB 2782, a bill designed to protect California's shrinking stock of affordable housing. The landmark legislation passed; as a result, no city or county may approve a mobile home park closure or conversion if it results in a shortage of affordable housing. This was good news for the approximately 700,000 Californians who live in the state's 400,000 mobile homes and 4,100 mobile home parks. Mobile homes, despite their name, are not truly mobile and are often cost-prohibitive to relocate.

For many, American suburbs symbolize social mobility and political conservatism and represent homogenous spaces of whiteness. *Suburban Refugees* challenges these assumptions. Contrary to popular perception, suburban inequality is expanding faster than inequality in rural or urban areas.[2] Half of America's population—predominantly families with children—live in the suburbs. Upon arriving, newcomers are more likely to settle in suburbia than cities, and over the past thirty years, suburban immigrants have become more likely than US-born suburbanites to experience material poverty.[3] In fact, immigrants living in under-resourced neighborhoods represent one-fifth of all suburban residents.[4] Yet, since the 1960s, federal and state investments in social safety programs have mainly targeted urban areas.[5]

This book grapples with systemic causes of rising inequality in the suburbs as well as opportunities for political change. Sơn wasn't fighting only to keep his home; he was fighting to keep Little Saigon, the largest enclave of Vietnamese refugees in the United States. *Suburban Refugees* shows how Orange County's Little Saigon has dramatically changed since its inception, with Vietnamese refugees creating a thriving community in a global and multigenerational suburb. In socioeconomically diverse suburbs such as this, refugees and immigrants are challenging bureaucratic and state violence that threatens to displace them from their homes. *Suburban Refugees* demonstrates why immigration to the suburbs is not an inevitable route to economic opportunity or upward mobility. At the same time, this book explores how suburban organizing presents unique and novel opportunities to resist displacement and strengthen refugee placemaking.

Little Saigon, set thirty-five miles south of Los Angeles in Orange County, is a global suburb of Vietnam and the capital of the Vietnamese American refugee community.[6] Orange County—known for luxury shopping, suburban tract homes, Disneyland, and surfers—also has some of the country's most diverse and fastest-growing immigrant communities. Originally planned as a white suburban bedroom community of Los Angeles, the county now has a population of over three million people and is the tenth most expensive place to live in the United States.

Home to more than three thousand Vietnamese-owned businesses, Little Saigon is more than just an ethnic strip mall; it brings in over $100 million annually in revenue. "This is not your grandmother's Little Saigon," noted a *Los Angeles Times* piece about the thriving restaurant and business scene spearheaded by 1.5 generation, Vietnamese refugees who arrived in the United States as children, and the second generation, the American-born children of refugees who are transforming and redeveloping Little Saigon.[7] On a typical day, children at DeMille Elementary School, as young as kindergarteners, are learning Vietnamese in the nation's first Vietnamese-English bilingual education program. Men sit outside at Coffee Planet, one

FIGURE 2. Bolsa Row, a mixed-use living, outdoor retail, and entertainment complex in Westminster, California (courtesy of IP Westminster, 2024).

of the many outdoor cafés and a diasporic relic of French colonialism, reading *Người Việt* and gossiping about Vietnamese American politicians. Phở 79, a James Beard Award–winning restaurant, is down the street. Here, patrons wait in long lines for a take-out bowl of phở or to sit inside to eat. A line of cars waits at the 7 Leaves Café drive-thru to get their famous salted caramel coffee, while others head to the Pickle Bánh Mì Company and select one of the types of fresh bánh mì listed on the Vietnamese/English drive-thru menu.

Little Saigon now stretches into six cities—Westminster, Garden Grove, Midway City, Santa Ana, Fountain Valley, and Anaheim—as it continuously expands its political and economic reach in suburban Southern California. The South Vietnamese yellow flag with three red stripes lines Bolsa Avenue for three miles. The Vietnamese American Chamber of Commerce, spearheaded by 1.5- and second-generation Vietnamese, is helping local store owners create virtual Google tours for their businesses. The Vietnamese directory, easily purchased on Moran Street, contains over four hundred religious organizations—including Buddhist, Hội Thánh Cao Đài, Phật Giáo Hòa Hảo, and Catholic—and over two hundred Vietnamese-owned bilingual law, dental, pharmacy, and accountancy offices. Local families still commemorate Black April, or the Fall of Saigon, sending their children to school wearing black ribbons in memory of their losses.

Vietnamese are recipients of the largest refugee resettlement effort in US history, and this story takes place in their community. After over twenty years of US military intervention in Vietnam, Laos, and Cambodia, the United States accepted nine hundred thousand Vietnamese refugees between 1975 and 2000 through a variety of policy programs.[8] Approximately 3.9 million Vietnamese soldiers and civilians were killed during the years of imperial warfare, exceeding 12 percent of Vietnam's population.[9] Of these deaths, over one million were Vietnamese civilians, including those killed in massacres by the US military at Thủy Bồ and Mỹ Lai. The United States dropped more than nineteen million gallons of toxins on Vietnam, including four hundred thousand tons of napalm and thirteen million gallons of Agent Orange.[10] Yet the imperial wars in Vietnam, Cambodia, and Laos were not limited to the years between 1955 and 1975. The effects overwhelm these temporal boundaries and mark the individual experiences and bodies of Vietnamese people and their children. Yến Lê Espiritu argues that having lost the Vietnam War, the United States was left without a "liberated" country of people to showcase.[11] Instead, the rescued Vietnamese refugees became a substitute, enabling Americans to remake the Vietnam War into "a just and successful war." Vietnamese people are the "featured evidence of the appropriateness of US actions in Vietnam."[12]

In 2024, the median household income in Little Saigon's Orange County was around $127,800 per year and the median home value was $1.37 million, exceeding the national median of $74,580 and $495,100, respectively. However, the county's overall affluence hides the economic inequities in income distribution; since 1960, it has had the highest median rent of Southern Californian counties. Popularized portrayals in films and shows like *The Real Housewives of Orange County*, *Selling the OC*, and *Laguna Beach* showcase a predominantly white middle- to upper-class suburbia of affluence, concealing the racial and class diversity of the area.

Financial advisers usually contend that a household earning around $125,000 per year can reasonably afford a home in the $475,000 to $580,000 range—far below the price tag in Orange County. While many Vietnamese have amassed wealth, many Little Saigon residents cannot afford a home, even one far below the median price range. Yet they live there, nonetheless. Images of Asians and Vietnamese in suburban Orange County reinforce the model minority myth as high-achieving problem-free minorities who outperform whites in terms of household income and education. In reality, Asian Americans have the greatest wealth gap of any ethnic or racial group.[13]

These paradoxes challenge Americans' imagined notions of suburbia as egalitarian spaces of social mobility and lay at the crux of this book. Who is Little Saigon for, and who are suburbs for? How does placemaking occur in unequal suburbs? This book addresses fundamental questions about the right to live in suburbia. Orange County has its own histories of forced displacement of indigenous Tongva communities; segregation and redlining; and now suburban gentrification. Despite this, refugees are collectively shaping Little Saigon's future, influencing decision-making and calling for change. While forces of government and capital shape the policies that affect who can and cannot live in a community, people have the right to shape their own community's future, too. This book examines the dynamic between structural forces and residents' agency, focusing on suburban city planning, food gentrification, housing justice, neoliberal immigration policies, and community-based responses.

The rally with which this introduction began exemplifies the changing American suburban landscape. Growing up in Little Saigon, I often went with my refugee father to marches on the weekends, protesting communism on street corners and in shopping plazas. Twenty years later, protests are still happening, but their causes have changed. Today, Vietnamese refugees and their children are mobilizing for economic and immigrant justice, protesting housing displacement and refugee deportation and demanding rights to the suburbs.

WHY SUBURBAN DISPLACEMENT AND INEQUALITY IN LITTLE SAIGON?

Today, more than half of low-income and very-low-income households in the United States live in the suburbs, as do most Americans with a high risk of eviction or displacement.[14] Despite this, studies of displacement and instability have only just recently looked beyond urban centers.[15] We know little about how displacement operates in suburbia, which mechanisms enable displacement, and which community strategies help prevent it.

In the popular imagination, suburbs are seen as spaces for the upwardly mobile, where each new generation has the opportunity to climb the socioeconomic ladder. But these rosy conceptions of suburban life differ from what takes place in most of America's communities:

- Since their origins, suburbs have been demographically heterogeneous in terms of race, ethnicity, and income.
- Suburbanization has further spatially segregated the nation's neighborhoods by class, ethnicity, and race.
- The majority of America's immigrant population lives in suburban areas. Since 1965, immigrants have been much more likely to make suburbia their first destination, bypassing traditional gateway cities like New York or San Francisco.

Misconceptions about suburban racial homogeneity obscure the suburbs' heterogeneity. Suburban diversification accelerated after the liberalization of immigration reform in 1965, when increasing numbers of migrants from Asia and Latin America began arriving in the United States. Since then, research on suburbia, including studies of Black middle class and Black immigrants transforming suburban New York, has taken racial and ethnic heterogeneity as its starting point.[16] By the early 2000s, more than 50 percent of the Latinx population were living in the suburbs.[17] Asian Americans, the fastest-growing ethnic community in the United States, also gravitated to the suburbs. An incredibly diverse group, the category "Asian" in the United States includes over thirty nationalities. In California, nearly 16 percent of the population identifies as Asian American or Pacific Islander. In fact, Orange County is home to the third-largest population of Asian Americans in the nation, with one in four residents being Asian or Pacific Islander.[18]

Research published in the 2000s documents the incredible diversity of suburbs. Wei Li's study of ethnoburbs showcases a new ethnic settlement pattern in the suburbs that includes wealthy immigrants from Asia living in historically white neighborhoods.[19] Studies of the suburbanization of nonwhites, including affluent and middle-income Asians, followed. For instance, Willow Lung-Amam examined how affluent Asians are remaking the high-tech suburb of Freemont, California, but they are still seen as symbolic trespassers in traditionally white spaces.[20] Wendy Cheng made an important contribution by documenting emerging nonwhite identity in the traditional suburbs of San Gabriel Valley.[21] She examined Latinx and Asian multiracial middle-income suburbs and showed how racial identities are influenced by place. These books challenge the assumption that suburbia is cookie-cutter and culturally barren, showing instead how suburban landscapes are diverse yet segregated while still being aspirational spaces of social mobility. Yet their

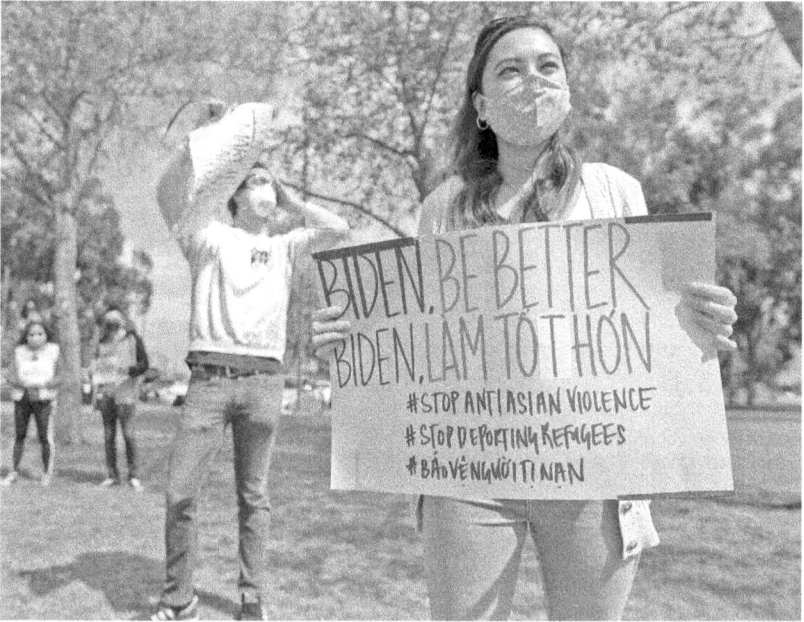

FIGURE 3. A rally in Little Saigon the day before ICE deported thirty-three Vietnamese refugees to Vietnam (photo by Tim Phan).

focus on middle- and high-income Asians tends to gloss over the socioeconomically diverse suburbs that are the focus of this book.

THE RIGHT TO THE SUBURB

The expression "Right to the City" represents the collective struggle of the working class, immigrants, and people of color to claim power to access economic justice, public spaces, services, and community institutions.[22] Activists, organizations, and scholars identify citizenship rights as including democratic participation, self-governance, and freedom from police and state harassment.[23] The right to the city is a way of claiming human flourishing, the right not to be excluded from decision-making while also having a collective right to place-making and to effect change.[24] This framework helps us understand Vietnamese refugees in Orange County as remaking their suburb to create a just space "in which public investment and regulation produce equitable outcomes."[25]

Although rights in the suburbs have historically been understood as white homeowners' rights, suburbanization since the 1940s demonstrates spatialized forms of racism.[26] Suburbs are part of the American dream, but they have become a symbol for white supremacy and heteronormative home-ownership and a "symbolic battleground for who has access to legal or natural rights in the United States."[27]

The financialization of housing relies on racial domination and privileging whiteness.[28] The financialization of housing is a product of using Black and Indigenous spaces for capital accumulation.[29] Misperceptions of the housing crisis assume a tenants' right crisis, not a housing crisis.[30] The Los Angeles Tenants Union refers to tenants as not only renters but "also the unhoused, all those who do not control their housing." The union explains why labels matter: "When we call this crisis a housing crisis, it benefits the people who design housing, who build housing, who profit from housing, not the people who live in it. . . . Humans, unlike housing, have race, gender, families, and history. Humans, unlike housing, have power."[31]

With more immigrants and refugees migrating to the suburbs, it is critical to investigate rights in the suburbs to more fully understand political access to the American dream. Suburbs are often stereotyped as spaces of conservative Republicanism where political activism is absent and residents are pacified by mortgages, shopping malls, and artisanal coffee shops—what one analyst calls "pacification by cappuccino."[32] This book suggests otherwise: immigrants and refugees are remaking suburbia through collective acts of suburban resistance. Refugees and immigrants are dismantling systems of colonialism, imperialism, and white supremacy in communities. They are challenging the dystopian ideals of consumption, material success, and excess that drive the American dream.[33]

In *Suburban Refugees*, I challenge sociological literature that frames refugee resettlement as a linear timeline presuming eventual assimilation and stability. This is not the case for many refugees; many refugees continue existing in a state of limbo, experiencing prolonged exile even after they are supposed to have been resettled. International aid organizations use the term *protracted displacement* to refer to refugees who find themselves in long-lasting, intractable states of limbo, facing "restrictions to their rights, deprived of freedom of movement, legal employment, and systems of justice."[34] While forced migrants today often experience prolonged displacement, I argue that unsettlement continues for many refugees, even after what is supposed to be permanent resettlement in a third country.

To expand the definition of protracted displacement, in the following chapters I turn to the structural forces that are often invisible that prolong displacement in the country of resettlement, the United States. This includes Vietnamese living with orders of deportation in suburban Little Saigon, waiting with uncertainty for their forced return to Vietnam. When the mark of a criminal record, no matter how minor or serious, creates a prison-to-deportation pipeline for Vietnamese refugees who came to the United States as children, we are talking about *protracted displacement*, or unsettlement. Though the United States was meant to be their ultimate place of relocation, the reality often ends up being far from the anticipated permanent and humanitarian resettlement.

Protracted displacement also includes the right to housing justice and economic opportunity. Many renters in Little Saigon are cost-burdened, unable to find adequate housing, and live with housing insecurity: suburban city zoning, occupancy codes, and exclusionary definitions of the family inhibit the right to home. Low-income households and older adults are also threatened to be displaced by the financialization of the housing market, which includes the significant expansion of corporate control of residential property. After fleeing war, some Vietnamese refugees experience other kinds of violence and uncertainty long after resettlement. Yet organizers and community members are also placemaking and reinventing Little Saigon. In the face of economic constraints and exclusion from labor markets, second-generation entrepreneurs are preventing their own displacement by returning to the community and engaging in creative entrepreneurship. Community members are also creating statewide policies and initiating campaigns to challenge inequality.

Using a Critical Refugee Studies (CRS) framework, I view refugees as social actors with complex personhoods. By interpreting refugees not as passive objects but rather as intentional subjects with stories, hopes, visions, and complex lives, this perspective challenges the prevailing "humanitarian narrative that turns refugees into dehistoricized objects of rescue."[35] Yến Lê Espiritu shows how the trope of the "good and grateful refugee" becomes a moral-political tactic buttressing the myth of America as a "nation of refuge," which makes Vietnamese refugees the "purported grateful beneficiary of US-style freedom, to remake the Vietnam War into a just and successful war."[36] Images of Vietnamese boat people enduring perilous conditions, risking death to flee a communist country and resettle in the United States, reaffirm the status of the United States as a nation of refuge, even if the government does little after resettlement.[37] *Suburban Refugees* builds on a burgeoning field of studies undertaken by Vietnamese American writers, scholars, and activists writing about Vietnamese lives and communities by and for refugees.[38]

ORANGE COUNTY'S LITTLE SAIGON

Orange County is the third most populous county in California, with the 2023 population estimated at 3.16 million people. It covers an area of 790 square miles and contains thirty-four cities and numerous unincorporated communities. Located one hundred miles from the Mexican border in Southern California, Orange County is sandwiched between San Diego County and Los Angeles County.

Economic Transformations

The area that is now Little Saigon was the original land of the Acjachemen people, later called the Juaneño by the Spanish, and the Tongva people.[39] At the end of the Mexican-American War in 1848, Mexico ceded California to the United States, becoming a state in 1850. Anaheim was the first town founded in Orange County; German migrants started the new community, which was built on winemaking, using primarily Chinese agricultural workers.[40] In 1868, the cities of Santa Ana, Westminster, Garden Grove, Tustin, and Orange were founded with farming as the backbone of their local economies.[41] Agriculture continued to dominate Orange County's economy before World War II, hence the name signifying the orange groves that dotted its landscape. In the post-World War II era, this radically changed as it became a part of Los Angeles's planned suburban expansion, with north Orange County, where Little Saigon is situated, growing particularly rapidly. Before Orange County became home to Little Saigon, Westminster was mainly a white, working-class town dedicated to family farms and light manufacturing.[42]

Between the 1960s and the 1980s, the West Coast amassed the most military expenditures per capita in the United States; California had the most military and defense payroll and pension dollars.[43] Aerospace-defense industries were the major catalysts for economic development nationally, and California was where most aircraft were built.[44] These companies included Northrop, Hughes Aircraft, Douglas Aircraft, Rockwell, and Ford Motor Company. Orange County was no longer a suburban bedroom community for Los Angeles; most residents who lived in the mega-suburb also worked there.[45]

Major employment growth in the 1970s in international trade, finance, and real estate diversified Orange County's economic activities, providing opportunities for its immigrant population, including Vietnamese refugees. These economic and demographic changes helped Orange County develop its cultural and economic autonomy, separate from Los Angeles. By the early 1980s, Orange County's economy was the thirtieth largest in the world, rivaling the economies of Portugal, Israel, and Egypt, with an output close to $70 billion. A population explosion ensued; the county attracted both skilled and unskilled labor, growing from 214,000 people in 1950 to 1.9 million in 1980 to 3.2 million today.[46]

In recent years, Orange County has received investments from Japan, Taiwan, and China. It has a large number of Asian-owned firms; California has 33.6 percent of all US Asian-owned firms, and almost half of these are in Orange County.[47] These companies include the US headquarters for Toshiba, Hyundai, Panasonic, Mazda, Kia, and Kawasaki. Global trade organizations spearheaded by local politicians and the diaspora in Orange County started with the 1967 World Affairs Council of Orange County, followed by the 1976 World Trade Association of Orange County and the 2001 International Business Center, among many others. These organizations have had a global reach, predominantly connecting with Asian and South American countries. Through these programs, transnational dignitaries from Latin America, Mexico, and Southeast Asia frequently visit Orange County to connect with their diasporas.[48] Scholars expect continued growth of well-paying jobs in technology, health care, and professional services through 2050, with the most significant expansion in the service sector.[49]

These changes yielded an increase in service sector and manufacturing jobs, which Vietnamese took advantage of upon their arrival in the early 1980s. The refugee population welcomed the availability of manufacturing jobs in Orange County. The irony here is hard to miss: the first jobs for many newly arrived Vietnamese were on the assembly lines of the same industries that produced fiberglass for US military defense contracts, which was used in the military violence that brought Vietnamese to Orange County as political refugees.[50]

Orange County is often called a global suburb because of its high-tech industry, diverse inhabitants, participation in the international economy, and cosmopolitan and metropolitan traits.[51] Many service and support economies have developed there, including its business and tourist sectors and many immigrant-based service economies. Today, the county is highly segregated by race and class between north and south Orange County: "Within the mental maps of developers and residents, Orange County divides into a north and a south with a veritable Mason-Dixon line cutting across the middle."[52]

Racial and Ethnic Transformations

Like the United States as a whole, Orange County has undergone a rapid racial and ethnic transition from a nearly homogenous 88 percent white population in 1970 to a nearly 62 percent nonwhite population in 2023.[53] Before 1965, the immigrant population in Orange County was dominated by Mexican laborers from the Bracero program. Asian immigration to Orange County did not start with Vietnamese refugees, of course. Chinese immigrants were in Orange County working on railroads and in agriculture and service sector work by the mid-nineteenth century. Professors Linda Võ and Mary Danico describe the great hostility, racism, and marginalization the Chinese community faced. For instance, in 1906 the Chinatown in Santa Ana, the largest Asian neighborhood in Orange County at the time, was burned down by city officials because of a supposed outbreak of leprosy in the community.[54] Japanese communities were also heavily concentrated and lived in Orange County before the Vietnamese came, and many of their communities were uprooted by forced relocation to incarceration camps after the bombing of Pearl Harbor.[55]

A confluence of factors helped make Orange County the Vietnamese capital of the United States in the 1970s and 1980s. Before then, the county primarily consisted of rental spaces that were relatively inexpensive compared to much of California.[56] Resettlement agencies took the refugees to Santa Ana, home to many Mexican immigrant workers and an increasing number of Vietnamese, because of its low-cost rent. This worked well for Vietnamese immigrants, who were attracted to Orange County for its warm and sunny weather, low-skill assembly-line jobs, and proximity to Camp Pendleton's defense-related jobs.

The area that became Little Saigon in 1975 included strawberry fields, machine shops, and dilapidated strip malls. Santa Ana and Westminster were dotted with undervalued commercial properties, especially along Bolsa Avenue, all ripe for development. In 1978, the first of more than three

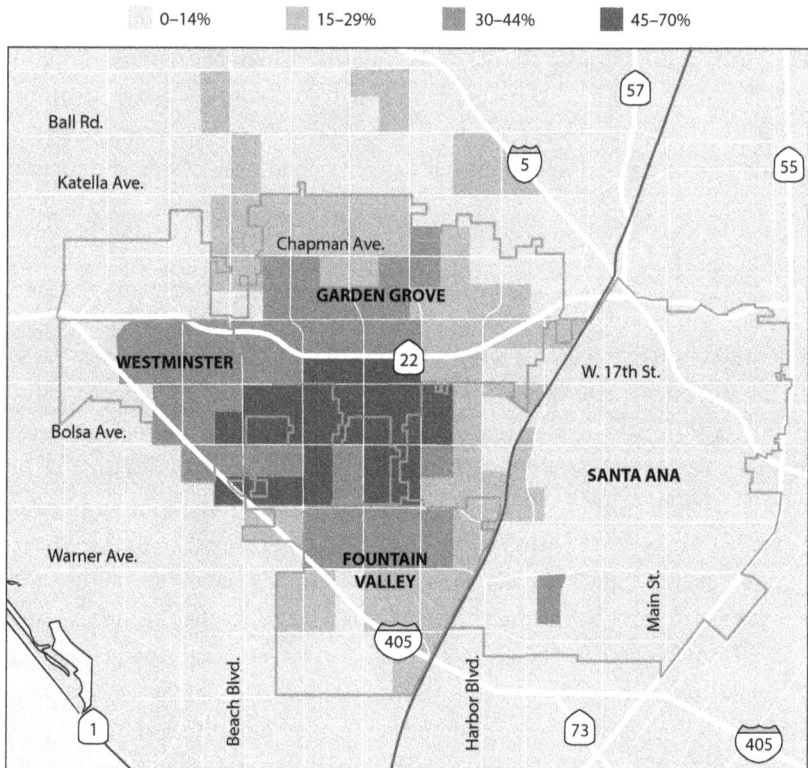

FIGURE 4. Density of Vietnamese residents in the Little Saigon area (*Orange County Register*, August 4, 2018).

thousand Vietnamese-owned businesses appeared in Westminster, including a produce market, medical office, pharmacy, restaurant, and real estate office. The boundaries of Little Saigon continued to spread, and by 1980 it reached Garden Grove and Midway City. Later waves of refugees came to change the enclave, including the second wave of Vietnamese refugees—boat people who fled Vietnam on fishing vessels and stayed years in refugee camps in East and Southeast Asia—who helped drive business along Bolsa Avenue.

Post-1965 immigration patterns continue to spatially inscribe new racial and class divisions within suburbia. The Los Angeles–Long Beach–Orange County metropolitan area is also home to the second-largest number of undocumented immigrants in the nation. Studies show that undocumented immigrants are much more likely to live in the suburbs of metropolitan areas than in the cities themselves, for reasons that include shifts in labor markets and family reunification.[57] The undocumented Asian population is the fastest growing in the United States, increasing from 7 percent of all undocumented immigrants to nearly 17 percent in 2022 alone.[58] The largest number of Asians without legal status in the United States reside in California. Political scientist Karthick Ramakrishnan estimates that one of five undocumented immigrants in California is Asian.[59] Asians with liminal legal statuses are often left in the shadows of policy debates and their experiences rendered invisible, as most researchers focus on Latinx residents and border security.[60] This book contributes to understanding how Vietnamese deportees experience living in suburban immigration limbo.

SOURCES AND METHODS

> This is the capital of the Vietnamese diaspora. There are so many of us here. We have so much political power in the county that's not being used at all for issues that working-class people are affected by.
>
> TRACY LA, *cofounder of VietRISE*

Tracy is one of the Vietnamese American organizers I met during my fieldwork who provided me with a helpful angle of vision on the local inequities and potential for activism. Through her, I came to understand how many contours of spatial inequality are hidden.

Drawing on archival research and fieldwork in both Southern California and Vietnam, *Suburban Refugees* incorporates ethnography, archival records, interviews with more than 101 Vietnamese refugees and their American-born children as well as interviews with 89 organizational leaders, and autoethnography based on my own experiences growing up in the community as second-generation Vietnamese. The appendix details my methodology, including how I met interviewees, the interview process, and reflections on my approach.

Historians often draw on archival research, including official records and personal papers, to create a picture of a community. To sketch a demographic picture of Little Saigon, past and present, I consulted the US Census and sifted through records and documents at the Southeast Asian Archive at the University of California, Irvine, a treasure trove of primary sources documenting the community. Newspaper archives and local publications like the *Orange County Register,* the *Los Angeles Times*, *Việt Báo*, and *Người Việt*, the most popular and widely circulating Vietnamese-language newspaper, helped me to understand changes in the community over time.

The lives of organizers like Sơn and Tracy are comparatively absent from these formal records. So, to understand Little Saigon and its contemporary fight against displacement pressures, I turned to the community and its residents. I contacted Asian American organizations such as VietRISE, Southeast Asian Coalition (SEAC), and Viet-CARE, among others, to learn about their projects and community resources, such as antideportation campaigns and mental health and housing assistance. Accessing adequate and affordable housing is difficult in Orange County. In 2021, Santa Ana became the first city in Orange County to pass rent control. To learn how this happened, I turned to coalition organizations such as Tenants United Santa Ana, whose work centers on antiracism and antigentrification. Much of the organizing for rent control has been ongoing for over twenty years; the aftermath of COVID provided me access to online meetings from suburban city councils and planning commissions. I also analyzed organizational websites and their social media on Instagram, YouTube, and Facebook. To contextualize this analysis, I talked to activists and organizers to learn about their organizations. I reached out to other organizations that focus on *crimmigration*—the deep connections between migration law and the criminal justice system—and whose work centers Asian Americans in California, such as API Rise and the Asian Prisoner Support Committee. I attended protests and marches on antideportation as well as teach-ins and press conferences for immigration reform, such as the proposed California VISION and HOME acts. For the chapter on housing justice, I created a flyer to solicit both tenants' and landlords' perspectives. I also interviewed local politicians, nonprofit leaders, and residents to analyze housing justice during this period after the passage of rent control in Santa Ana.

Being second-generation Vietnamese and from the community eased my access to different groups. As often as possible, I asked my father, a cultural liaison and war veteran who spent years in a reeducation camp, to accompany me on interviews; because of his age and Central Vietnamese dialect, people were nearly always respectful. This proved particularly advantageous when interviewing senior tenants and residents of the mobile home communities who generously welcomed my father and me into their homes.

Just as places have histories, so do writers and scholars. As a sociology graduate student, I originally planned to study Little Saigon from the perspective of second-generation Vietnamese, the children of refugees. However, after graduation, the reality of daily life in the community caused me to reconsider my research priorities. In the face of rising living costs and other outcomes of the Great Recession, my parents lost their small business. One cousin was deported to Vietnam. My uncle was living in a van behind Brodard Restaurant. My brother has been in and out of jail nine times—and my parents still don't know. I was struggling with being labeled a model minority as a first-generation college student, then an Ivy League graduate, and now a professor while my parents received food stamps. I wanted to understand how Little Saigon could maintain its reputation and space as the Vietnamese capital of America and for whom. As an assistant professor, I revised my research focus to how structures of inequality shape refugee lives years after resettlement, inequities within the community, and emergent forms of social justice activism beyond the praxis of anticommunism.

Growing up in suburban Little Saigon, I knew that the myth of suburban America as a homogenous and harmonious haven was just that: a myth. My father, a refugee who fought in the Army of the Republic of South Vietnam and escaped by boat to the United States, has been an American citizen for over forty-two years, but he rarely leaves the confines of our neighborhood. Growing up, I watched him experience racism and uneasiness when he did. The invisible borders of belonging and unbelonging that kept him in Little Saigon are exemplified by comparing Santa Ana and Newport Beach, two suburban communities in Orange County separated by eleven miles. In 2021, Santa Ana, the part of Little Saigon where I was born, had a median household income of $77,000. Newport Beach's median household income was $145,000. Newport Beach is 89.7 percent white; Santa Ana is 87 percent people of color. Moving between Santa Ana and Newport Beach induces visual and cultural whiplash.

The demographic story of Santa Ana and Newport Beach is the story of the nation's suburbs and counties at large. The country is both diversifying and segregating. California, the nation's most diverse state, and Orange County, a majority-minority county, are mythologized by popular media as either racial utopias or postracial spaces. While America and suburbia are more diverse than ever, census data at the block level confirms that most neighborhoods remain segregated and unequal.

When interviewing those who faced housing insecurity, I shared my family's story to let them know I understand their predicament and to explain my interest in how the community is changing. Afsaneh Najmabadi discusses the ethics of using family secrets in her research on love and marriage in Iran, noting that "memoir writers necessarily blur the lines between an autobiography and biography, self and other, especially when a child tells the parents' story."[61] Telling these stories is "to retrieve a past that is ours but not ours alone."[62] I have tried to integrate the CRS method of re-storying, a narrative form that "writes against humanitarian texts that reify condescending and depleted images of refugees that centers refugee stories that mix personal reflection with historical recollection that revel in beauty and survival, even when refugee lives are edged with precarity."[63]

The interviews lasted between one and three hours and were often conducted in locations respondents identified as most comfortable for them: people's homes, restaurants, workplaces, rallies, businesses, and schools. I digitally recorded and manually transcribed many of the first interviews; beginning in 2017, I recorded and transcribed using an online program, OtterAI.

THE ORGANIZATION AND THE ARGUMENT

How do suburban communities like Little Saigon survive in the midst of displacement pressures? How do refugees enact placemaking and fight for immigrant justice in the suburbs?

Suburban Refugees focuses on the structural conditions of displacement and community-based responses in a socioeconomically diverse suburb. I make three primary arguments: (1) immigration to the suburbs is not a guarantee of economic opportunity or upward mobility; (2) there are unique and novel opportunities in the suburbs to resist displacement and for refugee placemaking; and (3) definitions of protracted displacement need to be reconsidered.

Other authors have asked how, over fifty years, various waves of Vietnamese refugees have come to Orange County and built a distinct and recognizable ethnic community amid former orange groves in what was a quintessential white suburban environment. *Suburban Refugees* differs from these studies by identifying the current threats of eviction, mapping the spatial dynamics of inequality, analyzing immigration deportation regimes, and documenting community responses and organizing. This book asks how refugees manage to claim community space amid such external pressures. It explores causes of suburban displacement, such as city branding, and considers extra-personal forces like transnational capital, zoning laws, and population pressures that create housing insecurity. Recognizing Vietnamese refugees as active agents of their own futures, I ask how residents resist these multiple displacements and claim a politics of emplacement.

Chapter 1, "The Right to Placemaking," explores Little Saigon as a social and cultural construction that not only reflects the Vietnamese refugees who live there but also the practices of city developers and suburban planners who create a particular image of Little Saigon, marketing its Vietnamese identity. To illustrate, I use the case study of a food hall, Rodeo 39, and its artistic directors, two second-generation Vietnamese who are reshaping Vietnamese American foodscapes and transforming the business district from within. I show how Little Saigon increasingly depends on business models developed by the children of refugees. Vietnamese youths are actively creating unique spaces of cultural consumption, asserting their right of presence. By selling the city, the children of refugees are reimaging Little Saigon not as a haven for anticommunist refugees but as a site for drawing on their social and cultural capital to create new businesses, eateries, and development projects that value community reinvestment.

Chapter 2, "The Right to Home," shows how suburban displacement is not just a matter of city development, as discussed in the previous chapter, but also involves the right to housing. Of the thirty-four cities in the county, Santa Ana became the first to enact rent control in 2021. This chapter explores how rent stabilization passed after decades-long organizing and cross-ethnic coalitions of Mexican and Vietnamese community organizers. Strict land-use regulations in suburbia favor the maintenance and aesthetic of single-family zoning, promoting spatial exclusion. Here, I investigate differential access to rental units and the ability to maintain housing in Little Saigon, where the cost of housing is 356 percent higher than the nation's average. The suburban neighborhood of Little Saigon presents Vietnamese refugees with many barriers that limit their ability to stay in place—and equally as many community strategies to help them remain in place.

Chapter 3, "The Right to Organize," focuses on collective mobilization against displacement in Little Saigon. To this end, the chapter centers the experiences of mobile home park residents. Unlike most current research in housing that focuses on housing vouchers or public housing, I focus here on mobile homes, a mode of housing that represents a significant share of unsubsidized, low-income housing in the United States. In 2017, Vietnamese residents in Westminster faced the threat of eviction as their lot was slated to be redeveloped as a luxury condominium complex. The park's tenants are 80 percent Vietnamese, primarily seniors and disabled persons, and include veterans and refugees of the Vietnam War; more than half of households whose self-reported incomes were in the lowest income bracket. Residents facing the threat of eviction and dislocation successfully fought against the landowner and were thus able to remain in their homes. Examining the dynamics of the community's collective resistance against dislocation, I describe how the residents mobilized for three years, turning to the city council, organizing protests and a letter campaign, and creating statewide policy change.

Chapter 4, "The Right to the Suburb," shifts from city developers, suburban zoning, and community organizing to transnational states of limbo conditioned by state violence, including neoliberal immigration policies. Nearly one in five undocumented immigrants in California are Asian, and they are more likely to live in the suburbs of metropolitan areas. This chapter asks: Who has the right to stay in suburbia? Who does US immigration policy privilege? I use the method of re-storying to look at Vietnamese antideportation campaigns and draw on individual oral histories in Little Saigon that highlight trends of liminality in the suburban Vietnamese community. For instance, in one story, Minh Nguyễn tells of incarceration and activism while being one of eight thousand Vietnamese living in deportation limbo. This chapter shows how systems that provide refuge may also cause displacement.

The conclusion, "Suburban Organizing Playbook," reflects on the future of Little Saigon and the broader systems of banishment and inclusion, which are described throughout the book, and the conditions that shape refugee placemaking. I urge readers to brainstorm and develop a playbook for suburban organizing applicable to other immigrant communities, beginning with the lessons learned from Little Saigon. Suburban life is rapidly changing, and this chapter draws together new ways of conceptualizing this phenomenon and proposes interventions appropriate to a more nuanced exploration of suburban immigrant displacement and resistance. The experiences of suburban refugees diverge from the typical imaginings of suburbia and provide new opportunities for questioning inequality and gentrification and new ways to understand refuge and social justice outside the city.

ONE

———

The Right to Placemaking

ON THE EDGE OF THE Vietnamese community, in a formerly dilapidated shopping center that once housed a California Department of Motor Vehicles office and a movie theater, sits a new development: Rodeo 39 Public Market. Not far from the mom-and-pop restaurants of Little Saigon, the 41,000-square-foot food hall includes a floral boutique, apparel shops, a tattoo parlor, and sit-down restaurants. The food hall itself has seventeen different food concepts anchored by Phoholic, its most coveted eatery. Phoholic, a play on words highlighting the popularity of the Northern Vietnamese beef noodle soup, attracts long lines of patrons. This phở restaurant is known for its generous portions and two kinds of noodles, thin and thick. Another eatery brands its food as "Asian comfort food" and features a bilingual Vietnamese/English menu. Patrons have various seating options throughout the food hall, including long wooden tables, peacock blue velvet couches, and minimalist white dining tables with a QR code for ordering from the comfort of your seat.

Business mogul Andy Nguyễn and executive chef Michael Phạm, both second-generation Vietnamese, are the creative directors behind the new development. Their goal was to create a place that goes beyond "a transactional food hall environment." Andy says the market brands itself as more than a food hall, it's a "food and lifestyle center that is an experience space to hang out, a place where you can stay from morning to night."[1] To this end, in addition to its gastronomic offerings, the space caters to a young adult customer base with a retro arcade; cocktail bar; pop-up shops that sell clothes, sunglasses, and handmade jewelry; and a small stage for live performances. What makes this lifestyle food hall different? Nearly 80 percent of the stalls and stores are owned by Asian Americans who are overwhelmingly

FIGURE 5. Rodeo 39 Food Hall (photo by Cindy Trịnh, 2024).

FIGURE 6. Interior of Rodeo 39 Food Hall (photo by Cindy Trịnh, 2024).

Vietnamese and who serve popular foods reflecting this pan-Asian diversity: ramen, bánh xèo, phở, boba, Laotian barbecue, and coffee.

With the Rodeo 39 Public Market, we begin to see the effects of *food gentrification*, the process by which previously inexpensive staple foods and ingredients unexpectedly become trendy, costly, and eventually out of reach for communities that once depended on them.[2] Yet city officials, media outlets, and cultural elites praise the neighborhood's food scene as authentic, giving Little Saigon a growing cultural cachet as a foodie destination. Vietnamese food is now particularly appealing to consumers who use it as a marker to distinguish themselves and to suburban policymakers and city governments who rely on immigrant foodways to brand and market neighborhoods like Little Saigon as exciting and vibrant places to visit.

Food can be a lynchpin for power relations, signifying control and access. In Little Saigon, the politics of food are complex; food can be used by city planners and governments who support redevelopment projects to attract and brand spaces as tourist destinations for wealthier consumers, and it can be used by later generations, who, in the face of market constraints, turn to entrepreneurship to create new foodscapes through placemaking—but at what cost to long-term residents?

This chapter documents how the placemaking strategies of suburban city governments, business developers, and small business owners impact Little Saigon. A pandemic and two recessions, including the collapse of the housing market, have widened the fissures of suburban inequality. Income inequality has been widening in California over the past several decades, and Orange County is Southern California's most expensive rental market.[3] In 2024, the median price of a single-family home in Orange County is $1.37 million.[4] Nearly 29 percent of seniors in Orange County experience food insecurity, which means they do not have enough food, compared to 10 percent of households nationally.[5] In some Santa Ana and Anaheim schools, nearly 90 percent of children qualify for free or reduced-price meals.[6] Food insecurity tends to affect children, older adults, and low-income working families disproportionately.[7] Suburban city governments happily support redevelopment projects that attract wealthier consumers and capital that provide revenue from sales tax while displacing some long-term established residents who can no longer afford the community's amenities. The city of Westminster's *Little Saigon Blueprint for Investment* succinctly summarizes its economy-over-people priorities: "Orange County residents are younger, more ethnically diverse, primarily English-speaking, and have higher spending power and educational attainments. To appeal to these customers, Little Saigon will need to elevate its appearance and update sales and marketing tactics while diversifying offerings to include a mix of traditional and newer, trendier retail and dining concepts."[8]

I argue that in this process of place branding, the suburban city selects, commodifies, and markets which Vietnamese histories, identities, and aesthetics their target groups are most likely to consume, focusing here on Asian Americans, high-income English-speaking visitors, and middle-class Vietnamese residents. The negative consequence is its potential to displace established spaces for long-term lower-income members of the community.

At the same time, new generations of Vietnamese Americans, like those of Andy and Michael, are transforming the community by drawing on the cultural capital embodied in their refugee backgrounds to recast traditional foods into cosmopolitan culinary social capital.[9] This entrepreneurship results in new businesses, eateries, and development projects that intersect with state and private interests through the ideology of community reinvestment while also acting as potential forces of displacement. Unwittingly, this upscaling masks gentrification's differential impacts on Vietnamese of varying economic means.[10]

What is happening in Little Saigon suggests grassroots, Vietnamese-led redevelopment. By retooling gentrification as a bottom-up process that preserves culture, it is masked as less threatening to community members.[11] The transformations taking place are both beneficial and destructive. Beneficial in that community-building is still Vietnamese-owned and controlled. Vietnamese gentrifiers have diverse motives and may deliberately patronize existing local businesses to support working-class residents and support a social justice agenda.[12] Later generations of Vietnamese continue to use entrepreneurship as a way to ease their own economic integration in the face of weak job markets and discrimination. At the same time, placemaking is not equal. Unwittingly, this new form of placemaking has the potential to rewrite space, where Little Saigon functions as a site of celebratory ethnic consumption or as an "ethnic theme park," where "culture is choreographed as exotic, safe, and palatable" to attract a wider diversity of consumers.[13] This celebratory rhetoric masks ongoing and indirect class-based displacement where poorer residents who depend on the community may feel their sense of place slowly disappear as the familiar becomes unfamiliar.

"Isn't this place completely different from the restaurants our parents took us to?" I ask a friend as we sit in the food hall of the Rodeo 39 Public Market. The Little Saigon business community is undergoing a seismic shift. A *Los Angeles Times* headline proclaims: "An Update on the Vietnamese Dining Experience."[14] The story begins by telling us that Andy Nguyễn wants to "modernize Vietnamese food and the dining experience, so they are accessible to people of all cultures and generations." In addition to being the creative director of Rodeo 39, Andy is the innovator behind Nudo Nudo, a "modernized phở restaurant in the heart of Little Saigon."[15] He is a serial and celebrated entrepreneur in the food and beverage industry, widely known for his chain of ice cream shops with twenty-five locations across Southern California as well as other business ventures, including Ground House Burgers, the Ramen Bar, and Black Matte Coffee.

Andy spent his childhood eating home-cooked phở in Westminster and wants those outside the culture to experience Little Saigon without intimidation. He explained to a TV host: "A lot of these Vietnamese restaurants, if my friends outside the Vietnamese culture were to go on their own, they might feel uncomfortable because hardly anyone speaks English. They're not used to the type of service at typical Vietnamese restaurants where the workers aren't really interested in conversation. You go into an American fine dining restaurant, they're happy and welcoming. The Vietnamese culture is maybe bit more harsh, where it's just like, 'Here's your food,' and that's it."[16] Another *Los Angeles Times* article is headlined: "Not Your Grandmother's Little Saigon: Entrepreneurs Expand Enclave's Horizons."[17] "It's getting more bilingual, and it's not only an international destination for tourists, it's attractive to younger Vietnamese who are coming back to take charge because they're looking for a familiar environment, a comfortable place to raise their families," notes the president of the Vietnamese American Chamber of Commerce headquartered in Westminster.

Little Saigon is no longer a place where mom-and-pop Vietnamese restaurants are the primary options; it is now what one entrepreneur calls a "food mecca" for Southern California.[18] The district buzzes with stores offering innovative drinks and desserts. With the help of social media, fusion restaurants are flourishing, from ice cream–stuffed doughnuts, wagyu phở, and spicy miso carbonara to customized churros and Asian tacos.[19]

In every decennial census, immigrants and refugees are more likely to be entrepreneurial than the US-born. Nearly half of US Fortune 500 companies' founders are immigrants or the children of immigrants. Immigrant businesses account for a quarter of new businesses in the US, with diverse fields and sizes.[20] Immigrant entrepreneurship has long been heralded as a means of social mobility and a way to circumvent labor market discrimination.[21] For example, many first-generation Vietnamese who I spoke to pointed to labor market bias due to limited English proficiency and language skills and their educational credentials from Vietnam not being recognized by American employers.[22] The opportunity structures available in the United States and the co-ethnic context of Little Saigon are two critical variables favoring Vietnamese entrepreneurs and entrepreneurs in general.[23] The 1.5- and second-generation Vietnamese entrepreneurs who I spoke to described their motivations for engaging in a business start-up in terms of a creative enterprise.[24]

If Andy and these other 1.5- and second-generation Vietnamese were white, this would likely be described as gentrification. The various explanations and definitions of gentrification largely omit reference to race and ethnicity.[25] The popular understanding of gentrification holds that gentrifiers are typically white and that the residents who move out are generally people of color.[26] Yet, as we will see in the case of places like Little Saigon and suburban enclaves, ethnic gentrifiers are complicating this narrative of displacement.

The new entrepreneurial food and business models favored by Andy and other 1.5- and second-generation Vietnamese in Little Saigon suggest the makings of *ethnic gentrifiers*. Three main characteristics shape and construct this identity that results in upscaling and redevelopment led by affluent Vietnamese returning to the community. First, ethnic gentrifiers are conscious of being bicultural and growing up in multicultural and diverse neighborhoods. They can identify with Vietnamese, Asian, American, and local cultures; they are conscious of their identities as Vietnamese American and capitalize on their cultural capital. Unlike some of their first-generation counterparts, they speak fluent English (often without an accent), are educated in the United States, and can negotiate generational boundaries. Second, this capitalization of cultural and social capital results in new businesses, eateries, and development projects that intersect with the ideology of community reinvestment. In Latinx communities, this is referred to as *gentefication*.[27] *Gente* in Spanish translates to "people," thus gentrification "by the people." Finally, ethnic gentrifiers are often seeking a sense of community by staking claim to a space.[28] Other studies show that Black and Latinx gentrifiers "value low-income black and Latinx neighborhoods for the communities that live there as a form of cultural worth."[29] As individuals who work and spend time in spaces where they are often racial minorities, these gentrifiers desire communities where their racialized cultures are centered and valued. Their choice of neighborhood is often about "giving back" to the racialized communities that they came from.[30] By retooling gentrification as a grassroots process that "preserves cultural integrity, the process becomes perceived as less threatening."[31]

Communities of color often frame this reinvestment as a form of racial uplift that glosses over the negative impacts of displacement. While elite Vietnamese initiate residential and commercial investment and upgrading, this rhetoric depends on the notion that investment benefits all neighborhood residents, regardless of income level.[32] Studies of this phenomenon tend to rely on cases involving Black and Latinx communities in cities like Los Angeles, Harlem, Philadelphia, and Chicago.[33] These studies show that ethnic consumption and the commodification of culture are often key parts of the process that detract attention from the impacts of displacement on long-term working-class residents.[34] These formerly stigmatized neighborhoods often become recodified as exotic and up-and-coming for outsiders and middle-class residents.[35] Political scientist Michelle Boyd describes this type of ethnic or race gentrification as a form of defensive development, where "community building and economic revitalization strategies are designed to protect neighborhoods from control by white residents, city elites, and developers."[36] This case similarly illustrates how Vietnamese elites use upscaling both as a political strategy and as a response to structural constraints in the labor market, reflecting their class privilege and position in the racial hierarchy.

Similar patterns are also evident in suburban spaces of California, including Little Saigon. As the co-owner of 7 Leaves Cafe, one of the most popular coffee chains in Little Saigon, explained to a reporter: "The transformation you're seeing in Little Saigon is the second generation—or even the third generation—taking what was great and making it even greater."[37] According to Winifred Curran, an urban development scholar, gentrifying an immigrant city requires rewriting history; in this case, it is the second, 1.5, and later generations that are remaking and refashioning Little Saigon.[38]

The traditional logic of gentrification still underlies these glowing quotes as low-income Vietnamese residents are priced out. Ethnic gentrifiers ease their own assimilation process by taking advantage of the existing infrastructure of Little Saigon built by the first wave of refugees. This becomes the basis for creating new, expressive forms of entrepreneurship.[39] Ethnic gentrification, instead of being an intrinsically separate and more equitable approach to redevelopment, is often ambivalent and contradictory, marked by class and generational tensions.[40] While placemaking often evokes sentiments of inclusion, beautification, and community-driven processes of belonging, those left out of the community development process are often poorer residents.[41] Under the guise of revitalization and progress, placemaking can result in unmaking, perpetuating socioeconomic injustices like spatial exclusion for some.[42]

FOOD ADVENTURING

Upon losing her LA job in 2007 due to the recession, Tammy Lê, a second-generation Vietnamese, moved back to Orange County's Little Saigon to stay with family when she was twenty-four. A former model and teacher, the thirty-six-year-old now works in marketing and describes herself as an avid foodie. As we sit down for coffee, she describes a culinary renaissance in Little Saigon, where vibrant fusion foodscapes are emerging from the second generation:

> So, if you notice among Vietnamese, for our generation, a lot of things are popping up in the food industry. It's paying homage to our parents to preserve our culture by passing down food, but we're trying to make it more modern, traditional with a modern twist to it, like bridging the two gaps and generations together. So, our parents, they are like, "What is Phoritto [Phở + Burrito]?" They don't like the idea, but the fact that they're talking about it makes them curious enough. Our generation is always willing to try new things. Of course, we love the OG [original, highly respected], and no one can touch our mom's game. But we want to see how to innovate this into something else and make it even more delicious.

The 1.5 and second generations have transformed the food scene and the built landscape. I wondered how these later generations of Vietnamese decide to even start careers in food. Several studies report that entrepreneurship usually declines for the second generation.[43] While food can emplace and displace refugee and immigrant communities, it often reveals a space's transforming demographics and economic change.[44] Tammy explains the switch to creative entrepreneurship for many second-generation Vietnamese as an economic strategy in response to structural constraints of the labor market:

I think they're just unhappy in their jobs. I had a friend who wanted to become a lawyer go through law school and then realize being a lawyer wasn't her passion. So, I think a lot of it's because we pursue these careers because it's what our parents want. We do these things to please our parents as first generation, to make up for their sacrifice. But now, in this new generation, there is an influx of YouTubers, influencers, and people making six figures without having to go to school. It's like, why do we need to go to school when their job pays for itself? Yeah, so, in a sense, as millennials, many of us are very well educated; it's just we didn't have the resources to do better in our careers or do better financially.

Also, they want to do things they feel that bring them happiness. Who doesn't get happy when they eat? Food always brings people together. If I were to ask you: If you could redo this lifetime again, without hearing what your parents wanted you to do, what would you have done instead? I think a lot of them would have changed their careers and life aspirations.

For me, I went into education because my sister has Down's syndrome. So, I've always worked with kids with learning disabilities. I wanted to go into education so I can work with people like my sister, you know? When my mom found out all these teachers had been let go, she was upset. My mom doesn't understand English. She's like, "Why are all these people getting fired?" "No, mom, these teachers are not getting fired. Our government is too poor. The government can't afford to pay the teachers."

After being laid off as a special education teacher, Tammy found multiple gigs as an influencer and in marketing, where she stayed. In many ways she is typical of her generation, having come of age during and after the recession of 2008.[45] Between 2007 and 2009, the United States suffered one of its most significant economic downturns since the Great Depression: eight million jobs were lost, gross domestic product declined nearly 4 percent, and unemployment more than doubled from less than 5 percent to over 10 percent.[46] Economists estimate that since 2007, 16 to 32 percent of Americans have been making their living through nontraditional employment. Economist Alan Krueger found the sharpest increase to be a rise in what he calls "alternative work arrangements," which include the gig economy and self-employed entrepreneurs who work as independent contractors and freelance workers.[47] In 2017, those working in professional and business services like food service, health, and education represented half of those engaged in alternative work arrangements. However, although the recession caused many businesses to close or file for bankruptcy, economists note that the rapid rise in unemployment brought about increased entrepreneurship.[48] For many, the potential opportunities for opening a new business outweighed the alternatives to formal employment, spurring entrepreneurship. Foodie culture was one pocket of the economy that survived the Great Recession.[49] Financial instability did not slow this trend, which is characterized by an upper-middle-class mindset motivated by exotic status-seeking.[50] Thus, later generations of US-born Vietnamese turned to food and culinary culture and small business entrepreneurship in the community during this time, capitalizing on the infrastructure of Little Saigon and their cultural capital to create forms of expressive entrepreneurship.

When many 1.5- and second-generation Vietnamese were economically displaced by the Great Recession, they sometimes turned to their ethnic communities, creating class tensions with less financially resourced Vietnamese. Displacement manifests in multiple forms. Exacerbating affordability pressures and neighborhood resource displacement (changing the orientation of services) create a sense of social distance for long-term residents, even if they do not necessarily have to move.[51] As we see in the case of Little Saigon and other suburban enclaves, ethnic gentrifiers complicate this narrative of displacement.

In the case of Boyle Heights, a suburb of Los Angeles, Alfredo Huante shows the lack of agreement over whether or not gente-fication is a threat to the neighborhood.[52] Since the gentrifiers are not white but rather Latinx, their presence does not cause the cultural erasure that usually accompanies gentrification, as affluent Latinx residents will promote economic development and maintain racial diversity. However, local activists fighting gentrification contend that the new class of Latinx business owners is "still displacing and replacing long-term working-class Latinx residents who are also darker skinned."[53]

Scholars also note that displacement may not always be direct.[54] It can entail a loss of sense of place rather than a loss of actual space since low-income residents and other users might be deprived of their right to identify themselves with their neighborhood. In emerging communities with upmarket consumption, redevelopment can challenge long-term residents' feelings of inclusion and belonging. Things can start to look and feel unfamiliar. "They are modernizing some things," explains my dad's friend. "New restaurants are going next to the small businesses, but I am not paying $6 for a bánh bao," he says matter-of-factly, pointing to the new fusion bao restaurant across from his favorite coffee shop. My dad adds, "That place is just for young people." When I ask that we go, he replies, "I don't want to go in there." An OC culture and entertainment magazine describes its popular dishes, including cinnabao fries with whipped cream and condensed milk and the Bolsa bao with crispy pork belly. Dad observes, "These new stores and improvements are not meant for us."

"Watching this community start to change makes me understand how our homes are also part of our identities," a friend says. "Little Saigon is a place where my parents feel seen and welcomed, a place that reminds us of who we are." Loss can occur through seemingly minor occurrences, such as the closure of a local shop or traditional neighborhood services.[55] While most studies celebrate placemaking as inherently good, participatory, and emancipatory, this fails to consider the ways that placemaking can also be complicit in systems of erasure, gentrification, and socioeconomic elitism.[56]

Ethnic gentrifiers in Little Saigon often frame their business pursuits and products through a lens of cultural authenticity by highlighting connections to family traditions, their experiences growing up Vietnamese American, and the transnational space of Vietnam. For instance, news outlets describe 7 Leaves Cafe as the "Asian Starbucks" of Southern California.[57] The enterprise is named after seven brothers and friends who left jobs in accounting, finance, and law to start a coffee shop in Little Saigon. Launched in 2011, the chain has over forty-three stores spread out across Southern California and nationwide, with more than seven hundred team members. I first tried their beverages at a small drive-thru location that straddles Little Saigon; this strip mall, on a busy corner next to a major freeway entrance, also has a 7-Eleven and a tobacco shop. The first beverage I drank was iced mung bean—a gentle, foamy, sea-green drink with small pieces of mung bean, unlike anything from my childhood. The employees are first-, second-, and third-generation youths who speak Vietnamese and English with customers in the drive-thru, as there is no seating at this location. Crisp, clean, eye-popping photos of the drinks are emblazoned on the side of the building, advertising teas and coffees from around the world that they prepare with Vietnamese inspiration. Prices range from $5 to $6, typical for milk tea houses. Asked why he started the chain in Little Saigon, co-owner Sonny Nguyễn explained his business's connections to Vietnam to a local reporter:

> We grew up there. It's our community. Our family escaped Vietnam after the war and lived in the Philippines for a year until we got sponsored by a family. My dad found opportunities in Perris [in Riverside County, California], helping out with landscaping, but there was a language barrier. He needed to connect. He heard there was a growing Vietnamese community in Garden Grove so we packed our bags and moved. The idea for the shop came from

my eldest brother after he traveled to Asia. He said, "There's something that I'm seeing outside of the US that doesn't exist here. They're making these drinks and the preparation is so different from anything else. In Asia, they cook their drinks like soup."[58]

This co-owner of 7 Leaves Cafe sees himself as providing a food adventure in Little Saigon, the "mecca of food innovation," as he calls it, using transnational references to Vietnam. These references transform the space by assigning new meanings to familiar environments—the general look of the neighborhood changes as new cafés and restaurants serve expensive food and use bilingual menus that cater to clientele from outside the community. When longtime residents feel and perceive local spaces differently than before and when those spaces become sites of consumption, the neighborhood's identity transforms.

The new generation of Vietnamese entrepreneurs promises visitors a food adventure through Little Saigon, commodifies culture for profit, but resists exoticizing cultural differences. Rather, many see their participation in mainstreaming Vietnamese food as different than if it was done from a white or outsider subject position.[59] Sonny explained that the drinks he sells at 7 Leaves Cafe offer a food adventure for those not familiar with the culture: "We get a ten-pound taro root, chop, cook, and mash it up, and infuse it to make our taro milk tea. For our mung bean milk tea, we use pandan leaves, which people use to wrap and steam rice. It gives the drink a beautiful aroma. Our vision is to create drinks that represent different cultures. Before people might have been skeptical to try something new, but now people are like 'Let's go on a food adventure.' It's completely changed."[60] Thus, ethnic gentrifiers offer a food adventure by leveraging ideas of what Asia is in the United States, both to their detriment and advantage, by operationalizing aspects of their heritage for consumption by broader audiences and later generations of Vietnamese.

Ethnic gentrifiers also appeal to an optimistic, democratic multiculturalism that values the agency of people of color in championing and representing their own food.[61] I meet Nina and Thanh at Rodeo 39, and we sit down at one of the many tables to chat over boba and ube cheesecake. Nina, a twenty-year-old college business student, describes Rodeo 39 as a new representation of Vietnamese culture:

> I think it's exciting, honestly, because I feel like our parents' generation is a lot of mom-and-pop shops, and it is very traditional foods, which taste really

good. And for us, the second and third generations, we take our parents' recipes, and we mix it up with a modern twist, and we learn to make our foods a lot more expensive. Phở is really $5 a bowl, but here at the hall it's like twelve to fifteen bucks with tax and tip. I took my mom here to eat phở, and she was like, "Why? Why are we spending so much on phở?"

Thanh, also second generation and an MBA student, adds to the conversation:

> We are making Vietnamese food more mainstream. We're making it look more luxury. Like just by changing the seating or putting it in a luxury place like this food hall. It just ends up being more expensive, and people are willing to pay for it. So, I don't know. I think it's a good thing because I feel like as an Asian American growing up, I felt like it was really black and white. It's like you're Asian, you go to Asian spots, and then the American side of you hits the mall, and that's it, like we kept it really separate. And I'm glad that now we're kind of celebrating both sides and bringing it together in spaces like this food hall.

Even though they both feel a sense of pride in seeing Vietnamese food celebrated by becoming mainstream with an increased status, the change is also marked by tensions. Both acknowledge the upscaling of Vietnamese cuisine, with it becoming more expensive and set in spaces that may make some longtime residents feel like outsiders. This celebration of representation ties into the next section, which examines the diverse context of Orange County and how that influences Vietnamese entrepreneurs.

COSMOPOLITAN CRAVINGS

Dos Chinos, a Mexican-Vietnamese fusion food truck, is an example of the new type of cuisine flourishing in Little Saigon. Co-owner Hợp Phan grew up in the Santa Ana Vietnamese community where he helped out in his parents' phở restaurant. As he told a reporter, he was inspired by his Mexican and Vietnamese friends and classmates to open a Latin-Asian fusion food service: "My Mexican friends fed me cactus, and I was like, 'What is this? I don't know if I can eat this, it has needles and stuff,' but it's delicious. . . . And they fed me avocado with salt, and I was like, 'Avocado with salt?' Because in the Vietnamese community we normally eat avocados with sugar so it was the total opposite of what I'm used to. We're living really close together, cultures were intermarrying, we're best friends, growing up together—there needs to be a Vietnamese-Mexican something."[62]

Lok Siu argues that such Latinx-Asian fusion reflects the changing demographics of the United States, with Asians and Latinx being the fastest-growing immigrant populations. In areas like Orange County, these two populations have historically experienced strong interaction and exchange and continue to do so.[63] Growing up and attending school in Little Saigon, Vietnamese closely interact with first-, second-, and third-generation Mexicans and some Koreans, Taiwanese, Japanese, and Chinese. Little Saigon overlaps with Koreatown in Garden Grove and historic Japanese communities. Little Saigon crosses city borders into Anaheim and Santa Ana, which have large Mexican and Central American neighbors; in the 1980s, the area known as Little Saigon today had a larger Mexican population than Vietnamese. This, Hợp explains, is how he thought of a food truck offering tacos, burritos, and bowls combining the two cuisines, such as Vietnamese chimichurri chicken.[64]

Hợp started the food truck with his childhood friend, Việt. Although both are Vietnamese, they were always called Chinos by their Mexican classmates. "Every day, we ate from the food trucks after school," Việt told a reporter. "I used to follow them around . . . like literally when I was in high school, we would drive all over to try the best tacos."[65] Their love of food brought them success with their food truck, winning multiple awards; for several years in a row, they were voted Orange County's Best Taco and Best Burrito by *OC Weekly*, one of the most popular entertainment newspapers in the area.[66] Their food bridges the multicultural spaces of Orange County: some of their signature dishes are cheeseburger burritos, chorizo fried rice, and sriracha-Tapatio tamarind cheesecake. Their most popular dish is Bolsa Roast Pork, with salsa verde and Vietnamese pork belly. Việt explained in an interview, "My whole goal is to make food that would get a reaction from people. I was always the jokester growing up, always trying to make my grandma or brother and sister burst out laughing. Food is the same way. When people say my food is amazing, it's like a comedian getting laughs."[67]

Dos Chinos's hybrid Vietnamese and Mexican cuisine is a form of culinary multiculturalism that caters to the middle class and those with disposable incomes rather than the immigrant working class. For example, a reviewer on Yelp called the $12 Stoner Burrito "bad ass." One can also enjoy Lobster Elote for $27.50.

Fusion food often claims the assimilation of differences, which marks the coming together of different cultures, migrant collaborations, and cuisines to create something new. The assimilation of fusion cuisine can be contrasted with celebrations of liberal multiculturalism.[68] Multiculturalism based on the discourse of pluralism "asserts that American culture is a democratic terrain to which every constituency has equal access and all are represented, while simultaneously masking the existence of exclusion by recuperating dissent, conflict, and otherness through the promise of inclusion."[69]

These new fusion restaurants rely on celebrating multicultural cosmopolitanism. *Cosmopolitanism* refers to celebrating cultural diversity, including recognizing signs of cultural and transnational differences that are positive evidence of international and global cultural influences.[70] Jennie Germann Molz describes cosmopolitanism as an "adjective reserved for globalized and hybridized places through the multiple mobilities of people, commodities, and cuisines."[71] It refers to the "geography of the world on a plate that allows the curious tourist to travel the world without ever leaving home."[72] In *The $16 Taco*, Pascale Joassart-Marcelli explores San Diego's cosmopolitan food spaces and how they signify increased openness to diversity as a means of destabilizing racism; food provides "a means through which people connect with each other, breaking down stereotypes, and encouraging respect for differences."[73] While this exposes consumers to a wide and endlessly varying selection of foods that are globally linked to different countries and regions, Joassart-Marcelli finds that this optimistic celebration of multiculturalism can mask unequal access and erasure and produce a loss of place, even as people stay.

Just a hundred miles north of San Diego, Little Saigon in Orange County hosts the third-largest Asian American population in the United States. Many of the county's new strip malls and shopping centers have a pan-Asian feel as they draw upon the area's Asian communities, which include Chinese, Korean, Vietnamese, and Japanese populations. The loss of mom-and-pop restaurants in favor of new fusion cuisine creates barriers and inequities for some Vietnamese, making it hard for them to access the community as they once did.

By drawing upon cosmopolitan fusion, restaurants in Little Saigon market themselves to those outside and inside the community, affording higher prices, including many international and second-generation Vietnamese, white, Latinx, and middle-class Asian Americans. For instance, Loan Nguyễn is the creator of The Loop, sited in a strip mall in the heart of Bolsa Avenue in Little Saigon. The Loop sells customized churros with various glazes, dips, and toppings. According to Loan, as told to a reporter, "80 to 90 percent of my customers aren't Asian: we wanted to come up with a dessert that appeals to everybody."[74] Featured in *Cosmopolitan* magazine, Instagrammable desserts like her "mermaid glazed churro which features blueberry glaze and a mermaid sparkle sugar" come at the hefty price of $5 to $8 per churro. To attract the same clientele as places like Dos Chinos and The Loop, some traditional Vietnamese mom-and-pop restaurants have made the transformation to cosmopolitan fusion, adding Korean, Chinese, Taiwanese, and Mexican elements to their menus. The community has also slowly brought contemporary popular chains in Vietnam to Little Saigon, like Phúc Long Coffee & Tea and Trung Nguyên Legend, showing the transnational exchange between the diaspora and the home country and newer waves of higher-capital Vietnamese. This general shift has resulted in non-Vietnamese and new generations of Vietnamese using the space of Little Saigon, with Vietnamese entrepreneurs reorienting it toward their own experiences and outsiders.

Gentrification manifests itself in subtle but pervasive ways throughout cities and suburbs. As the 1.5 generation welcomes a wider audience into Little Saigon and caters to newer generations, they change the service, décor, and marketing to meet the expectations of these customers and, with it, the physical landscape and operational management style of the restaurants. As local businesses of the 1.5 generation cater to a multiethnic clientele rather than exclusively Vietnamese customers, they turn away from the traditional informal economy. For example, Apple Pay and credit cards are more widely used to give more people access to goods and services. Marketing styles also change. Older restaurants in Little Saigon compete for customers by placing advertisements in printed Vietnamese-language newspapers and hanging huge signs visible from the street announcing 50 percent off or "buy one get, one free." The second generation uses its media savvy to advertise discounts to those outside the community via popular social media platforms. These broad media campaigns encouraging different generations and others to visit and invest in their space end up benefiting businesses cross-generationally. As *Los Angeles Times* headlines state: "Little Saigon's Restaurant Scene Revives as Second-Generation Vietnamese Americans Mix It Up" and "The Next Big Thing in Tourism Could Be Little Saigon."[75]

HYPE CULTURE

In an attempt to create distinction through consumption, ethnic gentrifiers rely on an array of social media networks and digital platforms to appeal to

FIGURE 7. Line outside the grand opening of 7 Leaves Café, California (courtesy of Slique Media, Inc.).

trendy Gen Z, millennial, and Gen Alpha audiences.[76] Veblen's *The Theory of the Leisure Class* gives a classic sociological explanation of how people use taste to create status through conspicuous consumption, showing how hype happens.[77] Hype includes aspirational consumption through the marketplace—"status-induced consumerism" as a route of self-expression—so that brands, foods, and goods symbolically communicate social status by equating the possession of a limited edition or scarce materiality with greater self-worth.[78] Millennials and Gen Z are potent economic forces in the United States today, representing 30 percent of total retail sales. Studies show that millennials and Gen Z like sharing experiences with friends and are much more likely than Gen Xers to share their purchases on social media.[79]

Andy Nguyễn, creative director of Rodeo 39 and one of the founding co-owners of Afters Ice Cream, credits much of his success to online platforms and creating moments designed to go viral. His Vietnamese coffee ice cream and jasmine milk tea ice cream were inspired by his most-loved drinks growing up in Little Saigon. He recounted the need for fusion to a content creator:

> Jasmine milk tea is not supposed to be lavender but we're not using that brown color. We're going to make it lavender. Why? Because it looks a lot prettier on camera. We're part of that early Instagram generation and

applying a lot of our lifestyle in hip-hop music and EDM and, making it more
. . . more of a lifestyle and I think that's why it resonated and connected with
people. We took things that people are familiar with, like the donut thing,
people are familiar with donuts and we're giving our take on it. We are the
ones that put the Milky Bun item on the map. We created that thing off of
trying to be a little bit different. We were inspired by a lot of the fusion foods
at the time, though they had the cronut that was popular earlier in 2013. I
think we saw that and were like, "Okay, well, he's mashing up these items and
it's blowing up. This is the time for us to come up with something on our own
on the West Coast."[80]

Andy and longtime friend Scott Nghiêm began the successful chain in 2013.
Their goal with Afters was to add to Orange County's suburban nightlife,
which they found lacking. "There was a need for a late-night dessert place
that's cool and hip . . . like in Los Angeles," Scott told a foodie magazine. "We
used to hang out at all the boba shops, and jasmine milk tea was my go-to
drink. So I thought, can we turn that into an ice cream flavor?"[81]

Inevitably, the younger generation of media-savvy producers change their
neighborhoods when they draw upon and transform their ethnic capital,
such as jasmine milk tea and traditional Vietnamese coffee, into palatable,
cosmopolitan-approved food to attract new clientele: people outside the
community, millennials, Gen X, Gen Z, Gen Alpha, and higher-income
Vietnamese. In appealing to such consumers in this way, the suburbs are
replicating the styles and patterns of large cities. Social media sites promise
the democratization of food culture by enlarging the public sphere to expand
the audience and potential consumer base. Website reviews are critical for
sharing information and allowing ordinary people to give "honest and unfil-
tered opinions" about their food experiences.[82] This democratization of
information has shifted the power of food critique and its ability to influence
what constitutes good taste from the mouths of experts to ordinary consumers, who may well have different life experiences and food expectations.[83]

However, many small businesses are missing from digital platforms, leading to uneven representations, often with material consequences, changing
retail stores' and neighborhoods' aesthetics and composition.[84] The iron law
of upgrading shapes the choices and strategies of entrepreneurs and communities. Sociologists John Logan and Harvey Molotch describe this as the
economic development of neighborhoods pushed to cater to more affluent
residents to support changes in land and "use-values of the better-off at the
expense of the poor." In this case, it becomes necessary "to destroy part of the

neighborhood to save it," prioritizing amenities for more privileged residents.[85] The "community can only be saved by treating it as a commodity," whereby small suburban cities are locked into competition, making communities receptive to revitalization investment deals.[86]

ENTREPRENEURIAL MOBILITY

What are the larger structural forces and psycho-social emotional sources that redirect second- and later-generation Vietnamese back to Little Saigon like the generations before them? For some 1.5 and second generation, reimagining entrepreneurship is a viable economic strategy for economic integration in the current service-dominated economy. Accounts of neoliberalism by David Harvey and others see the rise of entrepreneurial activity as directly related to the informalization of labor and the dismantling of the traditional workplace over the past few decades.[87] Deindustrialization and the creation of the hourglass economy—a sharply divided economy with high-income at the top, an expanding service-dominated low-income at the bottom, and a shrinking middle class in between—have resulted in new challenges. From this, global command centers for finance, tourism, and technology have emerged in New York, Los Angeles, and Chicago.[88]

Entrepreneurial labor, as explained by Brooke Erin Duffy, masks pervasive worker insecurity in return for rationalizing neoliberal workers' investments of time, capital, and labor with the promise of eventual capital or future success.[89] Duffy conceptualizes this aspirational labor as "a mode of uncompensated, independent work propelled by the idea of getting paid to do what you love."[90] Even though individuals pursue the ideals of flexibility and autonomy through entrepreneurship, the rapid growth of independent employment is symptomatic of neoliberal ideologies and practices that shift organizational risks and responsibilities onto individual citizens and workers who then shoulder the burden of health care, training, and other costs that would come as benefits from formal employment.[91]

In the context of this changing economic opportunity structure over the last fifty years, the high cost of living and increased demand to live and work in California have created a land squeeze and escalating prices. Relative to job growth, California has not kept up with the demand for new housing construction, including affordable housing, and is ranked forty-nine out of fifty in per capita housing supply.[92] California gained almost 2.5 million jobs in the last ten years but built fewer than one million housing units, creating an imbalance between housing and job growth. Despite growth in high-paying jobs such as technology, increases in median income, and low employment rates, many workers still cannot keep up with the escalating cost of living in Orange County, where costs are nearly 90 percent higher than the national average.[93] To afford a one-bedroom apartment, a worker must earn around $29 per hour, just under $60,000 per year.[94] Nearly 60 percent of workers in Orange County do not earn enough to afford the median rent for a one-bedroom apartment with a single salary.[95] A worker that makes minimum wage in Orange County can afford to pay $575 monthly rent, but the median market rent for a one bedroom is nearly $1,600.[96]

In 2021, nearly one in three Californians were considering leaving the state because of the lack of affordable housing.[97] One cause of this lack is the high cost of building new housing developments on already overdeveloped, expensive land in locales where cities and local governments have little monetary incentive to build housing. Unlike in the 1950s and 1960s, when state and federal systems paid for the public infrastructure to build the suburbs, local governments today acquire larger revenues from taxes on commercial developments.[98] Some additional reasons for the exorbitant cost of living in the Golden State include single-family zoning laws, limited vacant developable land, cumbersome environmental reviews, and community resistance to new housing.

In this economic climate, new generations of Vietnamese are keeping control of their community through new endeavors in entrepreneurship. For many, this means continuing to invest in restaurants, the most popular type of business for first-generation refugees in Little Saigon.

But what about the mom-and-pop restaurants of the first generation? Finding myself in one such café on a sunny Southern California afternoon, I speak with Phương, a first-generation immigrant who owned a lucrative phở restaurant called Phở Kim Quy or Phở Kimmy for over twenty years. "Why did you decide to open a restaurant?" I ask her. "Well, it's easy. If you were a good cook at home, you can cook here."

Restaurants of the first generation overwhelm the space of Little Saigon with names that illustrate their specialty and the region in which their cuisine or ethnicity is found in Vietnam, such as Bún Chả Hà Nội (a type of grilled pork dish unique to the northern capital), Cơm Tấm Nha Trang (beef/pork rice dish from Nha Trang, a city in central Vietnam), and Triều Châu Restaurant. These names are recognizable to those who speak Vietnamese or are familiar with the culture; such a person would recognize that Triều Châu is a restaurant for food from the Teochew people. Restaurants owned by the second or 1.5 generation, however, have more cosmopolitan names, such as Garlic and Chives and Mama Tiêu's, or fusion-sounding Vietnamese names, such as Silk Noodle. Mama Tiêu's's menu includes a ragu bread bowl topped with cheese; watermelon basil lemonade; and traditional Vietnamese fare like phở and bánh mì. Second-generation restaurants also offer happy-hour bánh mì bites, an amenity unheard-of in traditional mom-and-pop restaurants.

For 1.5 and later generations, Little Saigon is a place of new economic opportunities, ripe for taking advantage of trendy youth and millennials who fetishize food and culture. In 2019, millennials, the largest generation in the United States, surpassed the spending power of baby boomers for the first time.[99] They have a strong preference for convenience, which includes eating at restaurants more than any other generation.[100] As Gen Z is now in the workforce, they are catching up with millennials, spending one-fifth of their income on food. They prefer quick-service, global, and fusion cuisine and rank atmosphere as important.[101] Their foodie adventures are likely to end up online, functioning as inadvertent branding tools.[102] Thus, larger sociopolitical and economic forces, together with the diversification of consumption opportunities available in a service economy, are driving the development of Little Saigon toward an entrepreneurship model for businesspeople with and without advanced degrees and for professionals who choose to leave traditional corporate jobs.

When second-generation Vietnamese engage in entrepreneurial activities, they often reimagine it as expressive or as part of the creative arts. Many of the second and 1.5 generations understand that working in Little Saigon wasn't a choice for their parents; the ethnic economy was, in many ways, their only option. They understand that their parents hoped to push them into jobs in the mainstream economy. For those whose parents pushed for professional jobs, a close link between higher mobility and education was sharply ingrained in them. As one second-generation entrepreneur described to me:

> It goes back to the language problem because for them, the older generation, whatever they picked as their occupation, it was always minimum wage regardless of career path. We have a wider range of salaries and opportunities. We don't have to be minimum wage. It has to do with parents' expectations [when] they push you to become a professional. They don't want you to work hard the way they did. That's why they are working so hard here, so their kids can have a better life and eventually take care of them.

After watching their parents suffer downward mobility upon arrival in the United States, many expressed a strong sense of family obligation and guilt. They expressed the need to repay their parents:

> My parents met after they got out of prison [reeducation camp in Vietnam]. They are older parents. That's the other thing—they were much older, so when they got over here, they didn't have opportunities to go to school or find better jobs, so they were stuck with kinds of jobs like seamstresses, so they emphasized education because they didn't have it either. My mom would bring home stuff from the factory to sew. I remember them dedicating this corner of the house to the sewing machines and staying up all night. After doing sewing for a couple of years, my dad went to work at Taco Bell, then my dad went to work as a cook at two to-go [restaurant] places on Bolsa.

Many of the entrepreneurs I interviewed said they first decided to enter professional careers but later turned to entrepreneurship either because they found their jobs in tech and medicine unsatisfying or because they were laid off in 2007 after the financial crisis. Their jobs in the professional fields were part of the mainstream economy that first-generation parents believed would buffer us from discrimination and provide stability. Sociologists have noted that first-generation Asian parents often encourage their children to pursue education and, in particular, technical fields as a defensive strategy against blocked opportunities and racial discrimination in the US labor market.[103] This rang true for many of my interviewees. As a second-generation Vietnamese lawyer explained to me over lunch, a key reason for entering professional jobs is stability and circumventing discrimination:

> When my mom first came here, she would have to do cherry picking, sewing, *hard, hard* manual labor where they would get paid below minimum wage, long hours. That's why my mom decided to do nails. It's not too bad, and you still make good money.
>
> They didn't talk too much about Vietnam, but every day, my dad would work late, so he would come home around 8 p.m., and we would have dinner. And my mom, anytime that I wasn't doing my homework, or I was goofing off or playing too much, she would say, "You have to work hard because you don't want to end up like your dad." So, sometimes, she would put him down to make me feel like I have to go further. My dad was a construction worker, and she didn't want the same for me. But I totally respected what my dad did.

Working in Little Saigon for many first-generation Vietnamese, in nails or as an entrepreneur, means that monthly income is variable, so many initially hesitate to tell their parents about their entrepreneurial work. One successful entrepreneur said he finally told his parents after he received a request to open a chain in Las Vegas. "I didn't tell our parents that I quit my job until we had three stores. Now that we have all this community support, my mom feels like, 'OK. This is cool.'" Or, as a freelance photographer explained to me: "[M]y mom finally came on board, but it took years. She finally saw that I made it when clients would fly me all over the world to photograph their weddings. She would brag to friends and her clients at the nail salon when I photographed Justin Timberlake. I know, because she has the photographs from wedding magazines at her station that I've done."

Noting a pattern in second-generation entrepreneurship, sociologist Patricia Fernández-Kelly coined the term "expressive entrepreneurship" to designate "the ways in which children of immigrants seek to circumvent labor market uncertainties through arts-driven business ownership."[104] Expressive entrepreneurship takes the form of creative self-employment, such as graffiti artists, bloggers, photographers, designers, etc.[105] The criteria and desires of second-generation entrepreneurs are no different than those of mainstream America: "Their search is not only for continued existence but also for wealth, recognition, and even fame. This path occurs when there is a convergence between (1) generational rises in aspirations, and (2) labor markets perceived by the young to offer limited paths to enact those ambitions."[106]

Entrepreneurship, then, becomes a new mode of labor market integration to circumvent weak labor markets. Children's entrepreneurial success translates into capital for status and well-being for the first generation in the community, many of whom work in unstable, low-wage jobs in Little Saigon.

Economists argue that young adults today have to be employable in labor markets that offer less for them than for previous generations.[107] In fact, millennials are the "first generation to have things worse than their parents."[108] Expressive entrepreneurship fits with the neoliberal idea of enshrining entrepreneurship as based on free choice and individualism. In this telling, the entrepreneur is part of an elite class that "accepts reward and punishment as an outcome of risk calculation."[109] It reaffirms the American myth of bootstrapping: that you can become what you want, and if it doesn't work out, it means you didn't want it enough. In the section above, multiple forces draw back later generations of Vietnamese to entrepreneurship; many are circumventing labor market discrimination and weak labor market opportunities to reinvent opportunities in the community and elsewhere, sometimes leading to displacement.

Other placemakers include Vietnamese entrepreneurs who are reconfiguring the business model of their parents' generation. Thus, while they might still be in the restaurant business, they now serve different food and brand it differently. Or, when a successful business is handed down to children, they often start using digital platforms to expand to a wider audience. Intergenerational entrepreneurship has long been heralded as a means of social mobility for immigrant families.[110] Since the late nineteenth century, immigrant groups and communities in the United States have contributed to ethnic economic niches, as with Italians, Eastern Europeans, Indians, Chinese, and Koreans.[111] However, not all follow the same pattern of small business ownership by generation.[112] Generational differences in entrepreneurship raise questions about the lifespan of ethnic economies such as Little Saigon, of which little is presently known.

Through informal interviews with business owners and formal interviews with the Vietnamese American Chamber of Commerce, I found that many in the 1.5 generation take over the family business or become entrepreneurs themselves in Little Saigon. This is unusual for second-generation immigrants elsewhere in the United States, as children rarely continue in the same business as their parents.[113] Those of the second generation who follow their parents to become entrepreneurs credit the financial and social capital their parents built up as motivation to choose the same industry. Pawan Dhingra shows this pattern in his study of motels in the United States, where the South Asian second generation, who experience racism in the mainstream labor market, often decide to return to their parents' businesses.[114] Most of the 1.5- and second-generation business owners I interviewed had graduated from four-year colleges or universities and majored in finance or computer science, earned an MBA, or attended medical school. Practically all had planned on having a career outside their family business before returning to reimagine Little Saigon.

Many of those I interviewed drew on the logic of gente-fication when describing how they were drawn back to the neighborhood to "seize an economic opportunity" or to try to represent the interests of the cultural community by "giving back" in a way that doesn't always lead to displacement and gentrification. Tâm Nguyễn is president of Advance Beauty College and on the board of the Philanthropic Foundation at California State, Fullerton. He is described as a force for community and entrepreneurial leadership in

Orange County. Tâm explained why he wanted to take over his parents' cosmetology business:

> I didn't have a career path except for the one that my parents wanted. In order to be a good obedient son, I figured that I should just become a doctor. . . . When I finished med school, I knew that I wasn't passionate about medicine. I got the MD for my dad and mom. I handed my degree to them, and I told them I saw an opportunity, I wanted to be in the family business. At first they said no. My parents' shop was not very sophisticated; it was very mom-and-pop. Even though it was the biggest one around at the time, the bar was pretty low; it was an ethnic community that was very mom-and-pop. The business was getting large in numbers but not larger in quality. Instead of doing a residency, I decided to get an MBA and help with the family business to help people in my community.[115]

Tâm expanded his parents' business, and today, two of their cosmetology schools are the largest in California. He estimates they have graduated over fifty thousand nail technicians over the years. The Garden Grove campus provides instruction both in Vietnamese and English, and a third campus opened in November 2015 outside Little Saigon in Laguna Hills. "I broke a boundary for being a male in the beauty industry; I'm an MD and MBA going back into the beauty profession. As a male, it seems like I would be more interested in being a manager of a firm or managing a hospital, except I own a beauty college in my own community." He explained the role of the Vietnamese community in his success: "When you build such a huge network in one industry, it will be able to help future Vietnamese Americans. So, any Vietnamese who came in the '80s, '90s, and 2000s clearly had a family member or someone close to them that was already in the industry." Their business also has a transnational focus that is not generally known; the family has invested in two schools in Hồ Chí Minh City and Sóc Trăng that train Vietnamese in the art of doing nails before immigrating.

People like Tâm challenge the popular belief that children of immigrant business owners generally leave the ethnic enclave and move into the mainstream labor market as they become college-educated and are presented with more job opportunities.[116] These trends do tend to hold overall for US-born Korean, Vietnamese, and Chinese children of entrepreneurial parents.[117] Yet, as my findings illustrate, the generational decline in entrepreneurial proclivity is not the norm in all ethnic communities; in Little Saigon, later generations are returning to revitalize the business district.

Phú Nguyễn provides another example of family entrepreneurship, handing down businesses from one generation to the next by taking over one's parents' successful business. He assists his father, who came to the United States in 1982 with "no English skills," managing Hoa Phát Money Transfer in Westminster. It is the first and largest wire transfer business in the Vietnamese community, with thirty US branches and over one hundred employees in Vietnam. He told the Vietnamese newspaper *Người Việt* that he estimates his family business has helped over five hundred thousand individuals with sending over $3 billion to families in Vietnam.[118] Phú explained to a reporter how his family business has helped the community:

> We sent probably over $3 billion to families in Vietnam. It's hard to quantify, but if you think about foreign aid to a country—and this is not him doing it, he's just a vehicle for them to do it—but I bet the amount sent may be more significant than US foreign aid or the UN or any government. [My father] came from nothing. He couldn't speak English when we arrived. But he was able to build up this business and help his people.[119]

Their office started in Little Saigon as the first US-Vietnam transfer system. Before the formalization of diplomatic ties to Vietnam, the family sent boxes of US merchandise worth a particular dollar amount for receiving families in Vietnam to resell. Phú's father explained how his business originally depended on the trust of the community:

> Back then, there was no such thing as [a] money transferring service between here and Vietnam. My family [in Vietnam] would sell the items from the merchandise that I sent home to them and give cash to the other family. It went both ways. People could give me $500 cash here, and I would send home to my family a package of merchandises worth about $500. My family would sell the merchandises off to get the cash to give to that person's family. Sometimes, my family would make a profit if they happened to sell the merchandises for $600. We used that profit to send more packages home. . . . The first year was slow, but people put more trust in me in the second and third year on. Then I started receiving orders that people didn't bother coming to check the package. They didn't care what was in there. They only need to mail to me asking for packages worth $500, $300, or $200. They sent money; we packed.[120]

Remittances through banks or formal money transfer operations, such as Western Union, are not popular in the Vietnamese community; instead, they use organizations or cash apps, such as Hoa Phát, Anh Minh, and Hong Lan, among others, that offer home delivery courier services in less than twenty-four hours, typically for only 1 percent surcharge.

Tâm and Phú's businesses continue the experience of providing transnational ties to Vietnam and training Vietnamese and others to integrate into the United States economically. Urban geographer Sharon Zukin describes a pattern of Black ownership in Harlem where more educated individuals with college and postgraduate business degrees open stores and create businesses in retail.[121] She finds that services and retail stores that long-term residents and lower-income residents depend on are sometimes eradicated as the social class of the neighborhood changes.[122] The discourse of returning home and giving back to one's community ascribes a value to the entrepreneur regarding what it means to be a good citizen responding to the needs of others and the community at large. This glosses over the gain of social and human capital for the entrepreneur and the logics of capital and power that result in the displacement of lower-income Vietnamese. These examples from the Vietnamese community, like Phú and Tâm, complicate this narrative. In some cases, "giving back" and "helping one's community" are still strategies for consolidating and increasing economic power, but they do not always lead to social displacement.

SUBURBAN BOOSTERISM AND BRANDING

While later generations of Vietnamese are capitalizing on Vietnamese American identity and culture, they are not the only actors involved in the transformation of Little Saigon. Suburban city governments have their own reasons for being invested in selling the city: commercial developments bring in large revenues from taxes. The role of local governments in reimagining the suburbs is crucial, as they are responsible for making important decisions regarding land use, granting permits, policing resident activities, and facilitating local development.[123] However, because suburban cities must compete with one another for growth opportunities, the last fifty to sixty years have left metropolitan institutional terrains in a highly fragmented state.[124]

Boosterism—promotional bombast to improve public perception—is one of the tools that cities use to reach their goals.[125] Perhaps one of the best-known examples of civic boosterism is the selling of the Western frontier by railway companies, entrepreneurs, and chambers of commerce. In the late nineteenth century, city leaders used sunshine and oranges to sell Southern California as the "Land of Sunshine."[126] Today, cities are still enmeshed in strategies to attract and compete for commercial capital investment, including the physical and symbolic reimaging and branding of spaces. Despite the lack of an established district-wide brand identity for Little Saigon, Vietnamese culture and the identity of the local people are clearly expressed along the corridor through historic landmarks, cultural emblems, design, and architecture, as seen in statues of war figures, a small museum of the Republic of Vietnam, and pagoda designs reflecting the architecture of old Saigon.[127] A Westminster city report highlights what they perceive as the need for unified cultural branding as part of their boosterism campaign: "The identity of Little Saigon is visually expressed through its cultural emblems, design, and, in some cases, architecture. Yet a unifying district brand is absent from growing recognition of the area. Creating a strong brand and visual identity is only the first step to raising awareness of Little Saigon and its offerings to the right audiences."[128]

The intended audience for this visual identity is largely outsiders—tourists and non-Vietnamese visitors. The city's emphasis on creating a unifying district brand to enhance the economic desirability of Little Saigon falls into a form of city branding. David Harvey describes this strategy as *urban entrepreneurialism*, a type of governance that encourages economic growth by allowing the private sector to thrive. This contrasts with *urban managerialism*, which focuses on delivering public services. Urban entrepreneurialism describes the shift in the global West in the 1970s, when cities started to become (or function as) commodities for business, focusing on attracting flows of capital and the "competitive conditions of existence of cities."[129]

In the context of place-marketing practices and the reimaging of Little Saigon, city branding is a strategic tool to elevate a space's appeal to businesses, tourists, and residents.[130] As a source of economic, political, and community development, it "communicates a city's competitive advantage, the quality of the place, its history, lifestyle and culture."[131] With globalization and the movement of capital, people, and goods, cities compete not only to become tourist destinations but also to attract financial investors, members of the workforce, and residents.[132] This manifests in how cities within a region are ranked and marketed when a blueprint for investment is created. From this perspective, in 2021 the City of Westminster rated Little Saigon as "unappealing and inconvenient" but also "unique and special":

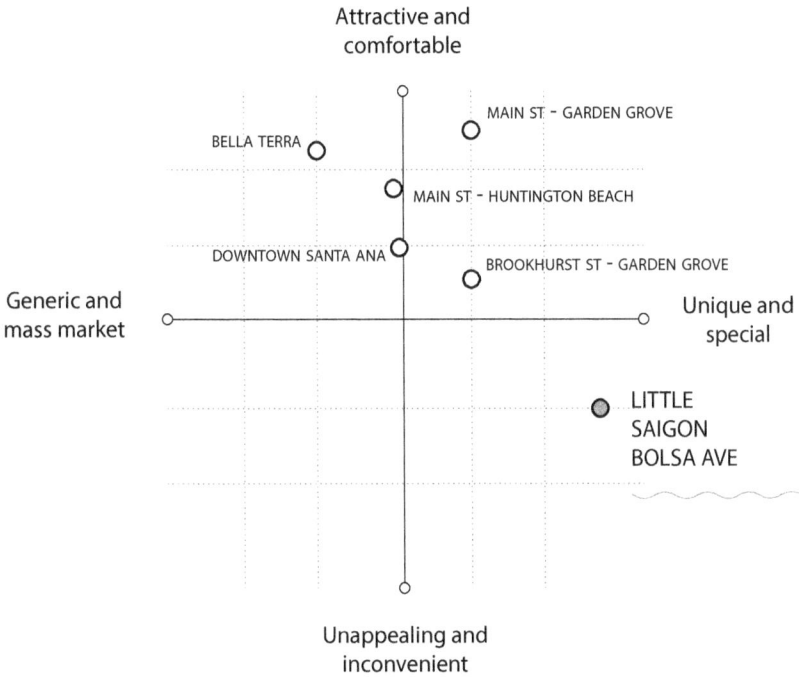

Attractive and
comfortable

MAIN ST – GARDEN GROVE

BELLA TERRA

MAIN ST – HUNTINGTON BEACH

DOWNTOWN SANTA ANA

BROOKHURST ST – GARDEN GROVE

Generic and
mass market

Unique and
special

LITTLE
SAIGON
BOLSA AVE

Unappealing and
inconvenient

FIGURE 8. Little Saigon Blueprint for Development, City of Westminster, California (staff report meeting, 2021).

The reality is that customers in the region have a wide range of destinations to select from when choosing where to shop, dine, and entertain. In particular, other commercial districts, downtowns, and retail destinations in the region have walkable environments with strong place qualities, including outdoor spaces for gathering and dining, as well as newer retail concepts and tenants that appeal to younger customers today. In order to remain competitive, Little Saigon on Bolsa Avenue will need to elevate its niche mix of small and local restaurants and retailers and create new opportunities for these businesses to better reach the customer base through marketing, branding, and physical space enhancements that impact initial impressions, customer dwell time, and return visits.[133]

The ideologies underlying city development form the basis for determining a locale's market positioning and ranking. Set up in competition with one another for scarce resources, each suburban city is rewarded according to its position on a hierarchy related to how it enacts policies related to factors such as walkability, public parks, and air quality. In Little Saigon, this intersuburban city competition for resources occurs in the larger context of US deindustrialization and economic restructuring, which began in the 1970s. A confluence of structural economic changes increased the need and intensity of city marketing and place branding. This includes rapid developments in transport and telecommunication technologies alongside liberalization policies that loosened federal control on capital mobility, including the growth of service- and knowledge-based industries.[134] Across the globe and the United States, this "caused an intensification of competition between regions and cities which are now more directly dependent on firms for jobs, taxes, and development."[135]

Strategies of community development that focus on branding are considerably more affordable for smaller suburban cities than public infrastructure investments: "Tourism and marketing were ways to make a 'fast buck,' requiring little expenditure, political debate, or legislation up front."[136]

"Unappealing and Inconvenient" or "Unique and Special"?

Little Saigon is spread out across disparate cities and includes different governing agencies, which can lead to conflict over claims of space. One example is the tension over hosting the annual Tết festival and parade celebrating the Lunar New Year. It is Little Saigon's most lucrative Vietnamese cultural event. In the span of three days, between two and three hundred thousand people descend on Little Saigon, with most visitors being part of the Vietnamese diaspora who now live throughout the United States and abroad.[137] The different suburban cities vie for these visitors through the annual Tết parade and festivals they offer. Westminster's annual Tết parade and festival attract nearly seventy thousand people each year.[138] In 2019, two thousand people marched down Bolsa Avenue wearing áo dài, greeting the crowd and each other in Vietnamese and English. The following day, in Garden Grove, four hundred people walked along Westminster Boulevard, marching with veterans or riding in convertibles and military jeeps. Nearby, the same weekend, a third Tết parade took place in Costa Mesa.[139] Garden Grove parade organizers said they are not competing with the Westminster parade. Rather, city councilors argued to a news reporter, "it's good for local businesses and to boost the city's image."[140] The annual Tết Festival at the Orange County Fairgrounds has been held since 1985, hosted by the Union of Vietnamese Student Associations. The festival includes arts and crafts, a cultural village, traditional Vietnamese performances, a beauty pageant, and carnival rides. Since the early 2010s, competing festivals have appeared in the nearby cities of Fountain Valley and

Garden Grove. The newer festival in Fountain Valley attracted 120,000 visitors in its first year, with revenue from sponsorships and vendor sales totaling about $300,000 in three days. Transnational tourism from Vietnam and the Vietnam diaspora shows how cities and their development processes drive and support suburban boosterism. Harvey and other scholars discuss this type of cultural regeneration and branding embedded in tourism as a strategic tool that cities employ to further suburban boosterism.[141]

Place marketing and branding activities are not only geared toward external visitors and transnational Vietnamese. Often, such activities are also directed at the local population to "create a sense of social solidarity, civic pride and loyalty to place and even . . . provide a mental refuge in a world that capital treats as more and more place-less."[142] This "mobilization of spectacle" is often "a subtle form of socialization to convince local people, many of whom will be disadvantaged and potentially disaffected, that they are important cogs in a successful community and that all sorts of 'good things' are really being done on their behalf."[143]

However, attempts by city developers to brand the area or create a unified visual identity have been met with local resistance. Little Saigon is also a site of struggle and contention over what type of branding model should be prioritized. For instance, in the mid-1990s, when a developer proposed building a pedestrian bridge named "Harmony" in the heart of Little Saigon as a symbolic landmark of the enclave, the community protested. They feared its Chinese-inspired design would destroy Little Saigon's Vietnamese character. "We don't want for our beloved Little Saigon to be turned into a Chinatown. The architecture of the proposed bridge is in the style and characteristic of Chinese. The Vietnamese have our own culture, our own architecture. We want this to stay as Little Saigon for the benefit of all who come here," explained Mai Công in the *Los Angeles Times*.[144] Mai, the founder of a social service organization in Little Saigon, and her husband formed the Ad Hoc Committee to Safeguard Little Saigon, a two-hundred-member committee opposed to building the Harmony bridge because of its design.

The proposed bridge included a thirty-foot-wide, five-hundred-foot-long structure joining the Asian Garden Mall to the Asian Village shopping center, two attractions on Bolsa Avenue held by Bridgecreek Development. Frank Jao, the "Godfather" of Little Saigon and owner of Bridgecreek Development, developed over one-third of Little Saigon. As a writer in the *Người Việt* newspaper said, "If we take away all the buildings and office spaces he built, we wouldn't have what we call Little Saigon. Little Saigon is basically a big master plan of real estate. He was the executor of that plan."[145] In 1979, Jao started a commercial empire one development at a time, beginning with the Far East Plaza. Within eight years, he owned at least half of the twelve biggest shopping plazas in Little Saigon.[146] His largest project, however, was centered on Bolsa Avenue: the Asian Garden Mall, known as Phước Lộc Thọ. When protesters rejected the artists' Chinese-style rendering of the Harmony bridge—pointing out that, among other design elements, Vietnamese temple roofs are red, not green—Frank Jao's response was: "All these people have done so far is to attack on the racial divisiveness issue and throw a lot of misrepresentation into the project . . . misleading the public by using radio, television and printed material."[147]

Other moments of contestation between Jao, an ethnic Chinese Vietnamese refugee, and the community included Jao's desire to rename the district "Asian Town" to attract more diverse visitors. This was dropped amid community protests at City Hall and elsewhere by residents intent on maintaining a visible Vietnamese brand. In the end, dreading acrimonious protesters, Jao did not complete the $3 million proposed bridge. In his defense, the mayor of Westminster, Charles Smith, praised the bridge as a symbol "that would have helped promote Little Saigon as a tourist destination."[148] As a result of the controversy, the city created its first design standards manual, codifying Little Saigon's architecture as part of its branding by enshrining an orientalist architectural design style in official city codes: "The design theme shall incorporate architectural elements similar to those found on buildings constructed in Vietnam in the early 1900s in the French Colonial Tradition or follow a traditional Chinese architectural theme because this style of architecture is used on many religious buildings in Vietnam."[149]

As a strategy to generate an influx of cash to revive their economies, the suburban city governments of Little Saigon actively choose to brand themselves in terms of architectural design as a form of place marketing, with the expectation that the city's cultural resources will attract tourists.[150] These examples reveal how various stakeholders—suburban city governments, residents, and developers—contest definitions and meanings of placemaking based on their own visions of Little Saigon.

CONCLUSION

The complex interplay of food gentrification and structural incentives for Vietnamese entrepreneurship, and the competing interests of suburban city governments in Little Saigon, indicate a community that is changing. At the same time, food is becoming a cultural and creative space for 1.5- and second-generation Vietnamese to define their cultural and racial positions internally and within the US population at large. Emerging fusion foods with roots in Vietnamese cuisine convey the heterogeneous, multiple, and dynamic histories of Vietnamese American identities. Refugees in Little Saigon "perform citizenship in their own ways by creating an ethnic culinary economy that allows them to feel like citizens in their community where they can work, cook, consume, eat, chat, and associate with others without feeling like racialized foreigners."[151] Vietnamese-run doctors' offices, real estate firms, tax preparation services, hair salons, supermarkets, and restaurants provide social and economic citizenship that empower Vietnamese materially and affectively, regardless of generation, even though Vietnamese-run businesses are no longer necessarily for all local Vietnamese.

This chapter also examined the structural incentives of local suburban city governments to brand and market Vietnamese cultural identity to appeal to non-Vietnamese and younger, upper-income Vietnamese Americans. In an effort to enhance city resources, politicians and local suburban city governments often capitalize and compete, commodifying Vietnamese cultural identity in their physical space, ignoring the fact that these place-branding practices, "targeted to visitors and gentrifiers, may exclude those for whom the symbols are most meaningful."[152] Thus, this chapter heeds the call of recent scholars to take race and ethnicity seriously in gentrification research since gentrification is closely bound to struggles for racial justice.

Some of the new Vietnamese-owned businesses by the 1.5 and second generation replicate a pattern that some call "home-grown gentrification" or "self-gentrification."[153] Many of these businesses are transforming the area, catering to a younger, more upwardly mobile Vietnamese and non-Vietnamese clientele, consequently excluding other Vietnamese. At the same time, these gentrifiers show a more direct effort to maintain their neighborhood's culture, but this redevelopment can contribute to further gentrification due to their class position and role as investors.[154] Historian George Sánchez argues that this form of gentrification may be "one stage in the more traditional process of gentrification, in which a new [Vietnamese] population are intermediaries before a white influx, with longtime residents still vulnerable to being priced out."[155] In this analysis, gentrifiers act as middlemen that set up the foundation for top-down gentrification and displace poor Vietnamese from their communities while giving way to racial and class change.[156]

It is not clear what will happen next in Little Saigon. Another possibility is reinvestment, displacement, and class-based polarization where immigrants are themselves among the gentrifiers. In this model, the community is upgraded by new or returning upper-class Vietnamese, and their children. DeVerteuil describes how Little Havana is being gentrified by returning Cuban immigrants who came to Miami in the 1950s and 1960s and their offspring, and some direct overseas investment from Cuba itself.[157] Little Havana is experiencing renewed investment that has little do with incoming whites. This is also the same for Los Angeles's Koreatown, where gentrification is intergenerational and transnational, including new build and planned housing financed by wealthy Koreans. Placemaking often generates economic capital for those who already have wealth without acknowledging the problematic processes of erasure, displacement, and destruction that some development brings.[158]

In response to the rising cost of living and housing, the business district is transforming from within. This chapter introduced the concept of ethnic gentrifier to explain the complicated relationship between some new models of ownership for later generations of Vietnamese. Little Saigon is increasingly depending on the business models of the 1.5 generation and the children of refugees. Some third, second, and 1.5 generations return to Little Saigon to ease their own assimilation process, given institutional economic constraints. They've created an ambiance that attracts consumers seeking an authentic experience through the omnivorous appropriation of Little Saigon for its restaurants, markets, and stores. At the same time, second-generation youths are asserting their right of presence by actively creating unique spaces of cultural consumption. By selling the city, Little Saigon's transformation to something other than a haven for anticommunist refugees is being forged by the children of refugees. Ethnic gentrifiers illuminate class tensions as they and other upwardly mobile Vietnamese assert their desire to stay in the community while lower-income Vietnamese experience community change that can result in displacement and removal.

One of the drivers of gentrification and displacement—ethnic and otherwise—is the cost of living in California. Since the formation of Little Saigon, the cost of living in California has increased dramatically, second only to Hawaii in the United States.[159] The next chapter examines the complex ways housing insecurity exists in the suburbs. In 91 percent of US counties, a full-time minimum-wage worker cannot afford a two-bedroom rental home; this is especially true in Orange County, where it would require an hourly wage of $44.69.[160] Like most of suburbia in America, more than 70 percent of Little Saigon is zoned for single-family residential housing, meaning only stand-alone houses designed for one household can be built. In Orange County, the vacancy rate for rental housing was 2 percent in 2021.[161] What do people do amid housing scarcity? How do Vietnamese in Little Saigon manage their right to a home with rising living costs? How are community activists mobilizing to fight for rent control in one of the most expensive counties in America when only a handful of states across the United States allow for rent control? In chapter 2, I delve into community strategies to countervail housing insecurity and the ways in which cross-racial and intergenerational coalition building is fighting for a right to home.

TWO

The Right to Home

I REMEMBER RECEIVING THE CALL on my cell phone on an early evening in 2011 as I was settling in at my desk to begin reading for the next day's seminar. "Con," my dad began, "we need $12,000." My mouth opened wide with surprise. "For what?" I asked. My father, in the twenty-three years of my life, had never once asked me for money. "The house payment is due," he said. "But how can it be that much? Can you have the business help?" I asked. My dad was an immigrant entrepreneur, running a small printing shop, and he often went back and forth between the shop and our house to pay bills in Little Saigon. "The business isn't doing well."

My dad had used the house as collateral for ten years, drawing on the home equity to pay for our basic needs and cover the monthly expenses needed to keep the family business afloat; my siblings and I knew nothing about this. For people with equity in their homes, a home equity line of credit amounts to an open checkbook. After the draw period, or the time you have to use the available credit, expires, borrowers enter a repayment period where they have to pay both interest and principal and can no longer draw on credit. The massive risk of taking out home equity loans is that your house will be foreclosed if you can't repay the loan when it comes due. I was a graduate student on a scant salary with little savings. I racked my brain, thinking of anything I had of value to sell—and came up empty. Within four months, we lost the house and closed the business. My parents were first-time homeowners, and the loss of the 1,300-square-foot house didn't just displace my parents and two brothers; it displaced my adult half-brother from the sunroom that had become his bedroom, my adult cousin from Vietnam who had a bedroom in the converted garage, and the college student renting my childhood bedroom. My dad went to live with my cousin in Anaheim, and everyone else scattered.

I quickly learned that, like many other families across America, the financial crisis of 2007 had had a profound effect on my family's ability to pay their bills. The crisis, which began years earlier with predatory lending (including cheap credit and lax lending standards), fueled a housing bubble.[1] The roots of the crisis included "the rush to lend money to homebuyers without regard for their ability to repay, including these new types of non-traditional mortgages, so-called NINJA mortgages (no income, no job, and no assets)."[2] Thus, in the early 2000s, the mortgage market expanded to those with low credit scores and homeowners who wanted to take out a second lien on their home or a home equity line of credit. The crisis led to the estimated foreclosure and loss of nine million homes for more than fourteen million Americans.[3] The resulting crisis created economic stagnation, saw family savings erode, home values plunge, and cities declare bankruptcy, while the ensuing recession created high levels of unemployment and left global markets in crisis. Unequal opportunity to rebuild wealth since the crisis has led to widening economic disparities.[4] The racial wealth gap, in other words, is now on track to compound over time.[5] My family was not only losing our home, but also our community. That community is Little Saigon.

I flew home from school in New Jersey to be with my dad in Anaheim as he figured out what to do after being forced to move. I had remembered my cousin's home being large with a pool on a tree-lined track. This time, it felt different. I entered the side gate of the driveway that led to the backyard, passed the garbage and recycling cans, and went through an unlocked white steel security door into the garage. But it was no longer a garage. It was now three bedrooms and a laundry room. There were no windows. A transparent blue curtain hid the washer and dryer. This laundry room was to the side of my dad's room. His room was narrow and looked oddly shaped, as if in cartoon-exaggerated proportions. The drywall did not touch the ceiling, so I could hear the clothes dryer and a TV playing in another room. The fan was running to drown out the noise and to cool his room, which felt warm. He sat on the twin bed, the only place to sit in the room, while I stood. The bold pink- and orange-flowered wallpaper cast a pink tinge on our skin. My dad's clothes and belongings were stacked in piles next to the bed. A small black mini-fridge was next to his bed, and the room was crammed with the fan, framed photos of us as kids, a photo of my grandmother, and a small bunch of bananas. My framed college diploma lay in one of the stacks on the floor. Usually, tenants pay $400 a month, including utilities and kitchen privileges, to rent a room in this garage-turned-home. Two Vietnamese college students, a male and a female, rent out the other rooms in the garage.

Many Vietnamese, like my father, rent small rooms in single-family tract houses and mobile homes in Little Saigon. No database exists that details the number of these shared spaces, but they are part of an established underground economy, an "informal network oiled by convenience, constant address changes, and cash with no contracts."[6] They are a means for those with few resources to find housing, a way for homeowners and subletters to pay their mortgages or other expenses, and a mutual support system for recent Vietnamese immigrants who financially pool resources as a down payment on the American dream. Rooms for rent, or phòng cho thuê, are advertised in the classified section of Vietnamese newspapers and range from $400 for shared rooms and makeshift garage spaces like my dad's to $1,500 for a one-bedroom accessory dwelling unit (ADU) or single rooms with private bathrooms and patios.

The rising cost of living and a housing shortage are not unique to Little Saigon; they affect people living in all kinds of households throughout the country. As researchers at UC Berkeley have shown, this crisis has deep roots:

> Over the past half-century, US households, especially renters, have seen a dramatic shift in their budgets. Rents have risen, incomes have not kept pace, and, as a result, renter households are spending a growing portion of their incomes on shelter. The share of renters who are rent-burdened—paying more than 30 percent of their income on rent—rose from less than a quarter in 1960 to nearly half in 2016. Even more striking, the share of renter households that are severely rent-burdened—paying more than half of their income on rent—rose from 13 to 26 percent during this period.[7]

Rising rent burdens result from a mismatch between income and rent growth, not just from rising rents.[8] This means many renters are paying a greater proportion of their income on rent in the 2020s than in earlier decades. As a result, when working-class households spend more than 50 percent of their income on rent, they might be left with $400 or less a month to pay for other family necessities such as food, health care, clothing, and transportation.[9] In Westminster, "74 percent of low- and moderate-income households experience a cost burden of spending more than 30 percent of household income on housing, and 42 percent face a severe cost burden of spending more than 50 percent of household income on housing."[10] Clearly, such cost and rent burdens make a significant difference in both short- and long-term health and well-being.[11] The creation of the informal rental market is fueled by weak federal, state, and local support for affordable housing and by the structural constraints that designate suburbia for single-family units.

Sharing housing legally and illegally in Little Saigon is one way renters mitigate the effects of rising rent burdens. The need for an informal rental economy goes well beyond personal choice or market forces. It is reinforced and buttressed by exclusionary local laws—that is, land-use laws and regulations that limit who can live in a given locale based on traits such as income, ethnicity, or race. Some of these exclusionary policies are found in what urban planners call the "arsenal of exclusion and inclusion."[12] Who gets to live where? And how do human-made design choices create inequality? These weapons include policies, practices, and physical artifacts that grant or restrict access to public spaces. Many of these laws are relics established more than a century ago, such as suburban zoning ordinances that privilege the nuclear family. Other weapons that should be denaturalized or critically understood are eminent domain, racial steering, and seemingly benevolent weapons like "no loitering" signs and cul-de-sacs that create exclusive suburbs. The politics of zoning is a form of public land-use regulation that has created a zoning straitjacket, freezing the public imagination of American neighborhoods into an idealized vision of single-family detached homes.[13]

Exclusionary social policies that control land use are further exacerbated by the fact that suburban municipalities designate the majority of land for the most expensive type of housing, *single-family*, while making it illegal in those zones to build more affordable housing such as duplexes, townhomes, mobile homes, apartments, or single-room occupancy units (SROs). As of 2022, 66 percent of Orange County neighborhoods are zoned for single-family housing and do not allow more high-density buildings to be built.[14] Little Saigon is more restrictive than many other parts of the county, with Garden Grove and Westminster reserving 76 percent of their land for single-family zoning and Santa Ana reserving 72 percent.[15] American cities first used such zoning practices in 1916; Berkeley, California, and New York City implemented zoning codes as a racist way to control Blacks and unwanted immigrants during the industrial building boom, such as the Chinese in Berkeley and Eastern European Jews in New York City.[16] Zoning codes were popularized on a national scale in the 1920s as part of an overt effort to segregate land and housing by race,[17] with state governments authorizing every city in a metropolitan area to adopt its own zoning and development policies.[18]

Anti-Asian and anti-immigrant sentiments have long been enshrined in California's housing policies. Berkeley ordinances introduced the first single-family zoning district in the United States, banning apartments and industry in areas deemed particularly suitable for residential use by whites. Charles Henry Cheney, a framer of Berkeley's 1916 zoning ordinance, didn't hide his reason for excluding certain types of businesses from residential neighborhoods: he targeted Chinese immigrants, racializing laundries as fire risks.[19] Anti-Chinese and anti-immigrant sentiments manifested in antilaundry legislation in the nineteenth century that included ordinances that targeted the industry in various ways, such as zoning policies to force laundries from white neighborhoods, taxes on laundries, and prohibiting drying racks on roofs, among other colorblind policies.[20] In a similar vein, a Berkeley city attorney characterized Berkeley's zoning proposal as part of a broader Californian tradition of segregating "heathen Chinese."[21] Los Angeles approved the country's first zoning ordinance in 1908 to "protect residential areas from industrial nuisances," meaning working-class immigrants of color.[22] Exclusionary zoning "legitimized the idea that upper- and middle-class white children should not come in contact with poor, immigrant, or Black culture."[23]

By the end of the 1920s, single-family zoning was becoming the norm with the help of politicians such as soon-to-be US president Herbert Hoover and legal cases such as *Village of Euclid v. Ambler Realty Company*. The 1926 breakthrough Supreme Court case from Ohio codified a racialized system of zoning on the belief that apartments are "mere parasite[s], constructed in order to take advantage of the open spaces and attractive surroundings created by the residential character of the district."[24]

The idea that an apartment is parasitic is enshrined in suburban land-use codes that privilege the single-family home as the suburban ideal. In Westminster city code, for example, that sounds like: "Maximum building height: 2 stories not to exceed 35 feet"; "Maximum Lot Coverage: 40 feet"; "Setbacks (Front Yard): Minimum 50 feet from the centerline of the street."[25] Zoning ordinances that limit the supply of higher-density housing are now broadly recognized as preventing the production of affordable housing and sustaining racial and economic exclusion and segregation. Not surprisingly, jurisdictions with a larger percentage of land zoned for single-family housing are more likely to have higher housing costs.[26] The extent of political opposition to non-single-family housing developments typically signifies higher housing costs, longer waits for permits, and a decreased likelihood of zoning

reform.[27] Rapidly gentrifying, suburban Little Saigon is home to such seemingly mundane land-use zoning ordinances that severely limit high-density
housing.

   This chapter explores what housing insecurity looks like in suburban Little
Saigon and various strategies organizers use to help stabilize housing. I explore
how housing insecurity is intimately tied to social policies such as single-
family zoning and antiquated occupancy codes that regulate the number and
relation of people allowed to share a home. Suburban communities continue
to be built upon policies designed with an assumption of single-family homes
inhabited by white American nuclear households with a female housewife, a
male breadwinner, and their children.[28] Vietnamese suburban refugees subvert that image and are remaking suburban life. What strategies are used by
community grassroots organizers, in conjunction with residents, to remake
racist and classist practices? In this chapter, I focus on one short-term means
of stopping displacement—rent control—and the strategies community
organizers used to win the fight for rent control in Orange County's Santa
Ana. Housing justice scholars argue that while scholarship often prioritizes
policy advocacy intended to pressure those in power, significant ideas of housing justice emerge from the bottom up in such sites of struggle.[29]

THE INVISIBLE RENTAL MARKET IN LITTLE SAIGON

I interview Phương, who tells me it is extremely hard to find a place to live in
Orange County for herself, her husband, and their two teenage children.
They currently rent a converted garage in Garden Grove. Bedsheets divide
the space into bedrooms and a kitchen with a hot plate, a full-sized refrigera-
tor, and a small table with four chairs. It is cheerfully decorated. As has
become increasingly common, Phương's family has turned the side driveway,
where one often finds a parked RV, into a garden with succulents and hanging plants. Elsewhere, this space might be converted into concrete gardens,
extra parking spaces, or the site of a legally permitted ADU. Although RVs
are allowed to be parked on driveways, they are not allowed to be residences.
Nonetheless, there is a growing informal cottage industry of households living in RVs full-time, though the practice remains somewhat hidden from
public view (and the law) when parked off-street.[30] RV living provides semi-
permanent housing and legal ownership, but it is increasingly criminalized
in public spaces.[31] Since 2021, only two of thirty-four cities in Orange County

allow RV or "oversized vehicle" parking on the street. This loss of an affordable housing alternative, so restricted by suburban zoning, has only exasperated the affordable housing crisis. The difficulty of finding a house or apartment is endemic in Little Saigon and most of Orange County. In 2022, fewer than 3 percent of housing units were vacant in Westminster, Santa Ana, and Garden Grove.

After seven years of waiting, Phương finally received notice that her family would receive a Section 8 housing voucher. Named after Section 8 of the Federal Housing Act, the Housing Choice Voucher Program is the country's biggest housing assistance program, supporting more than two million families in the private rental market.[32] The program started in the 1970s as an alternative to public housing. Unfortunately, its budget is insufficient to cover all who require assistance, leaving people to wait years before receiving a voucher—and knowing the whole time they may never reach the top of the list.[33] The vouchers permit tenants to pay just 30 percent of their income for rent, with federal funding paying the rest.[34] The vouchers can be used for either public housing or a privately owned residence advertised at or below the Fair Market Rent price.[35]

As ecstatic as Phương's family was when she received notice that their turn had finally come for a housing voucher, she tried to hold back her excitement because she knew they still faced two hurdles: In the midst of a housing shortage, could she find an apartment near Little Saigon that fell within the price range allowed by the voucher? And could she persuade a landlord to accept her family? In many states, source of income (SOI), including receiving public assistance such as a Section 8 voucher, is a protected category under the Fair Housing Act, making it illegal for rental property owners to discriminate against an applicant or deny an application just because they have a housing voucher.[36] SOI is a protected category in California since 2020.[37] However, property owners, landlords, and leasing agents continue to discriminate against renters based on their source of income, race, gender, familial status, age, and other protected categories.[38]

To make matters worse, Phương and her husband knew they only had sixty days to find housing before the voucher expired. Section 8 vouchers offer the recipient two to four months to find a place to live, frequently expiring before people can find housing. In Orange County, it is estimated that nearly one-third of Section 8 vouchers go unused.[39] She called me eagerly when she found a place. It is in a new housing development in Westminster. The location is perfect, she zealously explained, and close enough to her sons' current schools. The county assessor determined the rental value of the apartment to be $1,800, and the owner agreed to accept her voucher (although, of course, legally, he had to).[40] Based on her family's income, the government would pay $1,400, and Phương and her family would pay the remaining $400. Despite agreeing to this, the landlord later decided the rent should be $2,100. Understandably, Phương was upset but decided they'd find a way to pay the additional $300 to the landlord under the table by having her younger brother come to live with them, even though it's prohibited and being caught might mean losing the voucher.[41] The risk is worth it to them: "The market is too expensive. It is so hard to find a place and we only have one month left to find something close to the boys' schools before it expires."

The decline in affordable housing for Americans has not resulted in increased federal support. More than two-thirds of renter households who are cost-burdened in the United States do not receive any benefits from federal housing programs. In 2019, only 10 percent of eligible households nationwide received a Section 8 voucher.[42] High rents and low vacancy rates exacerbate the long waiting lists for housing aid. The Orange County Housing Authority manages approximately ten thousand active Section 8 housing vouchers.[43] Despite high need, the waiting list is closed in all Orange County cities. It was last open in February 2023, 2022, and 2005. In 2017, the waitlist for housing vouchers was over forty thousand.[44] Across the nation, wait times range from two to eight years; for example, in Indianapolis, the average wait time is five years, and in Wichita, Texas, two years.[45]

The US federal government provides funding for Section 8, but it puts much of the onus for supplying affordable housing on local housing authorities. The Orange County Housing Authority, located in the tenth most expensive place to live in the United States, does not offer site-based public housing; rather, it relies on an insufficient number of vouchers for private market housing that do not cover the need, complicated by the fact that not all cities in the county offer the same programs. Within Little Saigon, the city of Westminster offers 213 affordable housing units in twelve complexes, most with waitlists.[46] Midway City, with a population that is 47 percent housing-cost-burdened, has only two subsidized apartment buildings, both for specific populations: one for senior citizens, with a four-year waitlist, and the other with thirty units that are designated for unhoused persons.[47] Making it more difficult for renters, most affordable housing policies favor homeowners over renters; federal expenditures on housing programs support more mortgage-interest tax deductions on homes than project-based rental assistance or public housing funds for rent-burdened renters or tenants.[48] These structural failures of federal and local support for the housing insecure help create the necessity to rent rooms.

DISMANTLING SUBURBAN ZONING

Despite over 70 percent of the land in Little Saigon's neighborhoods being zoned for single-family homes and designed in the traditional tree-lined suburban manner, Little Saigon defies the suburban stereotype of nuclear home-owning families: it is primarily home to renters. To afford to remain in the area, many Vietnamese Americans invest in homes near Little Saigon and remodel them into room rentals. Renting rooms, both legally and illegally, is quite unlike renting apartments: there are no credit checks and no contracts. I was told by a renter, "You make a promise, and they make a promise. That's it." The 2020 US Census estimates that the number of renter-occupied units ranges from 48 percent in Garden Grove to 70 percent in Midway City—and this just includes those renting aboveboard. In Little Saigon, the actual number of renters is much higher, given the informality and temporality of room-rental living arrangements.

While renting private rooms in Little Saigon is often done illegally as an affordability measure, most forms of more affordable housing—such as apartments, duplexes, and single-room occupancies (or SROs, a private furnished bedroom with shared bathroom and kitchen facilities)—are often limited or outright prohibited in most residential zones in suburbia. Yet SROs fill a large need in Little Saigon. Historian Paul Groth explores their long and rich social history in the United States as a form of permanent housing. He points out that in 1990 more people in the United States lived in single-room rentals or hotels than in public housing.[49] The research shows how, historically, in the early nineteenth century, SROs were home to people of many classes, ranging from wealthy families in New York City living in palatial hotels to middle-class families who enjoyed the domestic convenience and easy access to employment. SROs also appealed to young adults who migrated to cities for work opportunities and lived in rooming houses designated for single men or women, migratory laborers and their families, and others in need of an inexpensive place to stay.

Today, SROs and their occupants are largely culturally invisible; they tend to be ignored and overlooked in development plans or framed as deviant. Yet, between 2001 and 2014, San Francisco had a 55 percent increase in families living in SROs, with nearly 40 percent housing four or more people in one unit.[50] They serve an important role in immigrant communities and ethnic enclaves such as Chinatown. Scholarly and public misconceptions about SROs still see SROs as crisis housing, only for the unhoused, disabled, elderly, and drug-addicted.[51] With the suburban single family as the codified cultural norm in the American imagination, the history of single rooms has largely been erased by sociologists and planners who seem to ignore the activism of SRO tenants fighting to maintain their rights to home.[52] Ironically, in places like San Francisco, tech workers and students are displacing many families from SROs as they are flipped for higher rents;[53] many of those displaced are Asian American immigrants and families.[54] In Santa Ana, renting a room, or what we might understand as an SRO, to a family member is considered a business, and homeowners "must apply for a fee-exempt family member rental license" with the city and show that the rents received do not surpass the expense of maintaining their home. The reality is, few know these rules and very few follow them.[55]

Another way of dismantling restrictive suburban single-family zoning is the California statewide initiative legalizing accessory dwelling units (ADUs) in single-family residential zones. Colloquially known as casitas, backyard bungalows, granny houses, or in-law flats, they are a strategy that enables more affordable housing and more income for landlords. California passed a law in 2020 that allows ADUs to be built in single-family zoned areas, superseding local municipal restrictions. Before this legalization of ADUs, they were used widely in Little Saigon, but the fragility of that use was clearly articulated to me by a Vietnamese realtor: "You cannot convert a garage into a living area most of the time. Most of the cities overlook this. They know the reality, so most cities don't enforce code. This is what I always tell Vietnamese homeowners in Orange County or in any county when you convert the garage into a living area: be nice to your neighbors. Because if your neighbor complains to the city, the city is forced to send an inspector to your house. So be nice to your neighbor, and don't park on their side of the street."

Given the recent ADU changes, garages can now legally be converted into an ADU across the state and get their own distinct address. As discussed later, renters in covertly converted spaces or who rent a room often do not have an address, which is necessary to help attain residency.[56] And most city ordinances regarding ADUs in Little Saigon do not use language that limits who constitutes a family for the purposes of living together, a problem also discussed later.[57]

While ADUs will help provide more affordable housing, they can only do so much. The reality is that with only a small proportion of qualified families managing to receive government housing assistance at the federal or local levels, the United States primarily relies on the private rental market to house low-income persons, leaving the landlord-tenant relationship at the crux of many tenant struggles. As we'll explore in the next section, tenant-landlord relations can be straightforward or complex in the informal economy of room shares and room rentals for international students, recent Vietnamese immigrants, elderly seniors on fixed incomes, college-educated millennials who don't make enough to rent their own apartment, and people like my dad who have ties to the community and have suffered financial loss.

CLASHING RENTER AND LANDLORD PERSPECTIVES

I meet Kim at her brother's dance studio in Little Saigon, a popular spot for ballroom dancing and karaoke. Kim arrived in the United States in 1980 as a refugee. Fifty-eight years old when we speak, she is a nail technician by profession and a renter and subletter for more than forty years. She has lived all across the country, first in California, then in Ohio, Maryland, and Arizona, and now back in Southern California. Like many of the renters with whom I spoke, she has rented rooms all over the Little Saigon district, including Garden Grove, Santa Ana, and Anaheim. In the last ten years alone, she has rented eight different places. A relentless worker, she doesn't remember a time when she hasn't worked fifty to sixty hours a week since coming to the United States. Kim is a proud grandmother and mother who raised three children as a single mother, all of whom have recently graduated college. At various points in her life, she has also rented a house and then sublet rooms to friends and relatives "because we are the first generation who just got settled in our new homeland and as political refugees, we are still going through hard times and challenges with a new life in the United States due to a new culture, language, and employment barriers." Kim describes the room rental market and her current rental at a distant cousin's house:

> I pay $500 a month to stay in a relative's house. I wasn't able to find a house or apartment for myself alone because it's too expensive. It's hard to live here

and the cost of living is too high, and my employment isn't stable. I work for a temp agency. Normally, people [landlords] don't want you to bring guests or anybody home. You have everything in the room and you don't have the privilege to use the other spaces in the house. You don't have a garage, you just use your room, and you share the bathroom with a roommate. I appreciate that I have a place to stay, but I feel limited.

It took my brother ten years to buy a house in Orange County. It is so expensive. He's a software engineer. He rented a room for ten years from his sister-in-law. He first worked in Nevada. He sold his nail shop and house in Nevada and still did not have enough money. He and his wife rented a room for ten years, and he just bought a house this year. Vietnamese live with their family and friends, and that is how we can save money.

In areas with a high cost of living, room rentals function as a means to save for a down payment on a house or to provide a private space for those living in a nonnuclear household. The informality of the arrangements, however, also translates into limitations on and fear of enforcing renter rights and protections in case of conflict. "Have you ever had any type of conflict with a landlord?" I ask. "And if so, how did you resolve it?"

This is a sensitive issue. As a renter, you have to pay them cash. And in most cases, they don't want to give you a receipt so you can't create a residency.... But because we need to help each other out, I had to take the offer that she [the relative] gave me because she was helping me out to have a place to live cheap and she also wants some extra income to pay her bills. But I wouldn't say I liked it, but I took it because I need a place to live.

With no residency, I can't get my driver's license. I can't convert my nail license [from Ohio to California] to do nails here, so I'm doing temp work. I mean, the landlord is helping me out by giving me cheap rent, but at the same time, she's generating money to pay her mortgage. I can't establish residency, and it's up to the landlord to give me proof of residency. I plan to move.

Kim's lack of state residency has significant financial implications as it limits her ability to do the work for which she was trained as a nail technician or even to get a driver's license. This propelled her to try to find another place to live. Having safe, stable housing lets a person "stay in their home as long as they would like to," which is important for securing a job.[58] Housing stability can have significant consequences on social mobility, health, civic participation, and financial stability.[59] As I heard from others as well, Kim looked for a room via Vietnamese newspaper advertisements, online, and word of mouth, and now has an informal verbal contract with her landlord. Housing privileges vary, but it is clear from advertisements that rent typically includes just a room with a single or shared bathroom, Wi-Fi, and electricity; use of other parts of the house is a perk, such as access to the kitchen, laundry room, living room, private entrance, or backyard.

I was fortunate to interview Kim's landlord, Hạnh, as well; she also looks for renters online and through social networks. We met at one of the many open-air cafés in Little Saigon. Hạnh is five-foot-two with medium-length black hair and wears a red beret with a matching scarf. She is fifty-two years old, divorced, and living with her three adult children and her disabled ex-husband. Hạnh was a teenager when she came to the United States as a refugee through family sponsorship and is one of eleven children. She founded and independently ran two successful businesses in the Vietnamese community: a restaurant and a video store. After sponsoring her brothers and sisters to immigrate to the United States, she employed many of them. Then tragedy hit. Her ex-husband, for whom she cares, had a heart transplant, and shortly after he recovered, she was diagnosed with a brain tumor. As a result of both severe carpal tunnel and two brain surgeries, she is no longer able to work; one of the surgeries left half her face paralyzed and emotionless. After becoming sick, Hạnh sold her restaurant. "It was too much. I ran the restaurant for seven years, and then I had to sell it before I had one of my first surgeries." I asked her when and why she started renting rooms:

> I had my first business in making Vietnamese CDs and videos. . . . You know, traditional Vietnamese music. . . . The media entertainment industry went down gradually after being affected by online streaming and the internet, so I have to close out that business. Nobody wants to buy it. So, I had to walk away. So, I purchased the restaurant so I could continue to make a living. I need to make some more money for living so I also rent out rooms to students. Sometimes, they were my daughter's friends who attended Cal State Fullerton and a few other students before her. I needed a more stable income because I still had a mortgage to pay.
>
> I worked for five years to pay for that house when money was good at the CD store. We didn't eat out or have vacations or travel, and we only had one car for the five of us. I saved enough money for the down payment on the house, which was $200,000.

Hạnh lived frugally for many years to be able to purchase her home, and after her and her ex-husband's medical emergencies, they decided to rent rooms to make ends meet. From the landlord and renter perspectives, renting rooms is a means to prevent displacement owing to job loss, medical emergency, or lack of public assistance.[60] Hạnh explains how Vietnamese rely on social networks and word of mouth and the invisibility of the informal room-rental economy as a strategy to build intergenerational wealth:

> Everyone posts their room for rent online. Everybody, a lot of people, I think the majority of people who rent to people do it online through the Vietnamese newspaper [*Người Việt*]. I would say for every ten houses here, at least five or six have a room for rent.
>
> In Asian culture we live in multigenerational families, so the young can save money, even save money for their parents, and the kids contribute to the rent. So sometimes we all live together, and with contributions from all family members, they can afford to own it.

This experience aligns with Nazli Kibria's research, which shows how many Vietnamese American families widen their structure of opportunities by using a patchwork method of bringing diverse resources into the household economy to attain economic goals like purchasing a home or establishing a small business.[61]

Since she is unable to work and does not have savings for retirement, Hạnh is contemplating filling in her pool, building an ADU in its place for her and her family to live, and then living off money from renting the house. Hạnh believes herself to be a good landlord, She says she's never had trouble with tenants and that they have never complained about the condition of her house. Another of her renters, who was positive overall, described their experience:

> We [renters, around three total] live downstairs, and Hạnh and her family live upstairs. The bathroom is in the main house right off the garage that we [renters] all share. Oh, now the bathroom. The first part of it is nice because it just has a sink so you can wash your hands, but then you open the other door and you went in. And, like, you can tell that it must have been like an add-on. And that's where they have a small shower and like some cupboards for storage and stuff. But it isn't very nice. I have to say that. You shower, and roaches come up. I told her about the roaches, and she just laughed and said she didn't know. It hasn't stopped the problem. At least we get to use the kitchen. In a lot of places, you can only store stuff and use the microwave in your room or you cook in the bathroom if it's clean enough. Also, she just rents to women, so you don't have to worry coming home.

The severe need for house renovations is a common theme in discussions of tenant-landlord relations. A Westminster city planning report states that

50 percent of households that are considered low-income in Little Saigon have "severe housing problems," defined as a home with at least one of four problems: (1) lacks complete kitchen facilities; (2) lacks complete plumbing facilities; (3) has more than 1.5 persons per room; (4) has a cost burden that is over 50 percent of the household's income.[62] Building codes increase safety but also the cost of construction and rehabilitation. Property owners often lack the funds to resolve violations and therefore are unable to get an occupancy permit from the city.[63] When owners cannot afford to meet the requirements, codes have the unintended effect of increasing the scarcity of affordable rental housing.[64] Thus, it is common for landlords who share their homes to avoid going through official channels altogether.

EXCLUSIONARY DEFINITIONS OF FAMILY AND OCCUPANCY

For many, renting a place and subletting rooms is a dream way to earn money for a down payment. But there are obstacles to this dream: a zoning code's definition of family; city ordinances that limit household size; and occupancy standards setting the number and relation of people who may legally live in a unit. These are some structural barriers to housing choice that have discriminatory effects. Journalist Hiếu Trần Phan explains in a local newspaper editorial that his first residence in the United States as a child was in a single-bedroom apartment in Garden Grove that housed up to ten people at one time. His mother rented out couches and bunk beds while their family slept on the living room floor. After a few years, they moved into a two-bedroom condo where they lived for more than fourteen years:

> "Heaven," I thought. "Now I'll get my own room." Instead, we sublet both bedrooms. I was assigned a couch in the kitchen. My family cooked, cleaned, and washed clothes for our renters. We swallowed a loss whenever they scrammed without paying a dime. . . . All that time, my family was breaking the law. We knew of city ordinances that limit household sizes for rental properties. We also understood that, since the late 1970s, many other Vietnamese in Orange County illegally sublet or rent out their houses, apartments, mobile homes, garages, sofa beds, or even a space on the living room floor. . . . Last week, I just paid the security deposit on a Westminster room for my cousin, who was moving down from San Jose. The memories of my own family's subletting history came back. Standing there, looking at the

humble surroundings, several thoughts invaded my mind: "This practice may be illegal, but no law should be absolute, and it's best not to judge others until you've lived in their shoes."[65]

Occupancy standards such as the ones discussed by the activist writer Hiếu have historically been used to exclude communities of color from housing. Occupancy codes are often based on a two-person-per-bedroom standard. Since the nineteenth century, these codes have been used to push out and control certain groups, such as Chinese, Jewish, Polish, Italian, and other immigrant groups. The earliest occupancy standards in the United States targeted immigrant groups and Blacks. In 1870, San Francisco adopted the first occupancy law in the United States, the Loading House Ordinance, based on cubic air space. The regulation demanded a minimum of 500 cubic feet of air per person in lodging buildings. Ellen Pader, a professor of regional planning, shows how rules developed by land reformers in the early twentieth century were created using middle-class English ideals and outdated scientific knowledge. These social ideals implicit in occupancy standards from the early twentieth century still underlie many of the current US design elements affecting the ethnic, racial, and economic structures of city and suburban life.[66]

Another tool that shapes suburban spaces with discriminatory effect is the use of a rigid and discriminatory definition of *family* based on a single, often heteronormative, nuclear ideal. Suburb municipalities often limit each residence to one family per unit, with the definition of family being contentious and shifting over time. In 1989, a *Los Angeles Times* article described how in some of "Denver's most affluent neighborhoods, 'living-in-sin' zoning locks out unmarried couples. In Poughkeepsie, New York, four or more people may not occupy the same rental dwelling unless they are related. In Chicago, eight couples living in public housing got married to avoid eviction."[67] In 1997, in Southern California's affluent suburb of Pasadena, a city councilperson argued that a family residing in a house should be strictly defined as those related by adoption, marriage, or blood, lest it "degrades the meaning of the term family," while those living in other relationships should be called a "housekeeping unit."[68]

Today, ordinances restricting what constitutes a family in terms of occupancy are still commonly found in suburbia.[69] In 2020, Arlington, Virginia, defined a family as "individual, or two or more persons related by blood, marriage or adoption or under approved foster care," or "a group of not more than four persons whether or not related by blood or marriage living together and sharing living areas in a dwelling unit."[70] These restrictions discriminate against groups of young people and single parents cohabiting with their children in favor of a family of two parents and two children.

In Little Saigon, the Garden Grove zoning code allows one "family plus any domestic employees of the family to legally live together in a home."[71] The explanation for this restrictive definition of family is to regulate density while limiting the likelihood of boarding houses, rooming housing, and dormitories.[72] Santa Ana specifically restricts occupancy of apartment units to one family: "An apartment is one (1) or more rooms in an apartment house or dwelling occupied or intended or designed for occupancy by one (1) family for sleeping or living purposes and containing one (1) kitchen."[73] In Westminster, the definition of family is more inclusive. There, family means: "An individual or two or more persons living together in compliance with the occupancy limits of Section 503(b) of the Uniform Housing Code, or any successor provision thereto as adopted by the city, as a domestic unit in a relationship based upon birth, marriage, or other domestic bond of social, economic, and psychological commitment to each other."[74]

While chatting with a Little Saigon code enforcement officer, I asked what the occupancy limits are for a single-family home or apartment that contradicts the legally enshrined suburban city definitions:

> There is no limit, ma'am. You know, single family, what does that even mean? Like, say, I'm a single-family, and I have nine children. Okay. Say, for instance, I have nine kids, husband, and my parents were living with me as a big family living in one single-family home. Who is anyone to say that should be legal or illegal? It is illegal to tell me I can't have that big of a family. A "single family" means one family, but there is no limit to my family size. . . . When it comes down to it, who's allowed to live in your home? It's your space. Sometimes you're friends through blood, but sometimes we're not blood, but we're family.

Even though it may not be legally enforced, offensive and limiting language still exists in restrictive occupancy definitions, expressing the official perspective on who belongs in suburbia. Renters, especially long-term renters, create new bonds of kinship outside the traditional norms and understandings of the nuclear suburban family. My high school friend's father, a former lieutenant in the Army of the Republic of Vietnam who escaped from Vietnam by boat, has been living in a family friend's converted garage since his divorce thirty years ago. In his mid-seventies, he and his landlords eat dinner, celebrate Tết, and watch Lakers games together. Their relationship goes beyond a monetary transaction; these are the people with whom he escaped by boat to America. After living together for many years, they consider each other family. Their living arrangement may be illegal and not meet the definition of family by some suburban city ordinances, but it is who they define as family.

RENTING IN THE SHADOWS

Not all room rental situations turn out so well. Renters spend a lot of money on basic shelter, sometimes under the constant stress of eviction. Without a formal contract, landlords can raise the rent and threaten eviction if the tenant refuses to pay the increase they demand.

Jessica's experience is typical in this regard. She is twenty-seven years old, a second-generation Vietnamese from Sacramento. She lost her job as a public school elementary teacher after the California budget crisis in 2008; when the state reached a $41.6 billion deficit, her Sacramento school district experienced an $85 million budget reduction.[75] She moved to Orange County, assuming she'd find more opportunities and a less expensive place to live. She found a job in marketing and moved three times during her first year. Whenever she needed to find a room in Little Saigon, she went to a Vietnamese newspaper directory.

> They were all month-to-month leases and word-of-mouth contracts. It's very Vietnamese. It's like a word of trust: I have your word that you will pay so and so. Thank God it was a month-to-month because my job wasn't stable, especially because I just moved. So that first year, I moved to Fountain Valley, but I just picked that place because I automatically thought, oh, Little Saigon must be a very cheap area. Because in Sacramento, the Little Saigon area is a low-income area like where my parents live, the area is like all people of color. And that area is very cheap still to this day. My parents bought their house in the early '90s for $80,000. But here, the Vietnamese community is around a very pricey land. And it was very expensive. So, I told my parents, "No, mom, like the Phước Lộc Thọ (Asian Garden Mall) area around Santa Ana and Fountain Valley is very expensive."
>
> Even though I had an agreement with the owner's family, they would keep raising the rent. They did it to me twice. When they would do that, I would say, "Okay, I need to move," and then sometimes they'll hound me for the

money until I threaten to leave. They were also really cheap. I remember I had drywall problems, and there were rodents. So, at night I would go crazy hearing all these noises.

The worst was the harassment from other tenants like, especially when I was alone in the place. This gentleman, another tenant, he is also a friend of the landlord, and he would wait for me outside the door. It was really uncomfortable. I would tell the landlord, and he would laugh and say he's harmless.

Jessica's description of her rental experiences highlights multiple vulnerabilities in her situation. Some renters face age discrimination as well. Room renters include many seniors drawn to the area, often because they prefer to speak in Vietnamese or cannot drive and need to walk to their churches, supermarkets, doctors, and pharmacies. However, as a second-generation Vietnamese social worker explained to me, even in the Vietnamese community, discrimination against the elderly can mean they have trouble finding a rental:

Many [landlords] do not want to rent to senior Vietnamese because they are afraid they will die in the house. The scary part is that many [renters] do not know their rights because everything is verbal. If a landlord does not want to give you your deposit back, then they can keep it. [Renters] have no means for fighting or advocating for themselves to get it back because there is no contract.

As these stories show, renters need protection from displacement; empowering them and enforcing antidiscrimination protection measures are key to this protection. Many room renters live in the shadows, not knowing their rights or the protections accorded them under the Fair Housing Act (FHA), part of the 1968 Civil Rights Act. Together with the 1980 and 1988 Fair Housing Amendments Acts, the FHA protects people from "being discriminated against in housing because of their national origin, race, color, religion, familial status (defined as the presence of children under 18), or disability."[76] It was originally enacted to combat segregation and enable integration. Passage of the FHA was encouraged by the Kerner Commission established by President Lyndon B. Johnson, which reported that residential segregation and unequal housing were potent reasons for civil unrest.[77] The 1988 amendment made familial status a protected category, as studies demonstrated the effect of landlords excluding families with minors from renting private housing.[78] Research showed that families of color were more likely to be affected by no-child policies, which thus "acted as a proxy for racial discrimination."[79]

In California, immigrants are often left out of rent relief programs that would prevent them from being displaced.[80] Despite many eviction protections in California, including those tied to pandemic relief, only tenants applying for rental assistance are protected.[81] But renters living in the most precarious conditions with nontraditional leases, including immigrants and senior Vietnamese who are monolingual or of limited English proficiency, have restricted access to online and digital technology. A common obstacle is that websites offer "poor translations from an overreliance on Google Translate and non-English-speaking applicants [having to] navigate various English-only websites before finding an application portal in their own language."[82] In response, a group of tenant advocacy organizations filed a complaint with the California Department of Fair Employment and Housing, charging discriminatory practices for tenants with limited English proficiency or disabilities trying to access rental assistance.[83]

As seen, renting rooms is both a way for landlords to diversify risk and an intergenerational and co-ethnic strategy to take care of relatives or friends who fall on hard times and need a place to stay, such as my dad. The need for affordable housing in areas with a high cost of living has made the informal room-rental economy a strategy for both landlords and renters. Despite how spaces are actually used at present, suburban housing instability continues to be shaped by the dominance of single-family zoning and antiquated occupancy codes and definitions of family. As federal housing assistance declines, local control and NIMBY (not in my backyard) policies often prohibit the building of affordable housing units in many residential neighborhoods.[84] To enable more affordable housing, policies and local control must change—and it is starting to. For instance, Minneapolis has eliminated single-family zoning, and California's new ADU law holds promise for increasing small-unit housing.[85] In Oakland, Just Cause eviction ordinances were passed in 2018 to protect all rental units built before 1996, including single-family units and condos.[86] And in 2019, Georgia passed a law protecting renters from being evicted for complaining about problems like mold, rats, and health or safety concerns.[87] Local suburban municipalities, such as Westminster and Garden Grove, have set aside money to fund unsubsidized housing renovations, with the goal of helping to make rents affordable on the private housing market.[88] The monies are limited; in 2022, they helped twenty households in Garden Grove.[89]

Rent control is one powerful tool to help renters avoid eviction and displacement and claim their right to safe housing, and grassroots activism is a key strategy of community organizations that work to empower residents. The next section shows the power of community organizers and grassroots organizations to mobilize a city council for rent control.

THE FIGHT FOR RENT CONTROL IN SANTA ANA

It was three in the morning on October 19, 2021, when Santa Ana council members voted four to three to pass rent control, becoming the first suburban city in Orange County to set limits on how much a landlord can raise rents. Rent stabilization policies are notoriously difficult to pass; only four states have any such policy on the books. With over three hundred thousand residents, Santa Ana is the second-largest incorporated area in suburban Orange County and overlaps with Little Saigon. Santa Ana includes many first-generation and immigrant communities; the population is 75 percent Latinx and 14 percent Asian, primarily Vietnamese.[90] The social and economic impacts of rent control for tenants, landlords, and rental housing markets are a focus of intense debate and disagreement among researchers.[91] Experts disagree over data, methodology, and how to interpret results. However, there is general agreement that in the short term, rent control can prevent people from being displaced.[92] California currently stands out as home to the most important rent-control battle in years. The rest of this chapter will explore strategies and tactics organizers used to pursue political change and win the fight for rent control in Santa Ana.

Access to rent control in the United States today is not widespread, but it has a long history dating back to World War I.[93] Historically, rent control has existed during wartime housing shortages and peacetime inflation when rents rise beyond the capacity of many tenants to pay.[94] During World War I, the US government focused more on threats to industrial production than housing access, leaving local jurisdictions to decide for themselves whether or not to adopt temporary emergency controls.[95] Of the cities that adopted rent control policies, Washington, DC, and New York City were the most notable. It wasn't until 1942, after the United States entered World War II, that federal rent control appeared as a national emergency measure. The US federal government imposed a temporary rent freeze in some areas designated for defense production.[96] Despite attempts by landlords and realtors to dispute the constitutionality of rent control, the Supreme Court upheld its legality as a wartime emergency measure.[97]

When the federal regulations that had passed during World War II started expiring in 1950, states and municipalities had the option of substituting their own rent controls or forbidding them altogether.[98] In the 1980s and 1990s, several states took away the ability of local governments to enact rent control. By 2023, thirty-three states prohibited their cities from enacting any type of rent-control legislation. Notable exceptions include California, New York, New Jersey, Maryland, and Washington, DC, which are places with the most active rent-control laws.[99]

In 2020, California's state legislature passed AB 1482, one of the strongest rent control laws in the nation, which limits annual rent increases to 5 percent plus local inflation or 10 percent, whichever is lower than AB 1482.[100] However, full implementation of the law is hampered by an earlier law backed by the real estate industry, the 1995 Costa-Hawkins Rental Housing Act, which prevents Californian counties and local municipalities from implementing rent control at the local level for single-family homes, condos, and any housing built after 1995.[101] It also prohibits vacancy control, so if a tenant is forced out of a rent-controlled unit or a tenant chooses to leave, the landlord can raise the rent however much they want for the new tenant.[102] Thus, in practice, the 2020 California law is limited to protecting tenants living in multifamily housing built before 1995 with some exceptions.[103]

At the local level, city or county policies can strengthen the renter safety net as local ordinances can sometimes override state regulations.[104] In California, the fight for rent control started long before the 2020 passage of AB 1482 and has continued since its passage, as cities have leeway to provide even more protection than the state law. I spoke to one of the main organizers from the movement, who explained, "This is a decades-long discussion because being a renter in a city like Santa Ana is not easy, considering it is a predominantly immigrant city." For decades, the local Vietnamese population in Santa Ana has understood the importance of rent control for the health of their community. Thái Việt Phan, the first Asian woman and Vietnamese American to serve as a Santa Ana council member, told a reporter that organizing for local rent control began over twenty years ago, in 2000, when senior residents, primarily Vietnamese, lobbied the Santa Ana City Council to help them.[105]

Councilperson Thái Việt Phan explained her thought process in the lead-up to the 2021 Santa Ana City Council vote on rent control. She spoke during a city council meeting about how rent stabilization policies would help current residents, who must often choose between home, groceries, and health care:

I did not initially support rent control. However, through the pandemic and in speaking to more residents, I looked at what can I do to help families who are on the brink of calamity.... First, I've been there. I've been in a place where I had $3 in my bank account. With $3 I couldn't buy food. Sometimes the only thing I ate was In-and-Out Burger and that's because I worked there and that's what I had for food. But you know what, I always paid my rent. In the Vietnamese community, you always pay your rent. And I imagine it's the same for most residents in our city because being hungry is better than being homeless. Not having health care is better than being homeless. And that's what our communities have done, and that is probably why we're not getting as many rental applications [for support] because people are still making their rent. That's why OC Food Bank still has lines, and we are still doing food deliveries to folks here in the cities. So that is a huge reason why I had to look at why rent control is important.... I asked myself, what tools do I have to help residents today, right now? And so far, I haven't heard anybody come up with any solutions as to what I can do today to help residents who might not qualify for rent assistance, who might not get all the paperwork ... because they don't have it or can't convince others to give it to them. And that one policy is rent control. And rent control is the one policy I can think of that will help current Santa Ana residents, not future residents, not outside residents, not new residents, but current residents in existing neighborhoods.

Comparing difficulties between renters and owners, the Urban Institute shows that "paying for housing, utilities, food, and medical care, renters are more likely than owners to report trouble paying for at least one of these basic needs."[106] Thái Việt Phan described what one renter told to her: "I always think about first rent, then I think about food. If we don't have enough, we cut back on food." With more than 50 percent of Santa Ana residents being renters, the win for rent control was a major victory for residents, providing important protections that could help ease material hardship.

In the victory for rent control, the Santa Ana City Council voted four to three to cap rents at 3 percent annually or 80 percent of inflation, whichever is lower, for buildings constructed in 1995 or earlier (per Costa-Hawkins) and for mobile home parks established in 1990 or earlier.[107] While California has statewide rent control, Santa Ana's ordinance is more stringent. The Santa Ana ordinances provided stronger protections than the statewide protections passed in 2020 at 5 percent annually, plus the local inflation rate, in one year. The Santa Ana law also includes language about Just Cause evictions that protects tenants and guarantees that landlords must provide an eviction notice in the language the owner and tenant used to negotiate the lease. Along with being the first city in Orange County to enact its own rent con trol law, Santa Ana was also the first to enact a rental registry that requires landlords to list their units on a city database, providing greater protections at the local level for Santa Ana residents.

Strategizing How to Pass Rent Control

While the Santa Ana City Council ultimately was the body that passed rent control, it was not the initial strategy of community groups. Historically, several organizations had focused on the potential power of the people of Santa Ana to put rent control on the ballot for voters through a petition process. A grassroots coalition of primarily Latinx organizations and residents drove the fight for rent control in Santa Ana. Tenants United, or Tú United, was the face of these organizing efforts, and at the forefront, but the fight took decades of effort.

In 2017, organizers canvassed and collected signatures to put rent control on the Santa Ana city ballot. Organizers collected nearly 9,299 signatures, leaving them 555 short of the needed 9,854 signatures to put rent control on the November ballot for city residents to vote on. Nonetheless, they were encouraged and submitted the petition to city hall.

Four community members and the organizers from Tenants United stood in Santa Ana City Hall in a meeting of the city planning commission, speaking in both English and Spanish to the female and primarily Latinx staff. With an iPhone, they filmed a tense interaction between the city attorney and the Tú spokesperson after the planning commission meeting, discussing the possible ways to legally pass rent control:

> ORGANIZER 1: Can you repeat the total number of signatures again?
>
> CITY ATTORNEY: The total is 9,299 signatures.
>
> ORGANIZER 1: And the total that was needed was how much?
>
> CITY ATTORNEY: 9,854.
>
> ORGANIZER 1: So, can you tell us, aside from the petition process, what are the other ways that rent control could become law in the city of Santa Ana?
>
> CITY ATTORNEY: There's different ways to make law generally in California; so you can make it either through the people—petitioning. . . . It can be done by the state, as the state legislature can make laws. And then the city council can make laws.
>
> ORGANIZER 2: Wait, for city council to pass a law, they can also put something on the ballot, correct?

CITY ATTORNEY: Yes, we don't have the exact dates, but it would be at the beginning of August 2020, which would be the deadline for the city to send to the county in the resolutions calling for elections . . .

ORGANIZER 2: Could we, say, tomorrow, start the process [collecting signatures to put rent control on the ballot] again?

CITY STAFF MEMBER: Sure, absolutely.

ORGANIZER 2: So that's one way [the ballot initiative], the other way is that city council can just take a vote, correct? To adopt it as law. How many votes are required for that?

CITY STAFF MEMBER: If money needs to be appropriated for the program, then you would need a supermajority, five out of seven [city council member votes].

ORGANIZER 2: But if they don't, it's four votes out of the seven?

In the wake of Tenants United's failed ballot initiative, the organization reformed itself. At that point, efforts to pass rent control in Santa Ana were more than twenty years in the making, and the group decided it was time to try something new. The struggle would soon be led by resident volunteers, unhampered by top-down bureaucratic organizing. Two organizers gave an update of their local rent control campaign via an Instagram and Facebook video on February 7, 2020: "We are launching a rent control campaign for the second time. In 2018, we gathered signatures; we were only five hundred signatures short of 9,854 needed. Since then, we've been learning from the last campaign meeting with the community and making the ordinance stronger than the first time. This time, we need eleven thousand signatures. And so, when we get eleven thousand signatures, it will go on the ballot for people to vote on. And so, we can give you a summary of the updated ordinance."

This second attempt at a ballot initiative through collecting petitions also failed as the COVID-19 pandemic broke out and door-to-door canvassing in the community became more difficult. I spoke with María, one of the main organizers from Tenants United, at an outdoor café in Santa Ana. Besides being a volunteer tenant counselor, she is also an urban planning consultant and active in multiple community grassroots organizations. Born in Santa Ana, she is one of six siblings and has fourteen nieces and nephews who live in Santa Ana. She explained her motivation to lead the fight for rent control:

I grew up in Santa Ana. I grew up in a single-parent household after my dad got deported. So, knowing the struggle and growing up not wanting kids to go with what you went through really was the push for me, and that also

constantly reminded [me] as I'm helping tenants stay housed, helping them
with their issues, while also fighting for rent control. [It's] a lot. . . . I had to
be really honest with myself and dive back to my own experiences. We don't
want kids to live like this.

Like many social justice organizers, María was driven by the disparities of
race, income, and power she witnessed in her own life to incorporate community members into public decision-making. This led her and other Tenants
United organizers to promote a rent control ordinance that made sense in
multilingual communities like Santa Ana. As María explained, "The beauty
of the ordinance is that you must provide whatever eviction or notices to
vacate you're providing in the language of the tenant, so it's not just in
English, because even that's intimidating. So, we are aiming for all types of
justice, including housing justice, language justice, [and] social justice, encap-
sulated into a whole action."

Thus, the fight for rent control in Santa Ana was resident-led, multiethnic,
and multilingual, including Vietnamese and Latinx youth from the city and
neighboring suburbs. After Mexicans, the second-largest population in Santa
Ana is Vietnamese. One of the key organizations facilitating the representation of Vietnamese in Santa Ana is VietRISE, which organized alongside
Tenants United in the fight for rent control. VietRISE was founded in 2018
in Orange County as a community organization with the mission to advance
social justice and build "power with working-class Vietnamese and immigrant communities in Orange County."[108] The next sections show how the
fight for rent control was both cross-racial and intergenerational.

Cross-racial Coalitions

> The burning down of Chinatown in Santa Ana in 1906 is a
> part of history that is rarely acknowledged, but it's important
> to acknowledge that Asian folks have existed and wanted to
> become part of the community here.
>
> INDIGO VŨ, *VietRISE organizer*

I first meet Tracy La, the executive director of VietRISE, on a sunny Sunday
afternoon in early June 2022 at Freedom Park in Westminster. At her feet is
a large banner: "Little Saigon for Permanent Community and Family
Unification." The rally is sponsored by seventeen local organizations and
nonprofit groups. Nearly one hundred people of varying ages are present,

from moms with children in strollers to senior citizens, but the crowd is primarily young people in their twenties and thirties, half Latinx and half Vietnamese. They are rallying to urge local officials to take a position on the VISION Act, which would end ICE (US Immigration and Customs Enforcement) transfers from local jails and prisons in the state to immigrant detention centers. The multilingual and cross-racial organizational statement reads, in Vietnamese, English, and Spanish: "We, in Little Saigon, want community and family unification, NOT more incarceration and separation! Right now, countless incarcerated immigrant and refugee community members are being double punished by the state. Southeast Asian, Black, Latinx, and Asian immigrants are being targeted in high numbers for ICE transfers and detention. We have the opportunity to end ICE transfers—but we need Orange County's senators to actually stand with immigrant communities. . . . We're so close to getting the bill passed—these three and their votes will critically decide whether we end ICE transfers this year or not."

A festive mariachi band plays to lift the mood and draw attention to the rally, framed by the Vietnam War Memorial, a six-foot-tall bronze Vietnamese urn where an eternal flame burns. Flanking the memorial are two fourteen-foot-tall bronze statues of soldiers, side by side, one Vietnamese and one American, dressed in fatigues and carrying rifles with the flags of the United States and South Vietnam waving behind them. Beside the memorial are photos of deceased Vietnamese soldiers from the war, along with offerings of flowers, cups of coffee, and cigarettes placed there by visitors. Tracy explains the purpose of the rally, communicating the need for multiracial solidarity and collaboration across communities: "We are rallying to make sure our state senators know what vision we seek for Little Saigon. It's a vision where our local and state leaders have the courage to confront—head-on—the lies that are said about our communities, all of our immigrant communities in Little Saigon and across Orange County: Vietnamese, Korean, Mexican, Cambodian, Caribbean, African and Central Americans, and actually do something about it. . . . In Little Saigon, our communities know that ICE has zero regard for our immigrant families, for our constitutional rights, and for our laws that guarantee equal protection."

The organization advocates for solutions through multiracial solidarity that do not perpetuate injustice at the expense of other communities. Tracy is a child of Vietnamese refugees, a resident of Ward One in Santa Ana, and has been a renter her entire life. She wanted to create an organization focusing on social justice for working-class Vietnamese. After living in Little

Saigon for six years, she saw the need to organize Vietnamese Americans on issues ranging from immigrant justice and housing rights to education about facets of Vietnamese history. Sitting on the grassy hill outside the rally, Tracy explained to me her motivation for helping lead the organization to focus on working-class Vietnamese:

> This is the capital of the Vietnamese diaspora. There [are] so many of us here, and we have so much political power that isn't necessarily being used for issues that affect working-class Vietnamese. My dad worked in a Vietnamese restaurant, and my mom was a nail technician, and sometimes I used to go to work with them. I worked as a cashier in the restaurant that my dad worked at. . . . I saw how my dad was treated, and he worked like twelve hours a day because the boss said he was the only one she could trust . . . These are my parents' experiences, and I think they are incredibly badass people.
>
> Growing up, the first house I lived in was full of family. It was like three bedrooms, six people in one room, but I loved it. It was all the people I loved, and for me, I didn't see that as an economic injustice, even though it wasn't necessarily good if you're a child growing up. By age six, we were able to move out because we were selected for Section 8 housing. Then I moved around with my family probably three times after that because rent kept increasing in certain areas. Then, when I got to Orange County, I experienced the worst rent situation.

Tracy points out an internal heterogeneity within the Vietnamese community that is rarely acknowledged. Like María, Tracy's experiences growing up motivated her fight for social and economic justice for working-class Vietnamese and other immigrant communities.

Intergenerational Coalitions

Intergenerational organizing was a critical resource in the fight for rent control in Santa Ana. Much of the literature on immigrant generations shows intergenerational tensions or gaps.[109] In contrast, the story of Santa Ana's fight for rent control shows coalition building and bridging between generations.

VietRISE served as a bridge between generations, ensuring a diversity of Vietnamese voices were included in the fight for rent control, as Tenants United did for the local Latinx population. Tracy described to me the importance of intergenerational leadership and organizing when speaking before the Santa Ana City Council to urge them to vote in favor of rent stabilization

FIGURE 9. VietRISE and community members prepare for public comments at the Santa Ana City Council meeting (photo by Vincent Trần, October 11, 2021).

in 2021. She further explained the difficulty of creating space to have senior Vietnamese voices adequately represented at city council meetings and how VietRISE responded to develop systems of genuine power sharing and representation at city hall:

> It is really difficult for senior, disabled, elderly Vietnamese residents to come to speak to places like this. Three years ago, these residents attended the city council meeting. They rented their own bus, stayed until 1 a.m., and had to wait until their time to speak. And I learned that [because they were there so much longer than expected] afterward many of them had to go to urgent care and had to go to the hospital because they missed their medications. And last time when they spoke, you know they couldn't even be heard.... There are Vietnamese residents in the city who are facing displacement and are in solidarity with the renters, and everyone else is facing this issue, too.
>
> So, as you can see, for the last several weeks, we have been organizing with the seniors from our community who've all been facing exploitative rent gouging. It has been a blessing to organize with them and learn their stories [and] for them to hear ours. We have joined together as members from multiple generations to fight to protect our elders, our seniors, and every generation of renters who come after those affected and would benefit from this rent control ordinance.

VietRISE ensured senior voices were heard when they could not physically attend city council meetings. As Vietnamese elders spoke over Zoom, VietRISE members held up photos and images of them. A VietRISE organizer explained, "In organizing, people are most moved when they see people's faces. During the city council meetings, when the senior residents called in, people said, 'Oh cool, Vietnamese seniors are calling in.' People aren't used to seeing Vietnamese people organizing or calling in. People generally don't think of Vietnamese people as fighting for housing issues. So, I saw in the [city council] audience, people were surprised."

Another tactic was for second-generation Vietnamese to act as a bridge, with the youths speaking as proxies for the seniors who could not physically attend the meeting. Speaking in English at the Santa Ana City Council meeting before the final vote to approve rent control was held, Tracy read a petition signed by seventy-one residents in the Bali Hi Senior Mobile Home Park in their own words:

> We, as residents of Bali Hi mobile home park, the low-income seniors in Santa Ana, hereby express our deepest gratitude and most sincere appreciation for the city's bold rescue measure in the form of its first rent stabilization and tenant eviction protection ordinance, especially for vulnerable constituents like us: (1) securing access to affordable housing; (2) struggling to make ends meet, month in and month out; (3) crying out everywhere for help; and (4) barely surviving, barely managing to survive on the brink of overlapping looming calamities that have posed critical, even life-threatening, challenges for senior residents of Santa Ana living on fixed income and limited financial resources for years.
>
> Many of our neighbors have succumbed to early deaths or have become severely ill from the unbearable toll of worrying about all sorts of housing insecurity and associated dangers. We're simply living precariously on the brink of physical, mental, and multiple breaking points that a single trigger event could render us totally incapacitated, isolated, and effectively homeless.
>
> This action shows that the city has finally heard the crescendo of cries for help and has come to the rescue. For those who voted yes, thank you very much for having the political will and being resolved to stand in a gap to rescue the poor, the sickly, and the most vulnerable. Santa Ana is the first, along with 55 percent of Little Saigon's resident population, who are renters who are financially overwhelmed with unreasonable rent increases. So, those who voted yes last time, you were doing the right thing the right way for all the right reasons. For those that vote no. You have the chance to turn back that no and vote yes today. Thank you.

María from Tenants United reflected on the role of VietRISE in the fight for rent control and having senior voices included in the debate:

> VietRISE was very helpful in connecting Vietnamese elders and having their voices be heard. And that's something that I did respect a lot because, you know, these elders couldn't make it to like a city council meeting in person. But they [VietRISE] did have like some of their employees go to their houses to help them; I think they all met at like one center or something and helped them be able to make their comments, whether it was virtual [or not], and that was significantly important, because, toward the end, the fight for rent control did become multiracial. VietRISE was a facilitator. The organization bridged the older Vietnamese residents to realize that they had the right to advocate for rent control. At the end of the day, VietRISE were advocates for rent control.

Organizing for Housing Justice

Dedicated to an inclusive and horizontal coalitional approach that empowers the voices of residents above organizations, both Tenants United and VietRISE adapted their approaches over time. María explained the power dynamics of the decision-making process in the first ballot initiative: "Volunteers and community members only had one collective vote during the first ballot initiative, but each nonprofit organization had its own vote, which is unfair given that residents are giving their time and energy. They should have their own vote."

For Tenants United, the first ballot initiative had a top-down dynamic, with the nonprofits and organizers at the top. As a result, the coalition reformed itself by empowering residents rather than organizations and changing the voting structure so that each resident organizer received a vote. María described to me how the residents initiated organizational reform by decolonizing organizational practices and shifting power to residents:

> The nonprofit organizations were also very private about decision-making, especially to volunteers, as if they didn't really want to feel like empowering volunteers and residents that spent their time there. And it was ... a top-down dynamic. A lot of the organizations have a savior complex. Like we're here to save you and you need to depend upon us; we're not here to empower you. It creates this dependence and if the nonprofit stops getting funding or disappears, what are residents going to do?

A second key change for both VietRISE and Tenants United was "intergenerational organizing to reach every resident," which meant "going to residents; not waiting for residents to reach us," as Tracy from VietRISE explained. VietRISE connected with Bali Hi Senior Mobile Home Park during a council chamber meeting and began organizing with the senior residents there in 2018. Tracy explained:

> I was texting directly with council member Thái Việt Phan during a city council meeting, and she was like, "Hey, here's the number for a resident in Bali Hi Mobile Home Park who's trying to call in." So, this . . . was a senior . . . trying to call in and talk during the public comments section of the meeting about rent control, but the translator who was supposed to translate her comments from Vietnamese to English was doing a very poor job so you couldn't hear that she actually had something to say. So, about a week later, we asked to meet with them. We had a meeting of about thirty people in a small mobile home talking about how we're going to pass rent control. It didn't only start there, but that's how we connected to Bali Hi. We don't give them talking points. They are already organized. It's always a conversation.

Both organizations used the power of co-ethnic intergenerational and collective leadership, including listening to elders and asking questions. Tenants United also practiced inclusive outreach protocols geared toward reaching all residents and community members. As María explained, this entails

> talking to people and making sure that you're on every platform and that you can reach people. And I really felt like Tenants United were nontraditional, and we would post flyers at laundromats; anywhere there was a cork board, we would put an announcement. We found it and we put it there to make sure that even if these people didn't want to be part of our coalition, they have the knowledge of knowing that we have resources available to them. They have the knowledge of knowing that they have a city council representative that is supposed to represent them versus the other way around. Our collective is intergenerational. The most active and powerful is probably the mom's group. Do you see that park over there? [She points to the new playground across from the outdoor café.] Those women organized and got the city to pay for that park.

Another mantra common to both organizations was "They are our family," evidenced during city council meetings where organizers provided food and resources so everyone could participate. As María described their community focus:

We wanted to make sure that people weren't hungry or needed water. Because we're very community focused. We are not doing this to advance our own personal agenda. Most of the organizers are from Santa Ana, and some are college students who moved and fell in love with the city. But we all realized these people are like our family members, and we can't consider them strangers. I tell people why I'm here. I ask them to grab some food, even talking about why I'm here, making sure it's inclusive.

It's also important to note that housing justice is only one aspect of the work of these organizers. Community organizations such as VietRISE simultaneously grapple with multiple and inevitably interrelated social and political issues. This includes youth organizing, immigrant rights, civic and electoral engagement, and COVID-19 responses. In recent years, VietRISE has developed a bilingual Orange County resource guide, distributed meals to senior community members, and hosted a seminar on small business loans to help those impacted by COVID-19. Their power also lies in the political arena and in garnering local support from community members who have come to trust them. Grassroots organizers such as VietRISE use community participation to leverage people-powered change to fight against systemic racism and for immigrant justice.

The night after the historic win, Tenants United for Santa Ana and VietRISE both reposted an Instagram post written by a VietRISE organizer: "We want to especially uplift and recognize the work that was done by many of these folks pictured here to make this win possible: weeks of door-to-door canvassing, announcements in Vietnamese churches, town halls in Vietnamese, passing out info to hundreds of neighbors, talking to fellow residents outside of grocery stores, weeks of newspaper ads in Vietnamese, and more. The movement to secure this community win was a culmination of bold and unapologetic cross-racial, inter-generational, and multi-lingual organizing. 🔥"

CONCLUSIONS: A PRECARIOUS SUCCESS

The success in Santa Ana was tied to the city's political environment and the mobilization of residents by grassroots organizers to support rent control. In the end, the Vietnamese- and Latinx-led organizations, working together, decided that the best way to win the battle for rent control was to share leadership with community members and take their organizing straight to the city council and ask them to vote on it. Although they were victorious in 2021 with a close vote of four to three, they are aware that this victory, unlike a ballot approach in which residents vote, is tenuous and dependent upon who is on the city council: new members can be elected who will vote against rent control.

Nonetheless, Santa Ana's historic win has had a broader influence: organizers and residents in the neighboring city of Westminster (the first major city to have an all-Vietnamese city council), other nearby suburban cities, and other parts of California have gained the confidence to try to mirror Santa Ana's victory. The hope among activists has long been that racial and ethnic political representation will bring about the necessary advocates and votes to wield resources that will directly benefit the city's immigrant and working-class residents. A new ballot initiative in Westminster is hoping to expand the city council from four seats to six in the hope of mirroring the win in Santa Ana. While organizers in Little Saigon fear that, in the wake of their Santa Ana success, a new mayor or city council could do away with years of work, they also know this was a monumental first step, both for rent control and for creating the grassroots scaffolding necessary to build more permanent and structural successes.

For people like Phương and her family described at the beginning of the chapter, rent control makes more than just a financial difference; rent stabilization means they no longer have to worry about unexpected large rent increases that will force them to cut back on basic needs, like health care and food, to make rent.[110] Housing stability translates into children's well-being, enabling them to not constantly change schools and to be able to stay in their community and homes.

Housing insecurity in Little Saigon, like much of America's suburbs, is shaped by the dominance of antiquated zoning laws and weak federal, state, and local support for building or otherwise providing affordable housing. The American ideal of the single-family suburban home has resulted in a strict land-use policy limiting the supply of alternative affordable housing. Yet the aesthetic of the single-family home does not meet today's reality or the community's needs. The informal room-rental economy in Little Saigon is a strategy landlords and renters use to diversify risk, make a down payment on the American dream, and stay in their community. The victory for rent control in Santa Ana was one that Vietnamese residents in Westminster and Garden Grove, especially owners of mobile homes, are carefully watching.

This chapter shows the racist history of zoning and how the racialized language of zoning has been made more colorblind or seemingly race-neutral, while, in reality, zoning codes still regularly enforce class- or economic-based segregation.[111] Today, all American suburbs and cities, except Houston, have a zoning authority. Almost universally, the single-family ideal has entrenched structural constraints on the ability to build more affordable housing in American suburbs.

Buying a home in a mobile home park is an affordable alternative to home ownership; owners buy the house and rent the land underneath it. But what happens when big companies buy up the mobile home parks in Little Saigon? How do residents fight against developers who wish to sell the ground beneath their homes to build luxury condominiums? The next chapter looks at grassroots activism by a Vietnamese-majority mobile home park in Westminster in the heart of Little Saigon and their fight against eviction.

THREE

The Right to Organize

ON AUGUST 21, 2020, Sơn Đỗ, a resident of Little Saigon, presented his testimony before the California State Senate.

> My name is Sơn Đỗ. I am a homeowner in Green Lantern Mobile Home Park—a representative of the Green Lantern Residents Association, and president of the Orange County Mobile Home Residents Coalition. Green Lantern Village has 130 mobile homes and about 250 residents located in the City of Westminster. The city also has seventeen mobile home parks, totaling 2,883 mobile homes, and is 11 percent of its total housing supply.
>
> Mobile home residents desperately need AB 2782 because our park owner wants to close Green Lantern and intends to pay us only $20,000 to $35,000 for our mobile homes, well below the market value of between $80,000 and $200,000 each. Ninety-two of the 130 households in our park are very low income, and our mobile homes are our only real asset. If this park is closed, we will not have enough money to replace our homes, and many will become homeless . . .
>
> In addition, 70 percent of Green Lantern residents are Vietnamese American people who live here because we are in Little Saigon. Being in Little Saigon enables many of us to rely on our families for support and receive care, such as medical services, from Vietnamese-speaking, culturally competent doctors. If we lose our park, it will destroy our community, make it hard for us to care for ourselves, and cause extreme cultural and emotional pain to our families. This harm cannot be quantified.
>
> For these reasons, I respectfully urge you to vote to pass AB 2782 to provide our city with the tools they need to protect our community and us and prevent most of us from becoming homeless. Thank you.[1]

Mobile homes are the largest source of unsubsidized affordable housing in America, yet their continued existence in suburbia is precarious.[2] Despite

FIGURE 10. A blossoming cherry tree outside of a home in Green Lantern Village (photo by Linda Tang, 2018).

their popular image as part of rural America, mobile home parks are more likely to be concentrated in suburban and metropolitan areas.[3] They provide stable homes for those who may not be able to afford a traditional house, allowing them to participate in the American dream of homeownership. People are often surprised to learn that these homes, which cost less than a quarter of a traditional home, are often quite spacious, enabling a family to live in a pet-friendly dwelling of 1,200 to 1,600 square feet, with a driveway, a small yard, and a community swimming pool or park. Approximately 700,000 Californians live in some 400,000 mobile homes in almost 5,200 mobile parks. In Little Saigon, fifty mobile home parks dot the suburban landscape.[4]

Affordability is a large part of the popularity of mobile homes. Nationwide, around 80 percent of park residents own their homes, but only 14 percent hold the land beneath them.[5] The remainder rent or lease their lots from the private landlords who own the land.[6] This puts homeowners in a tenuous housing situation in which residents are beholden to private property owners and private developers; the redevelopment of mobile home parks often displaces entire communities.[7] It is not easy to simply move to another site; despite being called mobile homes, they are not truly mobile and are often cost-prohibitive to relocate.

The dilemma of Green Lantern residents is playing out nationwide. Across the United States, private and corporate investors are demolishing mobile home parks and redeveloping them into high-end luxury condominiums and single-family homes.[8] After the 2008 financial market crash, investment and private equity firms rushed to purchase mobile home parks, buying out small family-owned parks and evicting existing residents. Corporate investors—such as Blackstone Group, Carlyle Group, Apollo Global, and TPG Capital—have purchased more than 150,000 parks.[9] In Missouri and Iowa, for example, out-of-state investment firms own about half of each state's mobile home parks; in Iowa, this adds up to nearly three hundred parks.[10] The Lincoln Institute estimates that between 2014 and 2020, Freddie Mac provided investment firms with more than $9 billion in financing to purchase 950 communities across forty-four states.[11] These financial actors, usually business organizations, increasingly purchase rental properties through anonymous limited liability companies. Unlike an individual landlord, this structure limits transparency, allowing property speculators to remain semi-anonymous, and minimizes investor liability while increasing housing disinvestment.[12] This is what happened at Green Lantern Mobile Home Park. However, the residents were adamant about fighting to keep their community when their corporate landlords threatened displacement by "demoviction."

Demoviction—residential eviction for redevelopment—is a powerful strategy of financialized gentrification. Corporate property owners seeking to gentrify an area consider a home in financial terms—an asset to be traded and managed or an investment for finance capital—rather than a site of shelter.[13] Certainly, they do not view it as a site of family or community, a location for memories and emotions.[14] Demoviction for redevelopment, then, is a tool by which property owners—who are often real estate investment and asset management firms working in suburban or urban communities with a high cost of living—facilitate the removal of existing residents before redeveloping and converting a property to a more lucrative use. Faced with corporate pressure to demolish their park and create luxury condos, the Vietnamese residents of Green Lantern Village spent the next three years organizing to keep their homes. Sơn's testimony at the beginning of the chapter is only one example of how residents chose to fight against eviction rather than be passive bystanders.

This chapter traces the resistance strategies of Vietnamese American residents in Little Saigon to fight against processes of suburban gentrification and understand a new enemy: the financialization of mobile home parks and the new phenomenon of large, often anonymous, financialized landlords.[15] As discussed in chapter 1, although gentrification was first understood and theorized in the urban context, research now shows its reach to the suburbs, with the displacement of vulnerable populations through demoviction orchestrated by private investors and aided by city governments.[16] This chapter shows how mobile homes are neither mobile nor temporary.

GREEN LANTERN VILLAGE

A quiet oasis sits off the major thoroughfare of Beach Boulevard in Little Saigon. In forest-green letters, the name Green Lantern Village (GLV) identifies the entrance to the mobile home park. Across the front of the sign is a white banner announcing "Spaces for Rent" in bold black letters. Another small sign at the entrance reads "Welcome." With nearly all the units mimicking miniaturized suburban homes, GLV could easily be mistaken for a single-family housing tract. Built in 1961, most of its homes are double-wide units, ranging from twenty-four to twenty-eight feet wide and up to sixty feet long, with two or three bedrooms and at least two full baths. This compares to single-wide units with only one bedroom and bath, which are usually fourteen feet wide and sixty-six feet long. Residents painstakingly care for the 130 homes set across ten acres. They are uniformly painted in muted browns, blues, grays, and greens, each with a unique mailbox, a shaded carport, and a small side garden for growing roses, Southeast Asian pomelos, kumquats, potted hydrangeas, dragon fruit, cherry blossom trees, and other favored plants. Despite GLV's location off a busy street, the sounds of traffic disappear as you walk farther up the circular driveway. In the golden hour, when evening arrives and the sun sets, neighbors walk the loop of homes and stop to chat; many residents sit on their porches and screened-in patios, greeting one another. Most residents are Vietnamese, primarily senior citizens and disabled veterans of the Vietnam War. For them, the location of Green Lantern Village is culturally significant as it is within walking distance of Little Saigon, where many residents frequent the senior center, visit their doctors and Vietnamese supermarkets, speak Vietnamese, and participate in cultural events. GLV is also less than one mile from Westminster City Hall and Freedom Park.

Ninety percent of Green Lantern Village residents own their homes and have lived in the park for over ten years. The rents for the lots on which the homes sit range from $900 to $950 per month, affording them a lifestyle that is increasingly rare in Orange County, where two- or three-bedroom apartments rent for $2,000 to $4,500 per month. Sơn has lived in Green Lantern Village for over ten years, and his thirty-three-year-old son and fiancé bought the home next to him. His decision to purchase a mobile home after living in an apartment was related to continual rent increases.

> Twelve years ago, renting an apartment was about $1,400 a month. . . . I had many friends who lived in mobile homes. At that time, purchasing a mobile home was around $30,000, and the land rent was only $700 monthly. It was an easy calculation. With the amount of money we pay in rent, we could easily purchase and own our home in about five years.

Sơn explained why he preferred to own a mobile home rather than renting or buying a condo:

> Mobile homes are more private than condos. We don't have to be next door or share a wall with a neighbor. . . . We can do more for the outside, including planting our flowers and garden, and the community in the mobile home park is very nice. I have nice neighbors, and we all know one another. We take care of each other.

For Sơn, his family, and others, mobile homes offer the opportunity for homeownership, a way into the American dream. Yet in recent years, predatory investors and forced evictions for redevelopment have increasingly threatened these communities.

DEMOVICTION: DISPLACEMENT THROUGH REDEVELOPMENT

Eviction is a powerful and harsh form of displacement, often a key mechanism in reshaping neighborhoods. One way that landlords can legally evict tenants is by changing the use of a property. The evocative terms "renoviction" and "demoviction" refer to this process, by which property owners evict tenants in order to renovate or demolish and redevelop their property.[17] Neil Smith's theory of uneven development and gentrification helps explain what is happening in Green Lantern Village. Smith argues that neighborhood change and gentrification arise partly from the ability of property owners and investors to obtain more significant profit from a land's redevelopment than from its current use. Owners oust existing residents through a combination of physical displacement (as properties undergo redevelopment) and economic displacement (as newer uses of land lead to increased housing costs). Existing residents are then gradually replaced by people with greater access to capital and the ability to consume new and renovated properties at higher rents.[18] The regional housing market can also create conditions for displacement, particularly in areas where housing supply has lower elasticity, creating higher prices due to demand pressures—as seen in chapter 2 on housing insecurity. The broader patterns of renoviction and demoviction are also intimately linked to the financialization of housing.

The deregulation and internationalization of finance that started in the late 1970s also had significant consequences for housing. A United Nations special rapporteur on adequate housing describes how the financialization of housing has transformed housing markets, treating "housing as a commodity, a vehicle for wealth and investment- rather than a social good."[19] The rapporteur says that "funds for mortgage lending now derive from national and international capital markets and not solely from existing savings and retail finance. . . . This process has been accompanied by the conceptual transformation of adequate housing from a social good into a commodity and a strategy for household wealth accumulation. Housing has become a financial asset ('real estate'), and housing markets are increasingly regulated to promote the financial aspects rather than the social aspects of housing."[20] This impact plays out in ongoing dispossession, including forced evictions and undermining of housing tenure.[21]

To make matters significantly more difficult for Green Lantern residents, even if they found another mobile home park close enough to Little Saigon to remain culturally connected, many of their homes are simply too old to move (due to structural concerns), and many parks do not accept mobile homes more than ten years old. As scholars have shown, policies regulating mobile homes can leave their owners in an unsettled state, with weaker renter protections compared to tenants in rented houses or apartments; often such homes are excluded from rent control and mandatory notice periods for rent increases or evictions.[22]

Mobile homes have a long history in the United States, where, more recently, the decrease in federal housing assistance has increased the popularity of purchasing mobile homes and mobile home communities. In

Manufactured Insecurity, sociologist Esther Sullivan traces the social history of mobile homes in the United States as an important form of affordable housing. During the Great Depression, mobile housing became popular by supplying affordable housing to a transitory workforce in a desperate search for employment. During and after World War II, when the country faced serious material and labor constraints, it again met aggravated housing needs. The increasing popularity of manufactured homes continued in the postwar years and into the modern era. As federal and state governments have withdrawn subsidies and support for affordable housing and shifted to private provisioning, manufactured housing production increasingly fills the affordable housing gap for families.[23] Given the US deficit of housing inventory and unaffordable prices, the Urban Institute has recommended including manufactured homes in the affordable housing supply as in the past; however, with the caveat that greater protections must be added. Manufactured housing is often segregated and financed differently from other housing, with less access to traditional mortgages and treated as a legal hybrid that is personal property (like a car) rather than real property (like most other forms of housing).[24]

EVICTION: CLOSURE AND CONVERSION

The first indication of eviction came in April 2017, when the Walsh family, owners of the Green Lantern Village mobile home park, mailed the Little Saigon residents a letter announcing their plan to close the park and redevelop the site into luxury condominiums. Stunned, the tenants worried they would be displaced and priced out of Orange County's housing market. They vowed to fight the move. Within hours of receiving the announcement, residents mobilized and sprang into action. They quickly translated the closure and conversion letter, written only in English, into Vietnamese and contacted popular Vietnamese news media and co-ethnic networks. Word traveled fast. Residents invited Anh Đỗ, an award-winning journalist from the *Los Angeles Times*, to cover their initial meeting with the Walsh family at Green Lantern. Anh, a second-generation Vietnamese and graduate of the University of Southern California, also wrote for the largest circulating Vietnamese-English newspaper, *Người Việt Daily News*, which, based in Little Saigon, her father founded, as well as the *Seattle Times*, *Dallas Star*, and other publications. Her front-page story in the *Los Angeles Times* caught the attention of

Vietnamese American individuals, organizers, and organizations nation-wide.[25] One organizer of particular significance was Linda Tang, also second-generation Vietnamese, who worked for a statewide, nonprofit housing advo-cacy group. After working on housing affordability for more than a decade, Anh's story in the *Los Angeles Times* was the first time Linda had seen report-ing on Asians and seniors. She brought in her friend, Lili Võ Graham, an attorney with Disability Rights California and also second-generation Vietnamese, who would later represent the residents and the Green Lantern Residents Association as their pro bono attorney before the city council. Linda explained to me how GLV was self-organized from the start:

> In terms of organizing, this was the first time I've worked with residents who were already organized independently. In my head, I was planning on telling them what to do the first time we met: "Okay, first, I'm going to tell them to outreach to the city council members and then reach out to their elected officials." But when I met them, they were like, "Oh, we already did that. We already met with city council members. We already met with the city attor-ney, the planning commission staff, and the city Board of Supervisors." They even reached out to our state senator. And what's also important is that they reached out to the media, so that's how the *LA Times* caught wind of this, because they were already on it. They already knew what they needed to do.

With the process of closure and conversion, or demoviction of the park into luxury condos playing out in Green Lantern, the community chose to respond in a very visible way: to engage in the political process by mobilizing and organizing door-to-door outreach efforts, contacting Vietnamese coun-cil persons, and spreading the word in Vietnamese and US media.

ORGANIZING AT CITY HALL: WHERE WILL WE GO?

Current laws on providing replacement housing after eviction for redevelop-ment do not consider a resident's disability or the importance of living in culturally significant places. The residents of Little Saigon emphasized these points in their testimonies before the Westminster City Council.

Public city council meetings and city commission public hearings were opportunities to mobilize and express discord with the closure. In the sum-mer of 2017, more than fifty residents and allies showed up at Westminster City Hall to speak during the oral communication portion of the meeting and advocate against the closure and conversion of Green Lantern Village.

Thirty-seven residents, speaking in both English and Vietnamese, presented their testimony before the city council, explaining what the park closure would mean in their lives. The room, designed to seat an audience of fifty, was packed, with additional residents and allies standing outside the chamber doors, peeking in and listening. Residents—who sat, stood, and chatted excitedly and nervously in Vietnamese—were recognizable by the large index-sized badges with forest-green lettering that they all wore on their clothes, declaring: "I am a resident of Green Lantern."

Like other local government structures in Orange County, Westminster City Hall sits within a civic center with a campus-like setting of identically stylized buildings with small gardens, fountains, and walkways.[26] I remember visiting the grounds of city hall with my parents over the years to renew their business license, pay fines and taxes, and for my brother to report to his juvenile probation program. Westminster Civic Park comprises plain, undecorated single- and low-level brick structures, with memorials that nod to the English origins of the city, erected in the 1960s when Westminster was 80 percent white. Inside Westminster City Hall is a large map of Westminster, England, along with aging street signs in Gothic script and a prominently centered miniature clock tower, resembling Big Ben.[27] The city council includes the three elected council members, the mayor, and the vice mayor, who sit in a U-shaped arrangement on a raised platform facing the speaker podium and audience. This live-theater arrangement makes it awkward for council members to converse among themselves; rather, the arrangement has the council performing to the audience.[28] Four of the five elected officials, including the mayor, are first- and 1.5-generation Vietnamese, representing a city that is more than 50 percent Vietnamese. Two city clerks sit on the left side of the room and announce via a loudspeaker who is next to come to the podium. Reflecting upon and watching recorded city council meetings between 2009 to the present sheds light on how the fight for Green Lantern unfolded institutionally in city hall.

Westminster Mayor Trí Tạ acknowledged the crowded room. He then requested that each person's time for public speaking be reduced to two minutes to allow everyone the opportunity to speak. The first speaker was Lili Võ Graham, a pro bono attorney with the Legal Aid Society of Orange County, representing Green Lantern residents. Wearing muted business colors and making eye contact with all the council members, she walked to the podium to speak about how the closure and conversion would be devastating to residents:

Mobile home parks in Orange County are important because we are in an affordable housing crisis. There is not enough affordable housing, which has led to an increase in homelessness. The mobile home park owners own the home they live in but lease the land space they're on. As I understand, Green Lantern Mobile Home Park's rent is between $900 and $950, and many people own their mobile home units. That means their total monthly rents are around $950. That is unheard-of here in Orange County. A one-bedroom right now in Orange County is about $1,600. A conversion of the mobile home park to luxury condominiums would be devastating to the residents at Green Lantern. The majority of the park residents are elderly, disabled, and on a very limited income. And many of them are very long-term residents. I spoke yesterday to a resident who's ninety years old. He's lived there for a long time, and he said: "No amount of money could ever replace my ability to live the rest of my life in comfort."

The City must take action and prevent the conversion of this park into a luxury development. These are residents in your community who want to stay in your community. This is their community. Last night one of the residents asked me where the city council was if I wanted to speak, and when they talked to each other, they said: "Oh, it's next to the senior community center where we exercise every day." This is their community. Their friends, family, and doctors are here.[29]

A buzzer sounded, indicating that the speaker's time was over. A voice booming overhead announced the next speaker. A woman in a vibrant sweater and blue pants, using a walker to get to the podium, was assisted by a security guard. She wore a large white name tag: "I am a Green Lantern Resident." Her gray-and-white hair was tied up with a black-and-white polka-dot handkerchief; her blouse was a mélange of yellow, black, and pink, like a sunset. Wearing glasses, she read in Vietnamese from a piece of paper she held:

I've lived here for thirty-one years, and I received notice that there is a conversion plan. Most residents are on a limited income. I'm worried because this is close to my doctors. I want to live in my community, and this is hard for us, especially since many of us cannot speak English. This is where I can communicate—I can read the newspaper, and neighbors and friends, my doctor, grocery store, and dentist all speak Vietnamese. This is where we can communicate and live our lives comfortably. Thank you.

The button buzzed to announce her time was over. Everyone in the audience clapped as she sat down and said "thank you" in English. A stout white man wearing gray slacks and a checkered shirt was next to the podium:

My name is Alex Granger. I've been living at the Green Lantern Mobile Home Park for fifteen years. I'm a seventy-year-old veteran living on Social Security and a fixed income. This proposed move would be financially and emotionally devastating for me. I had no plans whatsoever to have to move. I moved here fifteen years ago, and it was a senior-only park and that's since been changed to an all-ages park, but I'm just really afraid [voice cracks] that this move [stutters] would be [stutters] they would force me into a situation where I could not afford to move anywhere. And I do not want to become another homeless vet statistic on the street. This is, like it was previously stated, an affordable housing situation and [stutters] everything else in the area is impossible to move to because it's a higher cost. And I'm just barely hanging on now by my fingernails. When I heard about this proposed conversion, a month or so ago, I was just sick to my stomach at the prospect of being forced out of my home. I do not want to move, and I, along with all these other people, would greatly appreciate some help from the city council in trying to stop this proposed conversion thing. Thank you.

The next Green Lantern resident to speak was Thúy:

Hi, my name is Thúy. I am a single mom with two kids; one is three years old, and the other is nine years old. I live in Green Lantern for eight years. My daughter has a disability; she can't speak, she can't talk, she can't walk so she needs help. She also needs to see the doctors and specialists around this mobile home park and the special school around here. And she needs to go to therapy a lot, so I'm working around here. I am also caring for my mom and dad, so moving would be very difficult for my life and my whole family. I am the only one to take care of the whole family, so it is difficult for my life for my whole family. So, I don't want to move because my daughter needs a lot. I don't know what to do if we move out. We would miss everything around here. The school, the bus station, everything's around here. So, we don't want to move. I feel like I'm living in darkness. Please. Thank you.

The city clerk called the name of the next speaker. An elderly Vietnamese man walked to the podium:

My name is Daniel Nguyễn. I am seventy-six years old. I am a South Vietnam Army lieutenant colonel and was previously jailed by the Communist Party in Vietnam. Then I came to the US through the government's Humanitarian Operation program. When I first came to the US, I settled in Westminster and Green Lantern Mobile Home Park. Then it was only $450 for the land space but now the rent is very high. It is now $900 per month. I live on limited government benefits. Back in 2009, the owner told residents to leave, and the city council helped, and they could stay. I am asking for your help again to let us stay.

The crowd erupted into applause after each speaker. At this particular meeting, thirty-seven Green Lantern residents testified to the city on how the closure would affect them and why they needed to stay in the community. They explained that mobile homes are not easily mobile despite their nomenclature; relocation can cost up to $20,000. As noted earlier, even if they found another mobile home park close enough to Little Saigon to enable them to remain culturally connected, many of their homes were too old to move due to structural concerns, plus the reality that many parks do not accept mobile homes more than ten years old. Given these constraints, not even ten of the 130 Green Lantern units were relocatable. Thus, eviction would mean that, in the midst of an affordable housing crisis, low-income households—including Vietnamese elders, veterans, people with disabilities, and families—would lose their homes, their Little Saigon and Green Lantern communities, and any chance of accruing generational wealth, all in the name of creating more luxury condos.[30]

The mobilization of Green Lantern residents to speak at city hall is only one example of Asian American neighborhoods inspiring activism. Enclaves like Chinatowns, Little Tokyos, and Little Manilas have long been spaces and sites for social justice and oppositional resistance.[31] In the late 1960s, the Asian American Movement emerged from these environments, followed by other organizations that explicitly formed to mobilize around issues of working-class residents.[32] For example, there are now more than three hundred community organizations serving Little Saigon.

This collective mobilization in the political realm translates into electoral power. Vietnamese have a strong enclave economy with broad socioeconomic diversity, from which new activists and politicians from later generations are emerging. Sociologist Linda Võ shows that the "Vietnamese are a major voting bloc, and their residential and commercial concentration of Little Saigon has contributed to their political gain."[33] High naturalization rates (nearly 76 percent of foreign-born Vietnamese are naturalized citizens),[34] the dense concentration of Little Saigon, and help from the Republican Party have all contributed to the election of Vietnamese American politicians.[35]

Similar to the Cuban political machine in Miami, the Vietnamese are a political force within the local and state governments in California. The community has elected fellow Vietnamese people as city councilors, mayors, and sheriffs within suburban Little Saigon, and beyond the enclave as state senators and as members of the Orange County Board of Supervisors and California State Assembly. In fact, suburban immigrant communities have advantages over central city enclaves when it comes to electoral politics.[36] Once elected, suburban politicians often wield significant power due to the high degree of political autonomy that suburban city governments allocate to their elected mayors, city councilors, and school board members.[37] Sociologist Angie Chung compares ethnic political representation in the suburban Chinatown of Monterey Park, California, and Koreatown in urban Los Angeles. Chung found that the suburban location experiences a stronger residential and entrepreneurial presence based on its population size and related success in sending Chinese political representatives to office.[38]

However, intraethnic political tensions have arisen within the Vietnamese American community, reflecting generational, socioeconomic, and ideological divisions.[39] Thus, expectations that Vietnamese will automatically create a unified political bloc are too simplistic. Westminster, where Green Lantern resides, is the nation's first city council with a Vietnamese American majority—yet they still have not been able to pass rent control for mobile homes.[40] This is despite Westminster Mayor Trí Tạ, who left Vietnam when he was nineteen years old, residing in a mobile home park on Bolsa Avenue.[41] In the fight against the demoviction of Green Lantern, a resident told a local news magazine: "My mayor lives in a mobile home down the street. Maybe he's the next one."[42]

STRATEGIES AGAINST DEMOVICTION

Green Lantern Village Residents Association

"We have to organize; we need an organization to represent all of our voices. We are more powerful as an organization than just as individuals speaking." This was said by a homeowner at the first residents' meeting in 2017 about how they would organize to preserve Green Lantern Village from being closed and converted. Residents decided they needed to form a voluntary organization that would be front-facing and helpful during negotiations with the park owners and city council. After several informal meetings, residents decided to incorporate as Green Lantern Village Residents Association— a nonprofit 501(c) organization with the state—and to be represented by the Legal Aid Association of Orange County. The association's president, Lynn Trương, is an accountant who immigrated to the United States as a teenager. Her father had come after the war as a boat person and then sponsored the

FIGURE 11. Logo for the Mobile Home Residents Coalition of Orange County (courtesy of Sơn Đỗ, 2024).

other family members, including Lynn, her sisters, and her mother. From the first meeting with the park's owners (the Walsh family), Lynn challenged their decision to sell the property and evict the residents. I asked Lynn why and how they formed the Green Lantern Village Residents Association. "We created the organization in reaction to the park owner trying to close and convert the park. It was a reaction and fight against losing our homes. Being an organization lets us negotiate better with the planning commission, city council, and the landowner. A lawyer can represent us to fight better than just as one individual."

Besides publicizing their fight in local news media and speaking before city hall, the residents association enabled GLV to be represented by the Legal Aid Society of Orange County and Disability Rights California. Their approach to organizing and mobilizing follows the tradition of other immigrant-based social movements, such as the Association of Latin American Gardeners and other immigrant environmental justice activists based in Los Angeles.[43] The organizing efforts of the residents association were carried out by Green Lantern inhabitants and aided by second-generation Vietnamese interlocutors at the Legal Aid Society and Disability Rights California and organizers from Little Saigon community organizations like VietRISE.

Coalition Building

Many social movements include charismatic or coalitional leaders. Sơn is one such leader and organizer at GLV. "No one wants to leave here," he tells me at home as we sit at his kitchen table. A former second lieutenant in the Army of the Republic of Vietnam, Sơn served three years during the US war in Vietnam, fighting alongside the Americans. After the fall of Saigon in 1975, he spent six and a half years in a reeducation prison, followed by one year in a refugee camp, before he and his family arrived in the United States in 1994 as refugees through legislation known as the Humanitarian Operation program. His own experiences with dislocation motivated his work to prevent others from experiencing dislocation. Sơn says: "New people moved in just months ago, others just a few years ago. What choices do they have? How does anyone find a safe and affordable place in Orange County?"

Sơn tells me how, three months after the news of the imminent closure by the Walsh family, he printed three thousand flyers. "I took the flyers to seventeen mobile home parks in Westminster by myself, asking people to come to our park for a meeting with various organizations and some people from Buena Vista Mobile Home Park." I ask Sơn: "What is Buena Vista park?" He replies: "Buena Vista is a model case. The landowner had a plan to close the park, just like Green Lantern, to build condominiums. We wanted to learn from them." For five years, more than four hundred residents fought to preserve Buena Vista Mobile Home Park in Silicon Valley after the park owners announced their intention to sell the property to a developer. Even though leases are month to month, it houses long-term residents who have lived in the park since the 1960s. In the end, Buena Vista—one of the few mobile home parks in Silicon Valley—was funded and redeveloped as an affordable housing community through a three-way partnership between several local governments united under the umbrella of Santa Clara County, the city, and the county's housing authority. The park sits next to multimillion-dollar homes, has three billionaire neighbors, and is close to Stanford University. It is under the operating authority of the nonprofit organization Caritas, which purchased the mobile home park to keep it as an affordable housing property.

Sơn's strategic efforts in recruiting more allies included door-to-door outreach, late-night meetings, and meeting other homeowners throughout the city. After distributing his three thousand flyers, Sơn organized two meetings in the GLV clubhouse that led to the formation of the Orange County

Mobile Home Residents Coalition, a larger coalition of which the Green Lantern Village Residents Association is a part. He describes the meetings to me:

> Each meeting had more than two hundred people, including people from all over and their allies from Westminster, Santa Ana, and Garden Grove. In the meeting, some American families said: "We have lived here since we were born until now. We've lived in a mobile home park for forty or fifty years, and we want to form an organization, but we cannot do it in this many years." They asked us: "Why don't you form a group or organization, and we can get together from all the other mobile home parks in Westminster?" So, I said: "Yeah, why not?" With that, I decided to form the coalition, and we named it "Orange County Mobile Home Residents Coalition."

I ask Sơn: "What does OCMHRC do?" He responds:

> We keep bringing people together to fight for their rights from the landlord. We organize people to go to city council meetings and the city planning commission. We had a public hearing with the planning commission. We get the people together to talk because many residents want to speak out.

For over three years, the coalition has mobilized thirty to forty residents to speak at city meetings. Sơn hands me a business card. Written in the now-familiar capital letters in forest-green font, the thick white cardstock says: "Orange County Mobile Home Residents Coalition." Below in Vietnamese—*Liên Hiệp Cư Dân* Mobile Home Orange County—and their email address. "We send monthly emails and information to residents about their rights." I ask him about previous newsletters, and he tells me they are in his office. "Office?" I inquire. "Yes, I'll take you there. Follow me."

In the backyard behind his home is a detached studio office painted the same colors as his home. "It's like a shed, but now it's my office," he says. The ten-by-ten prefabricated structure is the headquarters of OCMHRC. It is insulated with drywall and has electricity and a fresh coat of paint. Above the door is a rectangular white sign with OCMHRC's logo and, in smaller print in Vietnamese and English, "Orange County Mobile Home Residents Coalition—Orange County," with the organization's email. Inside, the office has a desk with shelving; on the shelf is a copy of *California Mobile Home Residency Law*. Across from the desk is a pinboard with stickers from local nonprofit organizations and networks in the Vietnamese community, such as VietRISE and the Viet Film Festival, and an advertisement in Vietnamese for the 2020 US Census, for which Sơn volunteered. Also hanging are a framed letter of thanks from the California State Senate for his organizing work on mobile homes; the "I am a Green Lantern Resident" pin worn by residents at protests; cut-out news stories about Green Lantern and OCMHRC; and a story about Sơn, "a mobile home ambassador."

As we stand in the office, Sơn explains OCMHRC's structure—it has a board of representatives and a director—and why he decided to form the coalition:

> When I formed the coalition, I was sixty-seven years old. I'm waiting and asking many other people to help. I said at the meeting, "All men [who] are young men who want to be a leader come up and help the people," and I don't see anybody. And I thought to myself, why don't I do it? And that is the reason. I cry. Because not only am I helping the people, but I'm helping myself, my family, and my friends, and many, many others, and that's the reason why I stand up.

The coalition provided a means of sharing information across the county with other mobile home park tenants. It enabled GLV residents to learn from more experienced advocacy organizations when they started mobilizing to pass AB 2782 (as described at the beginning of the chapter), the California law recognizing mobile homes as a source of affordable housing and prohibiting them from being torn down and converted to other uses. After the attention from the *Los Angeles Times* article, Sơn led the Green Lantern Village Residents Association and OCMHRC in their collaboration with the Golden State Manufactured-Home Owners League—a statewide nonprofit homeowner advocacy organization formed in 1962—and Manufactured Housing Action, which works on statewide rent control. Other organizations specifically asked Sơn to give public testimony before the state legislature on AB 2872. The bill passed on August 25, 2020, exactly four months before the eviction letter. The bill is designed to protect the shrinking affordable housing stock by prohibiting any city or county from approving a park closure or conversion if it results in a shortage of affordable housing. Before AB 2782, it was optional for local governments to require a park owner to purchase the resident's home for a fair market buyout when residents could not be relocated to new housing. AB 2782 now requires park owners to compensate displaced residents by paying fair market value for their homes when relocation is not possible.

By joining forces with multiple coalitions at the local and state levels, Sơn and the residents of Green Lantern helped pass California legislation AB

2782, making it more challenging for developers or municipalities to change the land use of mobile home parks.[44] The victory was joyous but short-lived, as the next section will explain.

SHORT-TERM VICTORY

The passage of AB 2782 turned out to be a short-term victory for the Green Lantern community. Four months later, on December 24, 2020—Christmas Eve, exactly four months after the success of AB 2782—the Walsh family sent a letter to the residents of Green Lantern Village announcing that Green Lantern was being sold to a new owner: Civic Property Group, an investment company. The letter also gave a ninety-day notice that rent would increase by 10 percent, or $98 monthly. The news was devastating to the residents, who had hoped that the nonprofit organization Caritas would purchase and manage the property to keep it as an affordable housing development. Residents feared that the nearly $450 million price tag that was rumored for the property would mean a substantial increase in property taxes that the residents would have to shoulder. Their fear was warranted, as one resident explained to me one year later:

> The second increase in late spring came six months later to an increase of $150 per resident. When we asked the lawyer, they said we can do nothing. They do the right thing by law. By law, they can do anything because we do not have rent control. New residents to the park now pay $1,600 or $1,700 per month for lot rent. It was $950 before. And next year, we don't know how much the increase will be for everyone. We don't know what will happen next year.

Within eight months, the new owners had increased the lot rental price by nearly 25 percent for existing residents and 175 percent for new residents.

Although the residents could celebrate some victories—conversion and closure did not happen for a variety of reasons, including the passage of AB 2872, the residents' mobilization, time, and bureaucratic environmental impact permits—the new reality was that a developer had purchased the property along with the right to increase rents.

Son agreed to take me to meet with residents to hear what had happened in the last year under the new ownership of Civic Property Group when we met in 2021. Many of their stories exhibit what Peter Marcuse theorizes as "displacement pressures," referring not to actual displacement but the "anxieties, uncertainties, insecurities, and temporalities that arise from possible displacement due to significant rent increases and from the course of events preceding the actual rent increase."[45]

Trang's Home: "What We Need Most Is Rent Control"

An oil painting dominates the living room of Trang's home in Green Lantern. The painting is of a young woman in a purple áo dài, traditional dress, the wind blowing her long dark hair as her attention is focused on something in the distance. Plaques and awards line another wall. Photos fill the mantel of a cream-colored fireplace. We sit on worn, elegant, Victorian-style couches. Trang wears a black tracksuit; her hair is dyed a reddish auburn and covered with a stylish fedora cap.

She is seventy-eight years old and is the young woman featured in the painting. Trang is a celebrity in her own right in the Vietnamese diaspora, famous for her well-known political and entertainment radio station. She proudly says she can speak with Central, Northern, and Southern Vietnamese accents. "If I meet people from any particular region, I speak with them according to their accent." This is the story she tells me, matching the Southern Vietnamese accent of people in the room (who include my dad, Sơn, and me):

> I chose this place [Green Lantern] because I only had a limited amount of money, so I could not buy any house elsewhere, I could only buy a mobile home. I did not have enough money to buy a single-family house, so the mobile home was cheaper. When I first came here, it only costs $580 for the land rent, but now it costs more than $1,000 per month. The price has doubled. Land in Westminster is expensive. I was worried about the park closing when the Walsh family wanted to sell it. Even though they would compensate us several tens of thousands of dollars, it was still not enough to buy a house to live like living in this house. I cannot buy a house or even an apartment like this—with this many rooms or as big.

Mobile homes offer the opportunity for home ownership but come with housing vulnerability. Even though many homeowners own outright or have a mortgage on their mobile home, an actual mobile home community is almost always the private property of a landowner who runs it as a profit-making enterprise.[46] It is estimated that between 79 and 95 percent of mobile homes in the United States are never moved after being placed on their first site: the cost of moving a mobile home is substantial, including the cement foundation, porches, and landscaping.[47] In areas like Orange County, with tight housing markets and an absence of vacant spaces, it is virtually impossible to resite them.[48] Not surprisingly, the interests of those who own mobile homes and those who own mobile home parks are often in direct opposition to one another. Park owners want to maximize their return on the underlying land by raising lot rents, especially in areas with land scarcity and high cost of living, and residents want to stay in their community.[49] Trang expresses her worry about the ability to stay and where she would go:

> No one can afford to live here if the land rent keeps increasing. Many people will leave their houses because of that. The new owner has not given us any room to escape. If the land rent keeps increasing like that until we cannot pay for the land rent, we must leave our homes. We can move, but where can we move to? There is no place to move to.

In Orange County, as elsewhere in the country with a limited supply of housing, mobile homes in a park can be valuable, but mobile homes without a space are virtually worthless.[50] "Houses in this area [Little Saigon]," Trang explains, "are as expensive as Fountain Valley and Huntington Beach [whiter, more affluent cities in the county closer to the beach]. The price of a house starts at around $1 million here now." As discussed earlier, owners of manufactured homes who rent the land below them often lack the security of basic tenants' rights accorded apartment dwellers or conventional homeowners,[51] leaving them trapped by rapidly increasing rents. Trang describes the solution she and the Green Lantern Village Residents Association advocate:

> What we need most is rent control, because if there isn't, not just for ten years, but only in five years, I won't be able to afford to live here. . . . Most residents here are seniors and Vietnamese who only live on welfare, so how can they afford to live here? They have to move to live with their children and grandchildren or whatever, which I do not have.

Manufactured housing is an important option for elderly people on a fixed income; according to the US Census, nearly one-third of adults who live in mobile homes are sixty and older.[52] Trang and Sơn are well aware of how rent stabilization policies, such as the one recently passed in Santa Ana, would help them stay in place. As of 2023, ninety-two cities and nine counties in California have some form of stabilization policy that limits rent increases on mobile home park lots; Westminster is not one of them.[53]

In *Manufactured Insecurity*, Sullivan compares eviction experiences in Florida and Texas and argues that mobile homes are a privately developed and operated form of unsubsidized affordable housing where residents remain at the whim of the property owners. While liberal states such as California have made the conversion and eviction of mobile home residents more difficult through legislation such as AB 2782, residents still exist in a liminal state where property owners have the power to increase rents beyond what residents can afford. Most counties, local governments, and states have not enacted laws to regulate rent control—and when rent stabilization or rent control is passed, it often does not apply to mobile home parks, which are considered a special category. In California, private landlords have the right to increase the rent every ninety days for mobile homes. The displacement pressures of GLV residents' tenuous right to place are evident in the continued frustration and fear of the residents with whom I spoke.

Trang walks us to the door, and we say our goodbyes. She says to send her a copy of the book when it comes out, and we wave as Sơn leads us to Quyên's home on our visit to Green Lantern Village.

Quyên's Home: "We Cannot Go Anywhere. We Will Be Homeless"

Quyên's home is in the corner of the tract, where the road makes a U shape. The home is spacious and freshly painted; framed photos of her family hang on the walls, and a large, golden, embossed Buddha sits above the fireplace. Her recently remodeled kitchen has new, white appliances. An elderly woman with dyed black hair, she comes to the door using a walker. Inside, the living room has been transformed into a small bedroom; she recently broke her leg, she explains, and now must stay in the living room. She hobbles to the kitchen table. The room is immaculate, the floors spotless.

Quyên and I sit at the glass dining room table and chat in Vietnamese and English, while my father and Sơn sit in the living room and talk. Quyên came to the United States in 1990 at the age of sixty-two. She was a businesswoman in Vietnam from an upper-middle-class family. After the war, she and her "family were forced to move to a new economic zone in the countryside to work hard labor." She recounts being harassed for years by government agents, who would call and show up at their door weekly to interview them and request confessions. Eventually, the government forced them to move again into the mountainous area of Central Vietnam to work in another economic zone. She defied orders and moved her daughter to the Mekong Delta in the south, to escape by boat to the United States. She lives in Green Lantern with her daughter, Loan, who works at an electronics factory, and her granddaughter, Jenny, who is in high school. Photographs of her granddaughter's local high school sports teams hang on the wall and her trophies sit on a shelf. Quyên explains her difficulties in finding a job since she immigrated late in life:

> I came to California [from Vietnam] because my older sister was living here. I also went to work in a factory because my sister's child, my niece, was a factory manager. But at that time the salary was only four dollars an hour so at the end of the month we did not have enough money to pay for the bills because every four months we had to pay for the car and many other things, so I did not have enough to pay for all of that, so I only worked there for more than a year then I moved to San Jose, I had a friend there. There were a lot of factories there. When I first worked there [in 1992], the salary was $4.50 an hour. After working in that factory for several months, another factory offered a higher salary, so I left without any regrets, as long as the salary was higher. The factory there offered $5.50 an hour, so I stayed there. I worked there until the year, you know, the 9/11 incident, most factories in San Jose were closed. Then, we moved to Green Lantern. My daughter also works in the factory. I had a hard time finding a job then. Whenever I sent my job application, they all responded the same. The unemployment and state benefits were too little, so I tried to get a job. I sent my job application to many places, but no one offered me a job. I am seventy-nine years old. No one wants to hire me. I am too old.

Even combining Loan's full-time salary with Quyên's social security check, they cannot afford to stay in the mobile home they own, given the new lot rent—and their mobile home is too old to move to another park. Nor do they want to move.

> [What I like] most about Green Lantern is that I can meet Vietnamese people when I live here. They are also seniors, so I can talk or have conversations with them since I do not speak English. My daughter purchased this house for us. The problem now is that my rent is very high now. I must pay about $1,270. Ten years ago, the lot rent was around $800. It's too much. They said the price has gone up because the new landowner has to fix a lot of things.

Quyên continues talking about the mental stress of worrying about when they could lose their home:

> Under the old owner, when we heard that they wanted to build a condo in this place, we were so worried. We could not eat or sleep for days and nights because we did not know where we would move to. Whenever we talked about

it or whenever we closed our eyes, we were worried that when we opened our eyes we would have to move out of here, we were really scared. Fortunately, Mr. Sơn asked us to work together to talk to the landowner not to evict us from our homes. Most of us, as you know, living in mobile homes, are poor people. So, where [can we] move to, we will be homeless, so we fought against the landowner's eviction decision for many years. I attended all the city council meetings. I stood up and spoke at the city council many times to raise my voice. Before, we feared the park closing; now, the fear is how we will manage the rent.

We cannot go anywhere. We will be homeless. My health is getting worse and worse, so I only hope to live here for the rest of my life. I hope it will not be redeveloped again because most residents here have low incomes.

Eviction, in this case, is slow and psychologically unsettling. After years of her family being harassed and continually displaced in the wake of the war in Vietnam, she now finds herself reliving this stress in the United States, under the constant duress of not knowing when they will be evicted from their home and displaced again. To supplement her social security check, Quyên, who is nearly eighty at the time of our interview, attempts to find work under the table; yet it is not enough to maintain their home. Being a senior citizen on a fixed income of a little over $900 per month, the lot rent is now more than her monthly social security benefits and not affordable even with her daughter working full-time.

The specter of dislocation haunts Quyên even after the uncertainty of eviction and the park's closure is gone. Now, a slow eviction takes place as families are priced out and displaced over time by increasing rent hikes. These displacement pressures create psyche anxiety and uncertainty about the future and losing one's community. Matthew Desmond shows the real consequences of eviction: it can prolong families' residential instability, which begets economic instability, and periods of homelessness often follow eviction.[54] With continued increases in rent, Quyên and her neighbors' ability to maintain their homes is uncertain.

Phong's Home: "We Are Close to the Vietnamese Community"

The third home we visit, Uncle Phong's, is a couple of houses south of Quyên's home. A potted garden—with regal purple-and-white orchids, red and orange roses, and kumquats—lines the staircase to the front door. We sit at the glass-covered living room table, covered with photographs of his wife and three adult daughters on trips across the country. Phong has lived in Green

Lantern Village for fifteen years. He was in the South Vietnamese army for five years and then held in a communist reeducation prison for seven years. When he retired, he sold his house in Southern California and moved to Green Lantern after he worked out that it would be less expensive to spend his golden years in the mobile home park. At that time, the lot rent was $500. He loves Green Lantern because "people take care of each other."

> When somebody is sick, we inform others in the neighborhood. During the coronavirus, there are three hundred people living here, but no one tested positive.... We know many people died outside this neighborhood. We take turns driving each other for shots. I drove that lady you interviewed before here [Quyên] for her COVID shot.

Mobile home parks such as Green Lantern often have a strong sense of belonging and a supportive community. As one study found, they are "not transitional housing but places people live and plan to live for many years."[55] These social networks of support and community disappear once a household is displaced. This is the story Phong told about the eviction process:

> In fact, our displacement has two stages. The first stage, the first eviction, was to close this mobile home village to build new housing. However, in case of a closure, mobile home park owners must help relocate tenants' mobile homes within fifty miles. If a home cannot be relocated to another park because of its age or condition, then an owner should pay fair market value for the manufactured home.
> What the Walsh family was offering us was too low—only one-third of the house's value. The owner also said if we wanted to move our mobile house somewhere else, they could do it for us. But where could we move to? Here, we are close to other people, close to the Vietnamese community, close to doctors, and the Vietnamese market. It is easy to buy Vietnamese food here. Here markets are close to each other, only one mile from one another. For food, we only need to go to Bolsa. I only need to walk four or five minutes to the markets.

This sense of cultural community and place, the walkable co-ethnic services, and local social supports, cannot easily be replicated. Listening to the stories of residents exposed how eviction is slow and psychologically unsettling. Trang, Quyên, and Phong describe the lived experiences of housing vulnerability amid corporate control of GLV and financialized gentrification. In the face of rising rents, GLV residents once again put a plan into action to organize and subvert this attempt to displace them.

"THE NEW LANDOWNER IS A COMPANY": CORPORATE OWNERS VS. ALTERNATIVE LAND MODELS

Only eight states in the United States have policies to regulate mobile home park closures, and even where such legal protections do exist, they are not always followed. California's protections were not yet in place when the Walsh family first tried to evict GLV residents in 2017, leaving them to fend for themselves. Sơn describes the Green Lantern Village Residents Association plan to me:

> If the park was approved to close and be converted by the city council, the residents planned to protest. We would do a hunger strike. Some men said that they wanted to burn themselves in protest. That means we fight until the end. If we could not negotiate with the owners, and the city council approved the landowner to close the park, then residents would protest in front of the city hall. We would stay there for many days.

With the help of OCMHRC, they derailed the owner's plan to have the park conversion and evictions completed within the year. Sơn reminisces about that time and how residents rallied to fight the eviction.

> The landowner wasn't expecting the residents to fight or organize. We worked together with many other nonprofit organizations and lawyers who also raised their voices to support the residents' requests, and the city council extended their time. They never told us when we would have to move out, but in the end, it took much longer than the Walsh family thought.

The work of nonprofit organizations across the United States in creating alternative land ownership models for mobile homeowners has been vital in stopping demoviction. In some cases, nonprofit organizations have acquired mobile home parks for sale.[56] Pro bono lawyers for the Green Lantern Village Residents Association contacted Caritas, a nonprofit organization based in Southern California that is part of the alternative land movement. In partial fulfillment of their mission to "empower residents and preserve affordable communities," Caritas owns and manages more than thirty mobile home communities in California and Oregon,[57] including ones in other areas of Little Saigon, two parks in nearby Garden Grove, and locales in Santa Monica, Napa, and elsewhere across the state. Sơn explained:

Caritas met with us many times and they promised to try to buy Green Lantern at market price. Caritas is a religious nonprofit organization. It's a worldwide religious charity organization. However, Caritas could never get in contact with the landowners. The landowners refused to talk with the organization.

Instead, the Walsh family sold the property to Civic Property Group, a limited liability company. "The new landowner is also terrible," Phong told me. "No one understands why he keeps increasing the land rent so much. The rent keeps going up and up." Management practices of financialized landlord investors include raising rents; reducing maintenance, repairs, and services; and "transferring responsibilities such as paying utilities to the tenant," squeezing or extracting as much value as possible from tenants.[58] Sơn and Phong describe the extractive management practices:

> SƠN: One individual or family does not own the land. The new landowner is a company.
>
> PHONG: Well, yes, this company is terrible or as we say in Vietnamese the new landowner is *lưu manh* [insidious]. Before, when the former family owned the land, the average land rent increase was about 3 percent annually. But before they announced the closure plan, the land rent increased by 5 percent. The company sent another letter in June saying that the property tax was rising by thousands of dollars, which is divided by every household, meaning everyone has to pay $150 more for property tax.

Ownership of many mobile home parks has shifted from individual or family ownership to corporate ownership in the last two decades. Following the 2008 financial crisis, investment and private equity firms rushed to buy single-family homes and extended into other housing market areas, including mobile home parks.[59] Because it is difficult and expensive to move mobile homes, they are viewed as a stable investment. Typically, the new owners are out-of-state investment and private equity firms attracted to the high rate of return accorded by this form of housing—an investment strategy that exploits poor, elderly, and low-income persons.[60] According to Mobile Home University, a website that teaches investors how to buy and sell mobile home parks, "Mobile home parks yield the highest monetary returns in commercial real estate, higher even than apartment complexes."[61] After the transfer to corporate ownership, tenants' rent often increases by 20 to 50 percent within a matter of months, with corporatized ownership pushing out residents across the nation.[62] The rapidly increasing rents from corporatized landowners are not within reach of the Green Lantern residents. Sơn outlined the financial misfit between the new rents and residents' incomes:

> Most Vietnamese seniors here were in the army and came here through the Humanitarian Operation program. When they came to the United States, they only worked for about ten to twenty years before they retired. They also worked in low-paying jobs, so when they retire, their social security monthly payments are also low. Their average SSA generally is about $1,000 to $1,100. For couples, their SSA may be a bit higher, but for the singles who lost their husbands and wives, especially those who only have SSI, their monthly retirement benefit is only about $900, which is not even enough to pay for the land rent. So, fortunately, Vietnamese people, for example, someone like you, you are also Vietnamese, you may help your parents out. That's very common in the Vietnamese community. Some households here that I know, for example, the household over there, the uncle lives there alone by himself, and his retirement benefit is just about $1,000. So, most Vietnamese seniors need their children's financial support.

Across the country, giant Wall Street firms and private equity firms exploit and evict tenants and owners of mobile homes by mercilessly raising rents. The displacement pressure of potential eviction, alongside the long-term effects of personal trauma from the war, with its loss of community and home, create long-term stress as refugees continue to struggle for a decent life and financial security in unsettled circumstances. Phong further explained: "Many residents suffered from sleep deprivation, eating disorders, and [name redacted] even had a stroke shortly after the landowner announced the closure." Sơn nodded and said: "There are two other uncles I planned to introduce to you, too, but they are too weak recently, and both of them have had symptoms of early Alzheimer's. I think the closure plan caused their illness to become worse because they worried a lot and couldn't eat."

The material and mental consequences of financialized housing cannot be overstated; this new form of corporate ownership is deeply implicated in the loss of culture and community support and, at times, even an individual's health. The lack of adequate policy protections has left many Vietnamese refugees unsettled in the country that was supposed to represent resettlement and stability.

What will happen to the residents of Green Lantern Village? What lessons can we learn from their organizing and persistence? Homeownership is the American dream, and a home is often one's most valuable asset. Homeownership often leads to greater housing security and the accrual of generational wealth.[63] Yet not all homes are equal, and current housing law rarely protects owners of mobile homes. As seen, manufactured homes are unsubsidized affordable housing with weak protections for renters and owners. For mobile home park investors, however, "it's kind of a dream—inelastic demand. A lot of people own mobile homes but can't move. They must keep paying."[64] Large corporations buying mobile home parks are taking advantage of low-interest subsidized loans from Fannie Mae and Freddie Mac.[65] The government originally designed these programs to enable individuals to afford to buy a house to live in; however, that has changed. "They [still] do this for individual homeowners, [but] they also do it for big corporations that build or buy apartment buildings, condos, and mobile home parks."[66] When I asked Lili Võ Graham, the pro bono attorney for Green Lantern, what she envisions for the future, she said:

> There is never any true one triumph over capitalism. We are never going to be able to take down capitalism. It's more expensive for corporate owners to close the park again, and now more difficult than it's worth, so they will probably keep raising rents and pushing people out involuntarily with bad conditions. The land value will go up and up, and it's going to drive people out, so at some point, developing the land will be more lucrative than keeping people in place, so that's what we're seeing. The huge trend is driven by the market, which is unfriendly toward the poor and the aging.

In 2023, Congress reported that less than 5 percent of the US housing supply was accessible to older, disabled citizens.[67]

California housing advocate Linda Tang, who was active with the GLV fight, described to me possible next steps for residents in 2022:

> (1) Wait and see what happens as rent increases, the property could be again sold to another entity; (2) find a nonprofit housing developer to buy the property; (3) move; (4) campaign for a citywide space rent stabilization ordinance. [The city council can approve rent stabilization, which] is the easiest and least expensive route but needs a council majority to support, which is difficult, or gather signatures to place it on the city council ballot, which is expensive and time-consuming.

Residents can also build on the momentum of other recent success stories in Orange County to protect themselves from corporate landlords. As seen in chapter 2, Santa Ana residents rallied city council members to pass rent control and eviction protection ordinances that included implementing a rental registry for landlords that identifies households at risk of displacement. And in 2021, Fullerton and Anaheim passed AB 978, which limits mobile home park rent increases to a 5 percent maximum per year.[68]

When I asked residents what they see as the future of Green Lantern, many responded with both uncertainty and the hope of spending the rest of their lives there. "We can have a model co-op," or resident-owned community, replied a homeowner. There is precedent for this. In New Hampshire, residents saved several mobile home parks by pooling their money and purchasing the land beneath their homes. But what if the land is too expensive for the residents to buy?

In some cases, nonprofit organizations, such as ROC USA, assist owners of mobile homes to create cooperatives and raise capital to buy their communities from investors at fair market value. ROC comes from "resident-owned communities," a housing model that includes collective land ownership and shared governance, with residents setting their lot fees. ROCs result in lower rent increases and help protect residents from eviction.[69] Like a co-op apartment building, homeowners continue to own their homes but now have an ownership stake in the property, contributing fees for property maintenance.[70] ROC USA is a nonprofit organization that has spearheaded a network of more than three hundred resident-owned communities across the United States since the 1980s.[71] Like Caritas, nonprofit organizations can also acquire communities that are for sale. Alternative land ownership models, such as co-ops and nonprofit ownership, are crucial strategies to help protect mobile park communities like Green Lantern against eviction and displacement.

By studying how Green Lantern residents organized so effectively, we can learn how grassroots campaigns can challenge and contest local governments when faced with eviction and unjust laws. Green Lantern leaders and residents formally organized into a nonprofit organization, partnered with the local legal aid society, other Vietnamese-led organizations, and nonprofits focused on housing justice in the community, state, and nation. Residents mobilized and testified before legislative bodies, formed a countywide coalition by facilitating meetings with other mobile home parks, planned protests, lobbied city and state officials, and spoke to media in Vietnamese and

English. Second-generation Vietnamese pro bono lawyers and community members aided residents. Still, what mattered in the end was the collective will and action of residents who created symbols around which to organize, contacted city officials and the board of supervisors to make their voices heard, and overall defended their right to organize.

Despite the passage of AB 2782, the statewide bill that helped prevent the immediate demoviction of their park, Green Lantern residents remain in a state of protracted displacement as their corporate landlord continually increases lot rent. While the legislation might have averted demoviction in the short run, residents are thus slowly being displaced nonetheless. The story of Green Lantern is hardly unique to Vietnamese living in suburban mobile home communities. The financialization of property markets is creating a critical mass of disenfranchised residents who are losing their hold on suburbia.

In suburban Little Saigon, other forms of displacement are also occurring. More than eight thousand Vietnamese in the United States are waiting to be deported to Vietnam. In the final chapter, I explore further mechanisms of displacement, both visible and invisible, that threaten the community. I describe the protracted displacement of Vietnamese refugees who face immigration limbo as well as the efforts of community organizers in Little Saigon and Vietnam who are demanding the right to home and to stay in their community.

FOUR

The Right to the Suburb

IN MARCH 2021, Vietnamese American organizations in Little Saigon took to the streets to protest the Biden administration's deportation of more than thirty Vietnamese refugees. A bilingual sign declared: "Biden Be Better; Biden, Hãy làm tốt hơn: STOP Deporting Refugees; Ngừng trục xuất người tị nạn." A trilingual Vietnamese, English, and Spanish banner, with the signatures of twenty-five Vietnamese American organizations in Orange County, read: "Bring Human Rights Home: Rally and Car Caravan." The coalition's statement read: "Deporting Vietnamese refugees to a country that they have not known since they were young is an anti-Asian violent attack, not only on them as individuals, but on their family and our Vietnamese and immigrant communities across the country."[1]

Minh Nguyễn held a sign as an onslaught of cars honked. He is a coordinator and trainer with the University of Southern California Gould School of Law Post-Conviction Justice Project (PCJP), where he trains law students to work with incarcerated people. In addition, on weekdays he works full-time at a computer store and spends many weekends and evenings as a licensed dog trainer with his own dog-training business. He lives with a friend in a new apartment building in Little Saigon and does social justice organizing on the side with myriad postprison reentry programs; in addition to PCJP, he is involved with Human Rights Watch, API Rise, and the Anti-Recidivism Coalition. His goal, he explained to me, is "to change the laws to help people on the inside and for social justice reform." His passion for this work is personal, based on his twenty-five years of incarceration: "I was just recently released from prison in 2020. I was arrested in 1998 when I was nineteen years old. I was convicted and sentenced to life without the possibility of parole.... I was supposed to die in prison. Governor [Jerry] Brown noticed my change in prison [and] he signed a commutation and shortened my sentence from life without a possibility of parole to twenty-five years."[2]

Minh took advantage of all the programs the prison offered, earning his associate of arts degree, getting involved with the Catholic Church, reading voraciously, and, through a competitive selection process, participating in a job- and skill-training class to become a certified dog trainer. Since his release, he has led a purposeful and intentional life supporting his community, family, and friends. Despite this, he remains one of eight thousand Vietnamese who are undocumented—having lost their permanent residency status when they went to prison—and now living in deportation limbo in the United States. Minh is uncertain when the US Immigration and Customs Enforcement Agency (ICE) might try to detain and repatriate him to Vietnam, a country he left as a child and barely remembers.

What might surprise many people is that ICE can revoke the status of a lawful permanent resident (green card holder), refugee, or asylee—anyone not yet a citizen—and deport them if they have a criminal conviction. Several factors determine whether they will be deported, including what they were convicted of, their prison sentence, and when the conviction happened.[3] Noncitizens who receive an order of removal (also called a deportation order) from an immigration judge lose their former immigration status as green card holders or refugees and suddenly find themselves without status. Tín Thành Nguyễn, a Vietnamese American immigration lawyer, explained to me that "once you become deportable, you lose your status. Before, you were a green card holder, but now you have nothing. It is because of the history of war and diplomatic relations between Vietnam and the US that even if you have an order of removal to Vietnam, you will not get physically deported [immediately]." But nationals of other countries would be put on a bus or plane out of the country shortly after receiving an order of removal.

Since 1998, nearly seventeen thousand Southeast Asians have received final orders of deportation. More than two thousand have been deported to Vietnam, Cambodia, and Laos.[4] Many of these community members came to the United States as refugee children and were raised as Americans. Even though they have final orders of removal, many Southeast Asians are not immediately deported from the United States; instead, while waiting in immigration limbo, they start families and businesses, return to school, and get involved in their community. It can be months, years, or decades before they are deported.[5]

This chapter focuses on who has the right to stay in Little Saigon. How do federal immigration policies frame particular immigrants as desirable while banishing others? Who does the immigration regime welcome? Transnational refugee deportees show the limits and liminality of neoliberal immigration policies that bestow the gift of belonging. Transnational deportees are refugees who fled violence and war and then found themselves confronting further violence in the United States that precipitated their return to their homeland. US immigration policy stigmatizes them as "criminal aliens" for expulsion, negating that they have families, lives, and businesses in the United States, placing them in legal liminality and creating another form of protracted displacement.

Many theories of urban renewal and gentrification examine the physical act of displacement: the shift or break from one place to the next. However, as we have seen, other forms of community change and displacement underlie Little Saigon's story, such as housing insecurity, suburban gentrification, and the fear of losing one's community. Vietnamese in Little Saigon, with orders of removal waiting to be deported to Vietnam, are adrift in the American dream. The first part of this chapter focuses on Vietnamese deportees and shows how deportation is yet another way that cycles of refugee displacement persist long after resettlement. The analysis of deportees and their contemporary experiences in Vietnam shows who has the right to stay in suburbia—and the creative ways the community is responding to the deportation of family members to shape Little Saigon.

PROTRACTED DISPLACEMENTS AND REFUGEE
WAREHOUSING

When the mark of a criminal record, no matter how minor or serious, creates a prison-to-deportation pipeline for Vietnamese refugees in Little Saigon who came to the United States as children, we are talking about *protracted displacement*, or unsettlement. Though the United States was meant to be their ultimate place of relocation, the reality often ends up being far from the anticipated permanent and humanitarian resettlement. As novelist and professor Việt Thành Nguyễn writes: "The United Nations says refugees stop being refugees when they find a new permanent home. It has been a long time since I have been a refugee in the definition of the United Nations: 'Someone who has been forced to flee his or her country because of persecution, war, or violence.'"[6] Nguyễn poignantly questions the limits of the United Nations definition, because when does being a refugee begin and when does it end?[7]

Most refugees experience their condition as refugees indefinitely, across generations and space, through memories and experiences of being displaced or being the other, even in their new country of settlement.[8]

Protracted displacement is the experience of living in deportation limbo, uncertain where one belongs or whether one will be forcibly repatriated to one's country of origin. In this limbo, refugee law enshrines state violence and the broken promise of non-refoulement, which prevents the forcible return of a refugee to a country where they can reasonably fear for their life or their freedom. Since the mid-1990s, mass deportation and rates of deportation have been unparalleled, with the raw numbers of deportees significantly higher than in any previous period in history.[9]

As seen in the next section, the prison-to-deportation pipeline is a double punishment that separates families and negatively affects community formation in Little Saigon. The stories here build on foundations of systemic state violence that condition refugees' experiences long after they arrive in their countries of resettlement and illuminate the often hidden ways neoliberal immigration policies shape the suburban landscape.

The Prison-to-Deportation Pipeline

I interview Minh after having been introduced by a mutual friend, a Vietnamese American therapist and social worker in Little Saigon. Minh was born in Saigon in 1972 and describes coming to Orange County to live with his mother after they had been separated for six years. His father was a drug addict, and Minh grew up watching him abuse his mother, who escaped alone by boat to the United States in 1980, leaving Minh and his siblings in the care of his grandmother in Vietnam. Minh was eight years old when his mother left, and he did not see her again until he was fourteen. He explains how he felt abandoned:

> I felt like: "She just left to get a better life for herself. Why didn't she take us?" And at that time, I didn't understand it takes a lot of money to get us on the boat, and you know we were poor, and we didn't understand any of that. So, when I came to the US, I had a lot of resentment toward her already, like why she abandoned us, and now she's remarried to someone new with a new kid that I didn't know while I was over there [in Vietnam]. So, in the beginning, it was a struggle; she was a stranger. I didn't know who my mom was. I was eight years old, even when before I was eight, she wasn't around a lot. So, coming over here, I was a stranger to the culture, a stranger to the people, and

now even a stranger to my mom because I didn't even know who she was. So, it was hard when I first came to the United States.

Besides experiencing culture shock upon arriving in the United States, Minh had trouble at school, partly because he did not speak English well enough to understand the teacher, and the teacher did not speak Vietnamese. He was picked on at school shortly after arriving in the United States. When he decided to fight back verbally, four students beat him up. He was expelled. He remembers sitting bleeding in the school office, unable to explain in English that the other students were bullying him. He had no friends, but when he was forced to vacate school premises and empty his locker, a Vietnamese classmate came up to him, walked him out, and whispered at the gate: "Don't worry, we're going to get them for you."

> When I first moved to Orange County, I knew there were a lot of gangs here. Everyone was talking about the gangs in San Jose and Orange County. The next day, he [the classmate from the day before] and a bunch of his friends came to pick me up from my house after I got kicked out of school, and they said: "Ride along with us." So, I ride along with them, and we return to school. They told me to "sit out here. Don't go back into the school." I can't go in anyway because I've been expelled, so I sit in the car and wait for those guys to come out. They beat the crap out of them [the bullies]. And I felt happy; I was like: "Wow, who is this guy? Why did he come to defend me?" They just did that. We were laughing and high-fiving in the car; I felt like that's where I belonged, something inside me. I mean, I come home from school, and my mom is yelling at me: "Why did you get kicked out of school? It's your fault. It's your fault. Your fault." Now you have a group of guys who don't even know me but come to defend me, and they didn't even ask me to join the gang. They didn't try to pressure me to join. But at the time, I thought maybe this was something I belonged in.
>
> I spent time with them, and I became one of them. When I went to my next school, I could see that people feared me because I hung out with those guys. As a teenager, you are looking for acceptance. At that time, we called it respect. From the moment I set foot in school when I first came to this country, I was always picked on. I was always teased. By hanging out with those guys, I could go to school, and people respected me. This is what I want: going to school without fear.

Like many young Vietnamese in his position during the 1980s and 1990s, Minh joined a gang of other Vietnamese. This was a way to protect themselves from discrimination and "establish their own sense of identity and find ways to deal with their families' material conditions."[10] The emergence of

Vietnamese American street gangs coincided with the increasing racialization of youths of color in California and the nation more generally. The so-called War on Drugs that started in the 1970s and "tough on crime" legislation of the following decades precipitated an overpolicing of communities of color in the United States. The broader politics of the 1980s, including policies of mass incarceration, constructed Southeast Asian youths during this time as contentious subjects, as Kevin Lâm describes, subject to the architecture of the police surveillance state.[11] Consequently, many young Vietnamese arriving in the United States after the war became easy targets for gang recruitment and state punishment. By the 1990s, the arrest rate for Asian and Pacific Islander youths dramatically increased by over 250 percent over the course of the decade.[12]

The rise of youth gangs in California led to the enactment of numerous propositions and laws primarily targeting youths from working-class Black, Indigenous, and minority communities. Specific California state laws such as the Gang Violence and Juvenile Crime Prevention Act (Proposition 21), the Street Terrorism Enforcement and Prevention Act of 1988 (STEP), and the so-called three-strikes law of 1994 (Proposition 184) directly impacted gang members and nonmembers alike.[13] Police pulled over and profiled many youths of color who were perceived to be gang members, including Vietnamese. They were then photographed and placed in the state's gang database, known as Cal-Gang.[14] Minh describes his feelings at the time:

> I was looking for a sense of belonging. Once, I ran away from home for a month, and nobody went looking for me, not my mom or stepdad. I was sixteen years old. At that time, I felt like they didn't care if I lived or if I died. I felt like nobody cared at home. But every time I went to hang out with those guys, I felt like they do care because if something happened to me, they'd be there. If I needed clothes, they got me clothes. When I started hanging out with them and doing all the illegal activity, I slowly became one of them. But I didn't know ... I was in a dangerous game, and you go deeper. Looking back, I could have been dead at any time. Then, I thought it was a fun game. It was about respect, feeling like you belong, and people who love and respect you and will protect you, and that's what you're looking for: protection most of the time.

I feel connected to Minh as I listen to his story. My cousin Tim lived with us and had joined a gang after arriving from Vietnam as a youth. He left Vietnam at five years old, escaping by boat. As his family ran on the beach trying to reach the boat for escape, the police shot at and wounded his parents and sister; they never made it to the United States. My cousin spent three years in a refugee camp in the Philippines and then came to the United States as an unaccompanied minor. Now that we are both adults with kids of our own, I asked him why he never told me. He said some secrets and stories are never told: "You do not know what I have had to go through." At forty-five years old, he struggles with a gambling addiction and finding stable employment and housing. Another cousin who came when he was twelve years old is in prison, and we worry he will be transferred to ICE after he is released. Through Minh's story, I see my cousins' stories, how the system failed them, leaving many within our families and community to live every day in secrecy and with stigma. While ICE transfers are a national issue, they are more visible in California, which has the largest immigrant population in the country.[15]

There is something wrong when the systems intended to provide refuge and protection—here, the refugee resettlement program with its insufficient social, psychological, and financial support—become the cause of further unsettlement.[16] Heba Gowayed's study of Syrian refugees in the United States shows how "refugees arrive in the very countries whose foreign policies have subjugated them or people like them, and whose domestic policies are patterned by the same racisms that facilitated those foreign policies."[17] Comparing refugee policies in Germany, Canada, and the United States, Gowayed finds that US policies focus more on self-reliance. Although the US government takes responsibility for who may enter, once they are here the government expects refugees to be responsible for their successes or failures.[18]

In reducing Minh's prison sentence, California Governor Jerry Brown recognized that Minh had, indeed, taken personal responsibility to do what he could to set himself up for success, including participating in many programs of readiness for post-incarceration and presenting exceptional behavior. Minh's sentence reduction was part of a statewide reevaluation of inmate sentences, an acknowledgment of the "radical and unprecedented sentencing increases in the nation and increases in the prison building boom of the 1980s and the diminished role of parole in California's system of sentencing and rehabilitation."[19] Overall, the United States has one of the world's highest incarceration rates; despite having only 5 percent of the world's population, it houses nearly 25 percent of the world's imprisoned population.[20] I ask Minh: "How did you learn that you were being released? How did they tell you?"

So, it was Christmas Eve, December 2018, and they told me I had a phone call from the governor's office. I was like: "For what?" I go in, and the secretary from the governor's office says that they have reviewed my file and, given my interview and my work in prison, that I am a different person from when I committed my crime. The governor has granted my commutation and commuted my sentence from life without the possibility of parole to twenty-five years. It was Christmas Eve, and it was the best Christmas present ever. You know, it seems so unreal. I remember just like I couldn't sleep because I was afraid it was a dream. Because I dreamed about that day for like twenty years. I couldn't sleep at all, and I remember waking up at three o'clock in the morning, crying nonstop like a baby. It's just like the tears of joy and happiness, and you still don't believe it's real. It feels so unreal.

Even though Minh's prison sentence was shortened because he had proven himself to be a productive member of society, US immigration policy put him in the subject-to-deportation category. In November 2020, under the Trump administration, the United States and Vietnam signed a memorandum of understanding (MOU) creating a process for deporting immigrants who had entered the United States before the two countries normalized relations in 1995.[21] Most of these pre-1995 immigrants are refugees who left Vietnam as children, like Minh, or were born in refugee camps in Thailand or the Philippines. They were admitted to the United States as an aftermath of military intervention in Southeast Asia and subsequent allyship between the countries. This MOU superseded an earlier agreement that had prevented ICE from indefinitely detaining pre-1995 Vietnamese immigrants, even those facing deportation orders or orders of removal due to a criminal conviction. Instead, under that previous agreement, they were released under supervision orders, given work authorization in the United States, and required to check in periodically with an ICE office.[22]

The new MOU was foreshadowed in 2017, when the United States pressured the Vietnamese government to accept pre-1995 refugees for deportation. ICE started rounding up Vietnamese people around the country, including raids in Miami and Georgia, and issuing them final removal orders. Many of the Vietnamese refugees who were now subject to deportation had nonviolent offenses or years-old criminal convictions for which they had already served time.[23] Law professor Bill Hing Ong asks if justice is being served by deporting Southeast Asian refugees without consideration of their current life situation.[24] The review process for commutation is lengthy and rigorous, as Minh's experience shows. He describes going before the Board of Parole for a hearing and being questioned for four hours by a panel of three people. First, in a psychiatric review, a psychiatrist assessed whether Minh was a low, middle, or high threat to society. The deputy commissioner and other commissioners then interviewed him for nearly three hours. Minh had taken every self-help class available—such as Alcoholics Anonymous, Narcotics Anonymous, and anger management courses—and worked with University of Southern California law students on how to prepare for his parole interviews. "They want to know if I understand why I did what I did, what I have done to change, and what I will do in the future never to repeat that." Our conversation took place in 2020, and despite having served his twenty-five years, Minh was worried about what would happen next, given the political climate:

> So, it's a long process for me to come home, with many steps, and I will say that I'm blessed because the week before I know I will go home, I also know that I have an ICE hold or immigration hold. I know by the time I'm released, [ICE] is going to come pick me up and send me to the detention center, so I'm not really celebrating because I know I'm having to go to the next one and then be deported. I might never even see my family again. But, you know, thank God, and it is a blessing that it was during COVID. The detention center was full. They didn't know what to do with us. So, they released us and made me sign a paper to go home, and I got scared.... But thank God, nobody was waiting for me. Normally, ICE waits for you at the parking lot. As soon as you come out, they scoop you up.

Minh was lucky; he narrowly averted ICE detention and was able to return to his family and community. Research shows the importance of families for housing, financial, and emotional support to enable a successful reentry.[25] I ask Minh who was waiting for him when he got out. Was his mother excited? Minh had told me earlier that she had used her life savings to hire a lawyer for his trial, and now he reflects on his changed feelings about his mother:

> Oh, you know, the sad thing is my mom was killed when I was in prison. In 2004, she was killed by a drunk driver when driving home from work. So, you know, that's hard. Being in there, it's already bad knowing I'll never get out of prison. But losing her while I was there was the hardest thing I have ever gone through in my life. You know, even harder than when I received the death sentence or got arrested.... But that was like a wake-up call: I need to change my life. I need to return to the person my mom wanted [me] to be. That's the only thing I can do to honor her because I started to realize that my mom never abandoned me, you know, she had to go to [America] to get

a better life. She had to do this for me to have a good future. I was young then, and I didn't understand that. I resented her. I hated her. I was so wrong. When you grow up, you start to think of things differently. You know, I told her I was sorry. I was sorry for putting her through this.

Minh describes adjusting to life outside prison walls and the constant fear of being deported. This anxiety can manifest in what Angela García calls *legal passing*, a "strategic presentation of self to the outside world that takes on characteristics associated with the mainstream, US-born groups" to minimize the threat of uncertain immigration status.[26] This coercive assimilation and performance are not so much choices as forms of psychological and material survival, providing the illusion of cultural inclusion while hiding the reality of structural exclusion from permanent legal status. "Being in the system is hard," Minh tells me. "When we go in, ICE is going to interview us to see if we are US citizens, and then if we say we are not, they will put a hose on us [detain us]. And for me, I'm very blessed that I wasn't transported to ICE [straight from prison]. But they can still come back and get me at any time. It's always been a fear. A fear I've been living with constantly."

While Minh avoided the prison-to-deportation pipeline because the detention centers were full during COVID, that is not the case for most Vietnamese and others who are punished twice—serving a prison sentence and then ending up sentenced to an ICE detention center or deported to Vietnam. The next section explores the substantial impacts of protracted displacement on the families and suburban communities of those with orders of deportation.

Sentenced "Home"

Văn came to the United States as a refugee at the age of four, with his six siblings and his parents. He describes growing up in Southern California: "As a young child, you know, I did have dreams. I wanted to be an artist. I wanted to be in a rock band. I wanted to be a civil engineer, and my parents had expectations and dreams of me becoming a doctor. And to be honest . . . I was very capable." At sixteen, however, he was sentenced to life in prison as a juvenile. Văn describes how juvenile incarceration traumatizes people in a video on behalf of the Southern California Asian Pacific Islander Reentry Program:

> Prison is not a place where people heal. It is emotional punishment. We are a civilized society, and we have prisons as places for rehabilitation. But really,

it is there for punishment. And harsh punishment does not work. It is not effective. It does not make our society safer. My experience is that, being in prison, I was surrounded by so many people with no hope. And they were desperate in so many ways, and they needed help in so many ways. But we didn't get that help.[27]

Instead of healing and repair, the US system employs life and long-term sentencing, harming young people's physical and mental health.[28] The same abusive system that did not protect youths like Văn in the first place continues to haunt him and others while in prison and after release. Like Minh, Văn spent twenty-five years in prison before being released as part of California's program recognizing the systemic overpunishment of youths in the 1990s.[29]

> I didn't get to go home. I was taken into ICE detention. And I had to fight for my life. The life I knew here in America was the only one I knew. But ultimately, because of my mistakes from my teenage years, I was ordered by the judge to be deported. And being in there [immigration detention] was just like prison for me. We had cells. We didn't have programs to rehabilitate, which I don't see why if the people there haven't committed any crimes. They're only there because they're not documented. . . . I was a permanent resident, but I was ordered [to be] deported. So, I became undocumented. Overnight, literally. My whole family are naturalized citizens, and I never would have thought or imagined that I would be undocumented and treated as such.[30]

Detained immigrants lack many constitutional protections, and detention facilities are often indistinguishable from prisons and jails.[31] Detainees often experience physical and psychosocial mistreatment, including forced sterilization, poor nutrition, and inhumane conditions such as overcrowding and freezing temperatures.[32] They are often denied access to legal representation and telephone services to connect with the outside.[33]

After fourteen months, Văn was released from the ICE detention center. Like many Vietnamese who once had legal status to live in the United States, Văn was now undocumented, living in a continual state of protracted displacement with orders of removal looming. While waiting to be deported to Vietnam, many Vietnamese live under an order of supervision that requires them to check in one to three times a year with ICE. As a human rights lawyer explained to me:

> You have to check in indefinitely with ICE until they decide that Vietnam will give you a travel document. And that's what happened under Trump. All

these people have been checking for twenty years with no problem at all, then all of a sudden they get arrested at work or they are asked to come to the ICE office to update their address, and then they are arrested. They can stay here but are in no-man's-land.... It's like *Dead Man Walking*, especially during the Trump years.

With an order of supervision and by checking in with ICE, the newly undocumented can apply for a work permit for approximately $400 per year. They can use this work permit to obtain a Social Security card and a California driver's license—while they wait to see if Vietnam will agree to take them, in which case, they wait for ICE to arrest them. Văn has a job at a computer store while he awaits deportation from the country he has lived in for forty-two years to the country he only knew during the first four years of his life.

Immigrant incarceration and then living in the United States under orders of supervision are forms of *refugee warehousing*, the practice of keeping refugees in extended situations of restricted mobility and dependency, with their lives on indefinite hold.[34] Given the recent policy changes that allow the repatriation of pre-1995 Vietnamese to Vietnam, significantly more Vietnamese adults in Little Saigon who came to the United States as refugees fear deportation orders. Laws enacted since the legislative reforms of the 1990s criminalize fundamental immigrant rights, a form of legal violence that disproportionately impacts Southeast Asian communities and people of color. In particular, the Illegal Immigration Reform and Immigrant Responsibility Act of 1996 (IIRIRA) and the Antiterrorism and Effective Death Penalty Act of 1996 (AEDPA) criminalize people with immigrant and refugee status. These policies enacted in 1996 dramatically changed the consequences of having a criminal conviction, making it easier to arrest, detain, and deport people with permanent residency status who are not citizens.[35] While those without citizenship have long been subject to deportation for criminal convictions, IIRIRA made deportation for certain crimes *mandatory*.

In summary, these laws—that automatically place individuals in immigration detention following the completion of criminal sentences—doubly punish many Vietnamese for crimes they committed as youths, when they first arrived in the country and were navigating the culture, language, and their place in this new environment. Many young Vietnamese, like Minh and Văn, found refuge in a gang life they later renounced. Ultimately, the system that brought them here as refugees and then criminalized them as youths continues to haunt them as adults. Facing an uncertain future, they have become an invisible population in suburbia.

Living in Liminality

Vietnamese refugees held in ICE detention and then under orders of supervision are held in prolonged states of captivity or physical warehousing. This uncertainty of not knowing how long they will be in the United States before deportation leads to a great deal of stress for their families.[36]

Hoàng Trịnh and Vũ Hà, both of whom work at and run family businesses in Little Saigon, experienced more than eight months of immigrant detention at an ICE detention center in Orange County in 2017. The organization Asian Americans Advancing Justice filed a civil action lawsuit against ICE on their behalf to challenge the prolonged detention of Vietnamese refugees. Hoàng legally entered the United States from Vietnam when he was four years old. He is now a permanent resident and married with children. He was incarcerated for one year on drug charges, then arrested again two years later and put into ICE detention after police found a marijuana plant in his possession. He spent more than eight months incarcerated at the Theo Lacy ICE Facility in Orange County without a bond hearing.[37] If deported, he will move to a country in which he has no family to help him.

Vũ Hà, an artist and avid runner, was arrested as a youth three times between 2000 and 2005, with the most serious offense being robbery. Fifteen years later, he forgot to pay a traffic ticket and was taken to an ICE detention center, where he spent 180 days without even a bond hearing, awaiting deportation to Vietnam—a country he left as a refugee when he was ten years old.[38] Both Hoàng and Vũ still live in Orange County at the time of writing, uncertain if and when they will be deported.

Many immigrants at risk of deportation have no criminal record or only minor criminal convictions, with the most common criminal conviction being illegal entry, the second most common being traffic offenses (including speeding or DUIs—driving under the influence), and the third being drug offenses (including marijuana possession, which is still a federal offense despite its decriminalization by California and twenty-two other states).[39] In these cases, noncitizens are punished more severely than citizens convicted of the same crime.[40] As David Hausman, a professor at the University of California, Berkeley, School of Law, observes: "The longer a noncitizen has lived in the United States, and the stronger his or her ties here, the less deportation resembles a retroactive admission decision, and the more it resembles punishment."[41]

The state violence that designates which immigrant or refugee deserves to remain in the United States and how they are treated while both in and outside of detention has continued under the Biden administration. In response, Vietnamese activists and Asian American organizations have come together to fight for cases like Hoàng's and Vũ's.[42] To critique and address flaws with our immigration system and emphasize the double bind noted earlier, Critical Refugee Studies argues the necessity of applying refugee-centered epistemologies to understand the human consequences of indefinite detention. "Refugees and asylum seekers are often subjugated to state violence not only in the sending but also in the receiving context—by the very state in which they sought refuge. As such, migrants are often subject to the double burden of fear they encountered in their home country, which led to their displacement, and the fear that they allegedly pose to the host country, which vilifies them as a threat."[43]

This is not unique to refugees and immigrants from Vietnam; it also affects other racialized immigrants in the United States, such as Somalis and Venezuelans.[44] Since 1997, US immigration officials have deported Somali refugees convicted of felonies (including shoplifting and drunk driving) to Somalia even though the United States recognizes that there is no functioning government there.[45] Despite the 1990s immigration reforms that expanded the offenses leading to deportation, the United States did not deport refugees convicted of crimes to the communist-dominated countries of Cuba, Vietnam, Laos, or Cambodia until 2002, when the United States convinced Cambodia to accept the repatriation of a few of its nationals each month who had been convicted of aggravated felonies.[46] Like the Vietnamese, most of these adult Cambodian deportees fled as refugees; some fled the killing fields of Cambodia as small children, while others were born in Thai refugee camps. Until 2017, Cuban refugees had immunity from repatriation to Cuba; since then, thirty-four thousand Cubans were given final removal orders to leave the United States.[47]

Applying Cecilia Menjívar's concept of *liminal legality*, whereby the long-term uncertainty inherent in immigrants' legal status permeates numerous aspects of refugees' and immigrants' lives, we can see how profoundly this liminal state "delimits their range of action in different spheres, from job market opportunities and housing, to family and kinship, ... to artistic expressions."[48] Immigrant legal status shapes how refugees in limbo relate to others and structure their relationships with family and partners; it affects their ability to participate in local communities, combat domestic violence, engage in health-seeking behaviors, advocate for fair wages, and form self-identity.[49]

Double Punishment and Family Separation

Noncitizens like Minh and Hoàng who have served their prison time can be taken into ICE detention and deported to Vietnam at any moment. Hence, they are twice penalized through the association of punitive criminal and immigration laws.[50] This double punishment of refugees includes not only physical dislocation and separation but also the psychosocial apprehension of separating from and cutting ties with significant others, including children, romantic partners, family, and community. The fear of banishment marks not only the individuals but also separates and punishes their families. Mass deportation also tears apart communities, severing from them people who have formed strong ties in the United States. Tín Nguyễn came to the United States as a refugee from Vietnam when he was eight years old. His sentence—life without the possibility of parole—was commuted by the governor in 2018 and he was released in 2020. In prison, he graduated from the California State University, Los Angeles, bachelor's degree program, the first in-person program for incarcerated students in California.[51]

> Upon my release, I was detained by ICE. I still remember it. I remember my friend hugging his mom, kissing his wife, and hugging his family as he walked out that gate of freedom. The gate of freedom that we both worked so hard for, but yet I was shackled and I was handcuffed and I was placed in a van to be deported to Adelanto ICE Detention Center, where I spent the ten months once again fighting for my right to go home, fighting for my right to be home with my mom and my family.[52]

Despite Tín's transformation and exceptional behavior, he was "punished again by the government solely based on my place of birth."[53] After being released from ICE custody, Tín thrived, earned his MBA, and is now the immigrant justice program coordinator in Little Saigon for the Vietnamese community, helping to provide others with resources for jobs and support after reentry. He is currently applying to doctoral programs. Despite this, he lives under fear of deportation:

> I am currently under the threat of being deported back to Vietnam, and I still live with the dread that one day, I will be ripped away from my mom, my

family, and my community. At times, when I think about it, it still gives me anxiety when I think about the suffering my eighty-two-year-old mother will go through. For so long, she was waiting for me to come home and for me to become the man that she always dreamt me to be, and to be ripped away from her and to be sent back to the country that I know little of.[54]

For parents of the detained and deported, their children's experiences often bring back fears, anxiety, and trauma from their own refugee experiences.[55]

Women refugees face the same anxieties through double punishment. Lan Lý, age fifty-two, is a community organizer and mother of nine children. She fled Vietnam in 1981 and has lived in the United States for more than forty years. Lan explains at a press conference while advocating for the reintroduction of the Southeast Asian Deportation Relief Act to Congress:

> I want to be here when my children get married and have kids on their own. Even after transforming my life, I am afraid that ICE will rip me away from my family and community because of the mistake I made decades ago. My story is like many other Southeast Asian community members I organize with who are facing deportation. We have spent most of our life in the United States, and many of us have no ties or connection to the country from which we and our family fled. . . . Deportation is tearing communities and families apart.[56]

The effects of deportation can be devasting, not only to the deportee but to their family and communities. For example, more than seven hundred thousand US citizen children with noncitizen parents now live in Mexico with their deported parents.[57] According to sociologist Tanya Golash-Boza, the "DHS [Department of Homeland Security] deported more than 45,000 parents of US citizen children in the first six months of 2011, meaning that almost 100,000 parents of US citizens were deported in 2011 alone."[58] In 2021, there are even more mixed-status families, with nearly 5.8 million US citizen children living with undocumented household members who are in limbo; in 2023, nearly 22 million people live in mixed-status families.[59] It is a struggle to maintain relationships with children, partners, and other family members when removed.[60] In *Banished Men*, Abigail Adams describes the material and psychosocial consequences to families in the sending and receiving countries as carceral institutions ruin relationships and fray social ties with deportees who are often forced out of families as relationships deteriorate.[61] While exiled from work and family, deportees are stripped of their ability to trust that they will be able to provide caretaking and financial support, creating self-doubt and emotional suppression.[62]

The consequences of deportation also include the loss of the deportee's support for their family and communities.[63] Lan Ly is now an organizer and community leader supporting other Vietnamese refugees at risk of deportation to "come together to fight for a second chance for life and for justice."[64] When important community leaders like Lan and Tín are detained and deported, entire communities suffer along with their families.

Such deportations must be assessed within the context of the United Nations Convention for the Protection of Refugees principle of non-refoulement, which prevents countries from returning a refugee "to the frontiers of territories where their life or freedom would be threatened on account of race, religion, nationality, membership of a particular social group or public opinion."[65] As the United States is a signatory, its deportation procedures should be guided by this statement. Yet what happens when Vietnamese find themselves deported and separated from their families? In the next section, I turn to Vietnam to explore the experiences of deportees living in Vietnam and the grassroots organization fighting for their return home to the United States.

DEPORTATION AND THE RIGHT TO RETURN

In the Bình Thạnh district of Hồ Chí Minh City, Chuck's Burgers serves classic American burgers and double-fried french fries. It's the meeting spot for around twenty people plus five organizers deported from the United States, representing the Southeast Asian diaspora across the country: Orange County, Boston, Orlando, Charlotte, Atlanta, San Francisco, and Houston, among other locales. Born in Laos, Cambodia, and Vietnam, they are together for the first time, for the next three days, meeting under a giant baby-blue banner that announces: "SE Asian Family Reunion."

Cát Bảo Lê, the founder of the Southeast Asian Coalition (SEAC), is spearheading the event with her partner, an immigration lawyer, and their three-year-old child (and Cát is also five months pregnant). There is a team in the United States who is supporting from abroad. Over the next few days, SEAC will also hold a legal clinic where Vietnamese American volunteer attorneys will join via Zoom and in person to provide free legal advice. SEAC is the first organization nationwide to work both on the ground in Vietnam and with Vietnamese men in detention centers across the United States. Since 2011, three years after the United States signed the initial agreement creating a process to deport Vietnamese, Cát has worked under the radar with Southeast Asians facing deportation in the American South. However, her activism working against deportation started in 2002, when she participated in student-led protests and events against Cambodian deportation at UC Berkeley. She continued this work when she began working at the Asian Law Caucus in 2005, educating Vietnamese residents about deportation at Tet festivals, coffee shops, and community celebrations. Raised in California and North London by refugee parents who were Vietnamese boat people, her vision of SEAC is one of collective liberation, building people power through grassroots organizing around criminal justice, mass incarceration, and deportation. Speaking from the top of the restaurant's stairwell at the reunion, Cát reminds those congregated that they are a village united:

> We call ourselves a village, and the village consists of people that volunteer; the village consists of you; that's how we roll. Although we are an organization that gets funding, we try not to have that take away from how we relate to each other as family or human beings. Our logo is one family, we believe that when you see each other as family, whether you are Khmer, Montagnard, Viet, Black, or Latinx, you fight for your family. So if you don't see yourself as family, then you would be like, "Oh that's their struggle," but when you see each other as a family then you take it to the streets, you take it to ICE, you fight in court, and that's what important.[66]

In their critique of deportation, SEAC moves beyond focusing on the individual refugee to the role of the US state, the political context of refugee lives within US history, and the importance of cross-racial solidarity. At the reunion, a large poster presents a timeline showing how the US government has historically forcefully displaced Indigenous people, Black people, and migrants of color within the United States and across international borders.[67] Next to SEAC participants' names and years of deportation, the timeline includes critical moments in US history, such as the American Indian Movement, Black Power movement, Chicano Movement, War on Drugs, 1996 immigration reform, Black Lives Matter movement, 9/11, the creation of ICE, the Obama era, and the Trump era. "We are all interconnected," reads the poster's headline, highlighted with red stars. In this concise timeline, SEAC reveals the United States as an imperial state with geopolitical histories in Southeast Asia and globally—histories that continue to condi-

ONE FAMILY

FIGURE 12. SEAC organizational logo representing antiracist and anticolonial struggles (courtesy of SEAC, 2024).

tion refugee lives today. Deportees are profoundly affected by learning this history and the reunion itself, as seen by some of the responses to the SEAC survey below.

> "I am glad to be a part of this family."—Paul, age thirty-nine, North Carolina, deported in 2019

> Regarding the timeline: "This is the first time I'm seeing this."—Tim, age forty-two, California, deported in 2010

> "This was the best weekend I had since being deported."—Thảo, age thirty-eight, Florida, deported in 2018

> "Some of us have lost everything—our jobs, our lives, our families, and we are here now. I am so happy to be among these brothers and to support one another in this new life."—Jason, age forty-eight, Texas, deported in 2017

The reunion uncovered some of the unmet needs of both new arrivals and those who have been in Southeast Asia for years. Among the most significant findings was that Vietnam lacks an infrastructure for reintegration. Cát explains: "Basically, you get off the plane with nothing. That was one of our agendas for going back [to Vietnam]. If you had a backpack, what eight items would you need when you landed?" She identifies the most common priorities for new arrivals based on their survey of deportees: a place to stay, a smartphone, a toothbrush, cash, and someone to help process their paperwork for identification, since they have no ID.[68] Attorneys say deportees often struggle to obtain the identity cards they need to work or drive. The deportees sometimes face a hostile environment "because Vietnam does not want them back," says a former US ambassador to Vietnam.[69] On a case-by-case basis, SEAC will fundraise for someone in need of money to process paperwork or to cover basic living expenses.[70] As Cát explains to me, SEAC operates primarily through referrals. "It is hard to know how many siblings there are on the Vietnam side because there is no organizational infrastructure to capture them. So, you get lost in the sauce, so we only know the people who have come in subsequently from the people we know there. They say to us: 'Hey, another plane dropped down, and another brother wants to be in touch.' So, it's really anecdotal."

SEAC's work with Southeast Asians who have orders of removal took off under the Trump administration in 2018, when ICE agents across the nation rounded up Vietnamese and Cambodians to be interviewed and then transported to detention centers in Georgia, far from their families and community support. This required some quick pivoting for SEAC because the American Asian organizations and support infrastructures are in California and the Northeast, not the South. Cát explains, "Most Vietnamese nationwide were sent to Stewart Detention Center in rural Georgia during this roundup. . . . So as the only organization in the South working with Southeast Asians on deportation, we dropped everything, and in rapid response, we went to Stewart to work and counsel our detained brothers." SEAC mobilized a small team of Vietnamese American attorneys, aunties, community leaders, and other Black and Southeast Asian organizers to come and do legal intakes in ICE detention. There, Cát describes, "we bonded behind plexiglass with so many brothers and uncles. And they came from everywhere, so we connected with them and their families thousands of miles away for needs and news, and we still kept in touch. Some of them have been deported, even though they were pre-1995 people, refugees. So, the reunion was the first time we could hug them without plexiglass."

Stewart Detention Center is in isolated rural Georgia. More than half of the immigrants detained by ICE are housed in remote rural prisons where detainees face higher barriers to obtaining a lawyer and are more likely to have their asylum case denied and be deported.[71] That isolation follows them when they are deported to Vietnam. As SEAC's findings show, after ICE puts them on the plane to Vietnam, the returnees struggle significantly with basic needs and integration. Cát tells me that participants in the SEAC program have difficulty getting government documents; many live undocumented in the shadows, and they often require significant mental health support.

This corroborates other studies of deportation globally. Jeremy Slack's study of deported Mexican Americans finds that organized criminal groups and corrupt authorities prey upon deportees, subjecting them to kidnapping and recruiting them into organized crime and drug cartels.[72] In Jamaica, deportees struggle with financial and emotional hardships; they are often criminalized by the media and rejected by locals, with many ending up homeless or near homeless, depending on family remittances from the United States.[73] In the Dominican Republic, deportees are subject to further surveillance, with the reason for their deportation recorded and their deportation entered into their criminal and credit reports.[74]

Sociologist Tanya Golash-Boza finds that in Guatemala, Mexico, and the Dominican Republic, deportees are overrepresented as employees in the call centers where US customers are transferred when they dial the toll-free number on the back of their credit card. The US-based callers have no idea the call center workers are deportees, often earning less than a hundred dollars a week and working in dire conditions. Some deportees manage to launch small businesses or pursue professional careers, but this is rare. They often face "culture shock, lack of family ties, barriers to social integration, and stigma."[75]

Cát explains how readjustments in a home country barely remembered by most are really just a continuation of the symptoms fostered in the United States by violence against refugees and men of color, their lack of integration into larger society, and a carceral state that transnationally connects the US and Vietnamese experiences of refugees:

> They are adjusting, they are in a country that they can't leave. A lot of these brothers have been incarcerated since they were young, like children, you know, teens [in the US]. It's not like Vietnam has created this. It's already been broken in the US, living in the US under poverty as refugees, trying to survive with the police on your back because of all of these things that were happening around them—the War on Drugs, the crackdown on crimes, these gang databases— that is a lot of day-to-day stress. And not having a family that understands that because they're also struggling and then don't know how to navigate, life has all built up. It's an ongoing struggle. These brothers needed therapy since they were locked up in cages. You know they might not be in cages now, but they were treated like animals; that was their life for a long time.

The injustice of deporting refugees reveals the regimes of surveillance, criminalization, poverty, incarceration, and detention that conditioned refugee lives before their exiles and that still haunt them. Alan, exiled for twelve years, closes the first meeting of the Southeast Asian reunion in Saigon. He speaks about the significance of the reunion:

> I'm originally from Philadelphia. I've been back in Cambodia for twelve years, and I've been to a few community get-togethers like this, but this one is different. This one is not just different . . . it's special. It's not just a group of Cambodians, it's a group of us as a family and as a whole. This is something that gives me hope because it's not just Cambodia that is fighting, it's Vietnam, it's Laos that's fighting for our rights to return [to the US], and I think that's where the hope begins is when people of different backgrounds come together and fight for one cause. This is the beginning of something very exciting, and we hope that we will have the opportunity to be reunited with our parents and children.

As Alan explains, the fight against deportation and banishment is not exclusive to the nation-state; rather, it is part of a global system based on colonialism, militarism, and racial capitalism tying Southeast Asians together. Alan still hopes to be reunited with his family, to end living in liminality, and to be in the United States, which is home, not living as a transnational deportee. This is his hope for all Southeast Asians fighting for their right to return.

Initially, Cát was hesitant to talk to me about SEAC's work, as they've been underground for so long. Other than amplifying political education against deportation, some of their work has been intentionally underground to protect identities in the United States and abroad. But she decided there is a great need for transparency and organizing to help the deportees exiled to Vietnam. She hopes others will read this and be inspired to mobilize with Vietnamese deportees who thought they had finally found solace as refugees living in Little Saigon and the United States, only to find it taken away. Another organizer I interviewed said that for those "who struggle to adapt to Vietnam, this state of limbo becomes permanent." During their years living in the United States, the system that brought them there as children failed them and overcriminalized them; they were certainly never given the tools necessary to survive in exile. Displacing residents rocks the foundations of the community, severing relationships and, in many cases, causing family businesses to lose needed employees and community organizations to lose members who have much to contribute. In short, for deportees, the violence and US intervention in Vietnam that led to their departure from their home country in the first place continues in the United States, shaping inequities masked by suburban life.

To better understand the impact of living in a state of protracted displacement on transnational deportees and those living under an order of removal, it is helpful to return to the concept of refugee warehousing, originally developed to understand closed refugee camps. As articulated by the Critical Refugee Studies Collective: "Refugee advocates have traditionally promoted three solutions to refugee outflows: repatriation, resettlement, and permanent integration in first-asylum countries. However, refugee warehousing, the practice of keeping refugees in protracted situations of restricted mobility, has become a de facto fourth solution for unwanted refugees."[76] The impact of this fourth solution is inhumane, as it prolongs ongoing violence and masks the dehumanizing conditions of instability and uncertainty for Vietnamese living in deportation limbo.

While this definition of refugee warehousing was developed in reference to lengthy wait times within refugee camps, this chapter has expanded it to explore the protracted unsettlement of undesirable or unwanted refugees in both the asylum country (the United States) and, in the case of transnational deportees, the country of repatriation. Southeast Asian deportees like Văn and Minh are double punished for crimes committed in their youth while they were newly navigating life and culture in their suburban communities—communities that did not provide them with the necessary tools to succeed and become full US citizens. Instead, they, like other refugees who are deemed undesirable, have been thrown into the morass of refugee warehousing and protracted liminality.

CONCLUSION

The United States is often celebrated as a nation of immigrants that has welcomed foreigners throughout its history. However, as historian Adam Goodman shows, "the US has deported nearly 57 million people since 1882, more than any other country in the world. During the last century, federal officials have deported more people from the land of freedom and opportunity than they have allowed to remain permanently."[77] Who, then, has the right to suburbia and the American dream? Vietnamese transnational deportees show the limits and liminality of neoliberal immigration policies.

Deportation is the exercise of the state's power to control its unwanted populations. From immigration restriction to mobility gateways, immigration controls privilege particular immigrants and sanction others. This creates what Luca Mavelli calls a "neoliberal economy of belonging," where states include and exclude migrants "according to their endowment of human, financial, economic, and emotional capital."[78] The stigmatization of a criminal record gives the appearance of a legitimate and just process to people on the outside while normalizing double punishment and banishing individuals to a country they may not remember. This goes against international refugee law and the principle of non-refoulement. Minh's story, for instance, shows how lives cannot be reduced to "dispossession or abjection but are affectively rich, complex, and multidimensional."[79] Minh works two jobs and wants to start an organization to help Vietnamese reenter society after imprisonment and to do away with the stigma surrounding formerly incarcerated Vietnamese. He also wants to get married and start a family. Minh actively volunteers with Orange County's VietRISE and other organizations to work toward passage of the VISION Act (AB 937) in California "to stop the double punishment of immigrants and refugees transferred from prison and jails to ICE detention." With the closure of many detention centers in California, ICE is continuing to quietly transport Vietnamese and other Southeast Asian refugees to detention centers in other parts of the United States, too far away for relatives and friends to visit.

Deportation of Vietnamese refugees is a violent process of forced removal and disposal that considers neither the history of US intervention in Southeast Asia nor the imperial statecraft that led to their arrival in the United States as refugees.[80] While relationships like those the deportees built at SEAC's family reunion can safeguard them against some of the dangers they face, they cannot rectify severed relationships with families, significant others, and communities brought about by physical dislocation, social and legal states of uncertainty, and legal liminality. This chapter has shown how the criminal justice system, ICE, and detention centers harm refugees' and the community's survival. To better understand those factors, this chapter has used refugee epistemologies—how "refugees critique, engage, and evade" oppressive state institutions and state violence—to tell and reclaim their stories.[81] For some Vietnamese in the diaspora, life is still tenuous, with new forms of state violence following them; nonetheless, they continue to be active agents in their resistance. By centering the narratives on perpetual moments of displacement and how Vietnamese refugees engage and evade that displacement, the story of Vietnamese in Orange County's Little Saigon is the story of the past continuing to shape the present.

CONCLUSION

—————

Suburban Organizing Playbook

ON JULY 29, 2020, then-president Donald Trump announced, "I am happy to inform all people living their Suburban Lifestyle Dream that you will no longer be bothered or financially hurt by having low-income housing built in your neighborhood."[1] Just a week earlier he warned: "The Suburban Housewives of America . . . Biden will destroy your neighborhood and your American Dream."[2] During his run for reelection, Trump played on racist fears of terrorized white suburbs, calling on an outdated yet still popular image of suburbia derived from the 1950s.[3] Yet, as *Suburban Refugees* has shown, suburbs have long been racially and economically diverse sites of resistance. The book's larger story is not limited to Little Saigon or Southern California. Similar struggles over space and place are indicative of widening inequities and instability in suburbs throughout America.

This book was written during a time of mass tenant precarity, homelessness, and residential segregation. The predatory financialization that comes with Wall Street and corporations expanding their acquisition and control of residential property is manifesting in rent hikes, evictions, and demoviction of suburban communities. Despite these inequities, American narratives still reify suburbs as imagined spaces of opportunity for all who live there, as part and parcel of the quintessential middle-class dream. Equal access within and across places cannot happen without understanding the realties on the ground and acting to obliterate barriers to economic opportunity.

Suburban Refugees seeks to understand displacement pressures in suburbia, focusing particularly on housing justice and immigrant rights. From the outside, Little Saigon appears to be a space of affluence: a thriving and robust enclave economy, where the mayor and city council members are Vietnamese and multiple generations of ethnic entrepreneurs are transforming and revitalizing retail and business. Underneath this apparent American success story, however, people are losing their community, with many facing housing precarity or living in immigration limbo. This book attempts to put a human face on Vietnamese refugees by focusing on their everyday lives and sites of struggle, asking how we can learn from the people and activists in their communities and exploring how—nearly fifty years after displacement from their homeland—they continue to engage in creative modes of resistance.

Their experiences of resistance resonate beyond Little Saigon. New literature is critically examining other suburban immigrant communities and their struggles over space and placemaking as gentrification creeps in. For instance, articles are beginning to disentangle gentrification pressures in the inner suburbs of Toronto and Atlanta.[4] Willow Lung-Amam is researching suburban poverty and the politics of equitable development by examining inner-ring suburban neighborhoods of Washington, DC. Looking at how immigrant small businesses resist redevelopment and gentrification-induced displacement, her work provides insight into how coalitions can provide a critical platform for underrepresented business owners and residents in suburbia.[5] Alex Schafran's research explores suburban displacement as suburban resegregation.[6] For example, as central city neighborhoods gentrify in the Bay Area of Northern California, people of color are often forced to leave, fleeing in search of the suburban dream. Instead, they end up in suburbs where local governments refuse to develop adequate affordable housing or public transportation.[7] In another case study, George Sánchez shows how Boyle Heights, a neighborhood outside Los Angeles, is being transformed by two concomitant dynamics: increasingly high real estate prices and rising rents that are forcing working-class and Latinx immigrant families out of the community, and gente-fication in which homegrown, college-educated Latinx entrepreneurs are redeveloping the neighborhood, as we also saw in Little Saigon.[8] However, Boyle Heights has demonstrated resiliency against gentrification, and the gentrifiers have retreated, partly due to local, multigenerational organizations building on the hundred-year legacy of activism by Boyle Heights residents.

As significant as such community movements are within Little Saigon and beyond, they are only part of the story. There is no way to truly understand displacement or housing insecurity without also including the role of state and structural violence. In his book *Places in Need*, Scott Allard argues that "the competitive logics of local political economies powerfully dictate the policy choices of suburban governments. Pressures to maintain a strong business climate and an attractive community for homeowners often supersede any initiatives to help low-income households. Indeed, suburbs originated in the explicit or implicit exclusion of poor people. The fragmented suburban institutional landscape complicates efforts to coordinate programs of assistance across hundreds of municipalities, school districts, and township lines."[9]

Allard considers the suburbanization of inequality, which accelerated in the 1980s, to be one of the most significant demographic changes in US history, rivaling the Great Migration north and the suburbanization of US cities in the 1950s and 1960s. Population shifts are shaping this change due to greater numbers of Americans living in the suburbs and the economic changes in the United States since the early 2000s. A global pandemic and two recessions, including the housing market's collapse, have widened the fissures of suburban inequality. The economic recessions devastated low-skilled workers, who are now just as likely to live in the suburbs as in the city. At the same time, the labor market has become more service oriented, another factor implicated in the widening of inequality gaps.[10]

Displacement and gentrification must also be understood as systems of racial banishment; we must not sanitize these processes or pretend they are devoid of race. Ananya Roy's framework of racial banishment examines how eviction encapsulates other forms of racialized violence such as incarceration, slavery, colonialism, and apartheid.[11] This concept emphasizes state-initiated violence against racialized communities that traditional theories of gentrification and displacement ignore.[12] Dimensions of dispossession and displacement include housing grabs by Wall Street investors and private equity firms, unpayable rental debt, and the racial banishment of the unhoused through the criminalization of homelessness. Roy acutely identifies this as the new geography of poverty: "The American foreclosed suburb is . . . not simply an evacuated space but rather a territory, the normalized place where racialized and financialized impoverishment is enacted."[13]

In these final pages, I reflect upon the broader systems of banishment and inclusion described throughout this book and, based on this, urge readers to develop a suburban organizing playbook either as a class exercise or with other community members. The beginning of the playbook is here as a resource for students, organizers, and other readers to take the findings presented and adapt and extend them to similarly situated locales of interest. What lessons does Little Saigon provide for other communities? What are the systems of banishment and inclusion discussed so far? What is the future of Little Saigon and other suburban communities facing rising inequities? What conditions shape refugee placemaking? I then end with an organizing playbook that students and community members can create as a road map for their collective action, solutions, and best practices to mobilize.

SYSTEMS OF BANISHMENT AND INCLUSION

Suburban Refugees explores both the systemic roots of increasing inequality in the suburbs and potential solutions to rectify the problem from the local to federal levels.

Exclusionary and Inclusionary Policies

Exclusionary systems of banishment are conditioned and interrelated by violence at all levels of government. For instance, the local level is responsible for citywide policies that promote exclusionary rent control practices, single-family zoning, and building permits. The victory of rent control in Santa Ana demonstrates how state law can limit local-level policies; California's Costa-Hawkins Rental Housing Act restricts rent control measures for housing units built after 1995. At the federal level, the criminalization of immigration includes laws from 1996 that made people easier to deport. Furthermore, ICE transfers have become a means to double punish Vietnamese refugees and further the criminalization of men of color, separating family and people in the community who count on them. Deportation is part of a larger global system of racialized and gendered social control.[14]

We also find inclusionary practices that provide potential solutions to inequities at all levels of government. At the state level in California, for instance, AB 2782 sets the conditions for recognizing mobile homes as a source of affordable housing, protecting them from being torn down for demoviction. Advocates are working on other statewide legislation, including the VISION and HOME acts, which would protect noncitizens freed under criminal justice reforms from being transferred to ICE, meaning individuals like Minh, who received clemency, could restart their lives upon release from prison. Organizers are also working toward more widespread rent stabilization ordinances and resident-owned communities for mobile home parks, as described in chapter 3. Movement leaders and scholars are calling for the creation of a Social Housing Development Authority, a new government agency that would purchase distressed real estate, including multifamily rentals, while "financing its transfer to the social housing sector, including nonprofits, community land trusts, and public housing."[15]

Financialization of Housing

This book was also written in the context of the increasing financialization of housing nationwide, with corporate landlords controlling more of the rental and mobile home park inventory, as seen in chapter 3. In 1991, over 90 percent of rental properties in the United States were owned by unincorporated individual owners; by 2015, small landlords owned a shrinking percentage, with only some 75 percent of rental housing remaining in their hands.[16] This matters because landlords increasingly use limited liability companies, a structure that safeguards their assets and is notorious for its lack of transparency. Studies show that disinvestment and higher eviction rates are more likely to occur when owners hide behind limited liability companies.[17] This lack of transparency leads to a lack of accountability. Without understanding who owns the property, ensuring the safety and affordability of rental housing is extremely difficult. Housing advocates suggest that one way to rectify this is with a national registry of rental owners expanding on the model of those already established at the local level in Pittsburgh, Minneapolis, and Philadelphia.[18]

Easing the Burden

As this book shows, the significant cost burden of housing puts many Vietnamese families in precarious conditions, but there are also creative modes of adaption and resistance. For most families in America, housing is their single largest budget item. Despite this, most households who qualify for housing assistance will never receive it; only one in four eligible households receives federal aid.[19] There are solutions, but these take political will. For example, Jenny Schuetz and others argue that the government should put more money in people's pockets by expanding tax credits or creating mechanisms like a universal basic income.[20] Expanding the housing voucher program is another possible solution. However, without addressing the fundamental need to make affordable housing easier to find and accessible, these solutions are limited in scope and effectiveness. Affordable housing units can be challenging to find. Remember Phương in chapter 2, who struggled to find a place to live that was both within the permitted price range and rented within the time frame required by her housing vouchers? Across Orange County, there are more than thirty cities, each with its own unique public housing program. Proponents argue that technology can help streamline information sharing across locales by creating a national or state registry of affordable (income-restricted) rental units. In fact, organizations in Minnesota and Massachusetts are already developing relevant software and public interest technology that is accessible in multiple languages.[21]

More safe, affordable housing will require not just more units in communities of choice but also the policies to support them. Through the lens of Vietnamese refugees, we have explored how exclusionary zoning based on the ideal of the suburban single-family unit can be a barrier to housing development and integration, obstructing the premise of the federal Fair Housing Act. Currently, housing advocates are considering expanding manufactured housing to increase the supply of affordable housing across the United States.[22] This is a novel idea, but, as seen in the case of Green Lantern, it can only happen in conjunction with more consistent legal protections for both mobile home owners and renters. This includes eliminating exclusionary zoning in high-opportunity neighborhoods, protecting senior homeowners, and making co-op financing easier to acquire by mobile home communities.[23] A commitment to public or social housing will not succeed unless accompanied by policies that ensure access to other public goods like health care and education.[24]

Socioeconomically diverse migrant suburbs might have their challenges, but they are also rife with opportunities. The power of local governments in ethnically dominated city councils extends the likelihood that policies such as rent control will pass—as in Santa Ana, where Mexican and Vietnamese residents used cross-racial and intergenerational coalition building to hold their representatives accountable. As refugees and immigrants fight for their right to the suburb, many (although not all) are slowly moving closer to that goal, with coordinated organizing.

THE FUTURE OF LITTLE SAIGON

Text message exchange, 2 p.m., Friday, October 22, 2021:

ME: Hi, Ben, can I chat with your dad? Is he still living in Garden Grove?
BEN: No, he moved back to Vietnam.

ME: Wait, what? When?

BEN: Before COVID, he's living with family in Saigon.

After this text exchange, I phoned Ben, a friend since childhood. His father used to live in a mobile home park along Garden Grove Boulevard in Little Saigon, in a mobile home that Ben bought for him and still owns. The garden on the side is beautiful, filled with red clay pots of thanh long (dragon fruit) over five feet tall. I was more than a little curious to know why Ben's father had returned to Vietnam, given that he was even more staunchly anti-communist than my own father. In all the time I knew Ben's father, he refused to even purchase goods labeled "Made in Vietnam." "He hated them," Ben said. "They took our house. They took everything from us." Ben's father fought alongside the Americans during the war and does not speak English. Ben is now a successful pharmacist living in Arizona and splits his time between the two homes he owns in Arizona—one for himself and one he purchased for his mom complete with chickens and a large garden—and his father's mobile home in Little Saigon, where his aunt and father used to live. Ben's parents divorced when he was in high school; as an only child, he feels responsible for supporting both of them financially.

ME: How are you doing? How are your mom and dad?

BEN: Good; I'm back to my normal 8-to-5 job at the hospital in Arizona and then get Friday to Sunday off. Dad's OK. He said Vietnam is still controlling with COVID; they are quarantining everyone in the house.

ME: I wanted to ask about your dad's mobile home. I'm working on a project with Vietnamese organizers who are trying to work for rent control in Westminster. Was your dad's park bought out? Was his rent increasing? Why did he move to Vietnam?

BEN: Well, yes, when my dad lived there, the rent was stabilized from the 1990s to the early 2000s. But around 2010, the rent started increasing 20 to 30 percent every year. Every year it increases, and you have no control. The landlord can sell the land to a new [landowner] without your notice. Then, whoever owns the park can change the rules and the policy, and if you don't adapt, you get kicked out. So, my dad was the last person with the cheapest rent. His rent was $1,400 monthly, and everyone else's was $2,000 and up. My mom and I had this hunch; they've been doing it all over California, they end up building condos or houses. We are always worried that, whoever they sell it to next, that person, who wants more money, will develop housing on the land, a gated community, and then we lose our mobile home [because we won't have a place to move it to].

ME: Why did your dad go back? Growing up, he was so anti-Vietnam, but now he's back in Vietnam.

BEN: He wants to live in California, but it's not possible. I helped my mom buy a house, I bought one myself, and then I bought my dad a mobile home, which makes three. That's insane. I feel like I could be broke at any moment. What happens if I die? Who's going to take care of things? I told my dad he could live with me, but he doesn't want to live in Arizona. I mean, he's permanently living in Vietnam but not permanent. He has to travel every now and then because he doesn't have Vietnamese citizenship. So, he has to keep moving like a traveler, to show the US he's still not stagnant, but each country has different rules. So, I told him to just move to Thailand back and forth every month. So, he has to go to Thailand every month and then come back to Vietnam.

ME: Does your dad live with relatives?

BEN: He lives with my grandfather and his brothers. My grandfather is 103 years old.

ME: That's incredible. Once COVID is over, will you go see him in Vietnam? What did you say to your dad? Did you have to tell him that he had to move [out of the mobile home]?

BEN: My mom finally did that. They went back and forth. And he didn't want to go. And we're like: "Hey, man, we have to be realistic here." Because once my aunt moved out, I thought I could live there temporarily and drive back and forth from Arizona. But then I realized now I'm forty years old. Driving this distance every time is taxing. So, what's the point of me living there? I don't have time to hang out with our friends from high school, and they don't either. Plus, the traffic is so bad.

I was surprised that Ben's father had decided that if he couldn't live in California's Little Saigon, his only other choice was Vietnam—that he'd chosen that in preference to living in Arizona with his son. I tried calling Ben's father, but I couldn't reach him.

Two years later, I found out from Ben that his father's health had deteriorated, and he is now in a wheelchair and paralyzed. The doctors don't know what happened, and Ben is convinced his father can receive better care in Vietnam than in the United States. Ben still hasn't seen his father but calls him weekly.

For many elderly Vietnamese who have spent thirty or forty years in the diaspora, Vietnam is the place they choose to go to when the cost of living in Little Saigon exceeds their income. But do they really *choose* to go? Or is it just the only viable option? The number of Vietnamese refugees returning to Vietnam for their retirement is unknown. My father always says he will return to Vietnam after my mother dies. He dreams of a homeland that only exists in his memory; Vietnam has changed radically since he last saw it. "I can hire someone to take care of me there. I don't want to burden you." Even his saying that produces a deep sense of burden within me. Like many second-generation adults, the heaviness and emotional debt I feel for his sacrifices never leave me. International refugee law promises the idea of non-refoulement: people cannot be returned to a country where they do not feel safe. In the context of structural inequalities, elder Vietnamese refugees forced to return for financial reasons continue to face uncertainty and insecurity in both countries in terms of their residency status, insurance status, and legal regulations pertaining to income.[25] While the principle of non-refoulement doesn't legally include financial reasons, it practically has the same result.

REFUGEE PLACEMAKING

What is the future of Little Saigon and other refugee communities facing rising inequities? In the future, how can Little Saigons and other refugee communities share their lessons of placemaking and community building, including those lessons articulated in *Suburban Refugees*? Similar to Cubans who settled in Miami, Iraqis in Detroit, and Somalis in Minneapolis, many of the first Vietnamese exiles came from the educated professional class, with invaluable entrepreneurial experience gained in the homeland.[26] In the United States, they mobilized their skills and co-ethnic networks to begin new enterprises and entrepreneurial endeavors, creating a wide range of work opportunities for others in the community. This social and economic capital played a critical role in building Little Saigons across the country, helping to create the array of professional and service businesses in the United States that serve these communities.[27] What makes Vietnamese American entrepreneurship unique is the high rate of female business owners; nearly 50 percent of Vietnamese entrepreneurs are women.[28] What will happen over time to Little Saigons as the new generations come of age? Will it become a Disneyfied touristic site of consumption, in tune with the goals of the city planners discussed in chapter 1? How will second- and third-generation Vietnamese continue to envision and remake Little Saigon?

This case study has much to teach us about designing public policy for working with refugee populations settling in the United States and the power of community organizing. As the number of refugees worldwide surges—particularly populations from Ukraine, Syria, and Afghanistan—it is essential that we understand the rationale, successes, and failures of the Vietnamese refugee settlement program, the longest-running such program in US history, as the United States embarks on subsequent refugee response endeavors. The Vietnamese case highlights how a positive context of reception or institutional features of the receiving country can shape the depths of integration.[29] Generous federal and state benefits for Vietnamese refugees, including access to loans for higher education and small business creation, helped shape the emergence of ethnic niches often identified with this community, such as the nail industry and commercial fishing and shrimping. These benefits also enabled many first-generation immigrants and their children to access trade programs at community colleges and dedicated trade schools. The federal government's emphasis on families immigrating together was an important factor in shaping Vietnamese refugees' successful integration and the enclave economy. Nazli Kibria's study of Vietnamese in Philadelphia substantiates the importance of family and social support by describing the "patchworking" efforts of Vietnamese families.[30] This evocative term refers to how families bring together or merge different kinds of resources within the household, similar to income diversification, as a means to deal with risky economic contexts. The transfer of economic and cultural resources depends not only on the size of the household structure, with larger Vietnamese American households faring better economically, but also on families with diverse age and gender compositions. For example, families with different generations and genders living together have greater exposure and connection to a broader variety of sources of social networks that provide small loans and information about jobs. This broad-ranging access helps households to gather enough capital to open a small business.[31]

The migration of families as a unit has other important implications; by 1982, just seven years after the initial wave of Vietnamese refugees to the United States, two-thirds of Southeast Asians in the United States were sponsored by Vietnamese relatives.[32] This meant later waves of refugees often had more established Vietnamese family members to rely upon for social, financial, and logistical needs. And a strong refugee enclave provides a context for grassroots organizations and mutual assistance associations to develop to fill local needs in a culturally appropriate way, as we saw with VietRISE in chapter 2, which is mobilizing working-class Vietnamese in Little Saigon. The power of cultural capital through mutual assistance associations that offer services like job placement, English language instruction, and small business loans cannot be overestimated.[33] Vietnamese residential density in the suburbs and small business economic concentration translated into political clout for the community.[34] Yet the seeming success of the Vietnamese entrepreneurial economy as a model minority obscures the inequities within our community while also providing greater nuance for developing resettlement policies using an intersectional approach more generally.

Before arriving in the United States, many refugees spend years in protracted displacement after the war. As we've seen, this protracted displacement can continue in the United States, the most poignant example being formerly incarcerated Vietnamese living with orders of deportation. The United Nations High Commissioner for Refugees identifies protracted displacement as a situation in which refugees live in extended exile: "one in which refugees find themselves trapped in a state of limbo."[35] As explored in chapter 4, refugees can remain in precarious situations for prolonged periods after becoming displaced, be it in terms of access to economic and legal opportunities or being deprived of freedom of movement, employment, or systems of justice.[36] Revealing another layer of the US past and ongoing military colonialism, some Vietnamese refugees spent more than twenty years in refugee camps in Hong Kong and Guam before coming to the United States.[37] Refugee camps in the aforementioned countries are all sites of the American and British empire. Many of these refugee camps were former military bases used in the US-Vietnam War that incited the refugee exodus in the first place.[38] Unsettlement, or protracted displacement, is intimately tied to empire building, leaving Vietnamese unsettled throughout time and space even before supposed resettlement in the United States.[39] This book shows that displacement and instability for many Vietnamese, despite ultimately being resettled in the United States, last long beyond resettlement.

Suburban Refugees substantially redefines protracted displacement, exploring it as a complex phenomenon rather than a straightforward, linear process of moving from one refugee camp to another to eventual stability. Displacement, as seen here, often continues in the country of resettlement. Even with the promise of redemptive US citizenship, "the cycle of refugee displacement can persist long after resettlement."[40] Thus, it is imperative for policymakers to understand the dynamics of structural forces, the agency of displaced people, and how people shape the conditions of their displacement. From this perspective, we can question the wisdom—and likely success—of targeted refugee policies that don't take into consideration the effects of protracted displacement on newcomers. For instance, the nearly eighty-five thousand Afghan refugees who arrived in the United States as "humanitarian parolees" before September 2022 were not even given refugee status; they were only given one year to apply for asylum and ninety days of government support.[41] As I've worked with Afghan refugees for the past two years in South Bend, Indiana, as a volunteer and board member of a local nonprofit, it is clear from the lessons learned in the Vietnamese case that the lack of support Afghans experience today will carry on with them, as they potentially live in the limbo of protracted displacement in the United States. In this case, new amendments such as the Afghan Adjustment Act of 2023 would change the legal status of Afghans from parolees on a path to more permanent resettlement. As in Canada, Australia, and many EU countries, to succeed, immigrants should be given legal counsel or representation by the state to help navigate a complex immigration system.[42] Afghan families and individuals are still displaced following the longest US war, and tens of thousands of Afghans are trapped in legal limbo in the United States, despite this being their supposed country of redemptive resettlement.

AN ORGANIZING PLAYBOOK

Engaging people who live in Little Saigon and other similarly situated communities—with their varying experiences and histories—and the larger structural processes that impact inequality is a first step to creating more just communities. A next step is for organizers, scholars, students, and policymakers to apply those insights and develop organizing principles that other communities can adopt, with the goal of replacing protracted displacement with strong, more equitable communities. A playbook is a resource to support communities with actionable tools to navigate suburban inequality. Such collaborations have led to networks of movement-based and university-based scholars focusing on housing justice. For instance, in 2018, the University of California, Los Angeles, instituted a program called the Housing Justice in Unequal Cities Network, spearheaded by Professor Ananya Roy. The program focuses on housing justice situated in the "struggle for freedom on occupied, colonized, and stolen lands." It recognizes the logics of racial capitalism and that the theorization of "lived histories takes place in poor people's movements rather than in the rarefied realms of academia."[43] The network examines emergent practices of housing justice, including creative solutions to help upend housing instability. It has also created a tenant power toolkit in Spanish and English that includes steps for those facing possible eviction and rent debt to fight for their rights.[44] Other programs across the country focus more specifically on other forms of local injustice—such as economic, environmental, and cultural—while acknowledging the interrelationships. I encourage readers of this book to go online, read about organizing being undertaken in communities across the United States that are experiencing resegregation and displacement, and check out what is happening in your own or nearby communities.

This playbook is a start. The next step is to speak with friends, family, significant others, colleagues, and community members to evolve this list further by identifying subsequent steps. Opportunities for action are enormous, and this book has told of just a few. Get involved and learn about strategies for organizing, such as:

- eviction blockades
- community land trusts
- noncitizen voting
- housing cooperatives and commons
- tenant organizing
- debt unions
- unhoused tenant unions
- social rent
- land value tax

Suburban Refugees shows that underneath the idealized images of wealthy suburban neighborhoods lie inequities in access and stability. However, perhaps more importantly, it also shows the power and potential of refugees, immigrants, and allies to take a stand and fight for the right to determine their own means of placemaking and community organizing to create the communities they want to live in through intergenerational and cross-racial alliances. We can learn from communities and movements on the front lines of displacement by placing residents at the center as active participants and partners. Rather than seeing residents as passive recipients or beneficiaries whose presumed needs are managed from above, we need to ask communities to share their collective visions for change and development. The path to more equitable suburban development must start with empowering residents and community stakeholders. The housing justice movement and scholars have rallied around "homes for all," a slogan expressing housing as a public good and a human right. Another world is possible through creative organizing that demands the right to the suburb, the right to organize, and the right to placemaking, thereby actualizing immigrant rights.[45]

When does a refugee stop being a refugee?[46] Is it when they find their home? How one answers this influences future opportunities for other immigrant communities fighting for social justice in unequal suburbs. *Suburban Refugees* attempts to unveil displacement pressures created by structures of capitalism and advocates the need for sanctuary spaces and a right to home for all immigrants and refugees.

———

A Personal Note on Methods

BACKSTORY

"Where do I park?" My father nervously looks in the mirror, checking the blind spot.

"Anywhere you see an open space," I respond. I am surprised and slightly annoyed by his question since we're running fifteen minutes late for our reservation.

"How about right here?" he asks.

"Sure, looks good," I affirm.

He asks again, "Are you sure we can park here?"

"Yes, I don't see any signs that say otherwise." A sense of impatience starts to well in my throat, but I try to project a placid voice and face.

"Do you have a reservation?" the hostess asks when we enter.

"Yes . . ." I answer, taking charge of the situation. As we are led to our table, I notice that my father has become visibly anxious. His left eye is twitching.

"Can I come back and pick you up?" he asks after we are seated.

"What? What do you mean?" I respond. This is supposed to be a special dinner at a nice restaurant with my favorite person—my dad. I'm a senior in high school, and we're celebrating my scholarship to attend UC Berkeley in the fall with a gift certificate I received at my high school awards ceremony. "Why? Please, let's stay," I plead.

"No, no, I'll come back in an hour and pick you up," he says. The candles give off a soft flickering of light reflected on the white linen cloths.

"I'm not eating alone. Let's go," I say. By the time we are outside, exasperation is set in my voice. "Why can't we just have a nice dinner? I wanted to go with you." My adolescent whine is not attractive.

He breaks down and yells, "I don't want to go in there. I'm not rich, and I'm not white. I don't know how to use the tableware. I don't know what or how to order. This isn't my neighborhood."

We drive home in silence.

I write this book because my father, a refugee who fought for the Army of the Republic of Vietnam, was imprisoned in a reeducation camp, and escaped by boat to the United States, has spent more than forty-two years in the United States as an American citizen but rarely leaves the confines of our neighborhood. Growing up, I saw his discomfort and experiences with racism and xenophobia outside our neighborhood. His experiences are not unique. As a graduate student in sociology, I studied residential and racial segregation, but that research was primarily written about segregation in terms of Black and white populations living in central cities. Segregation is not a story exclusive to central cities; this book and work by urban geographers and social scientists now show that racial and class separation are the reality for Americans in suburbia.[1] At that high school dinner in Newport Beach, I saw the dynamics of geographic and social segregation mapping itself onto suburbia. As a graduate student, I originally planned to study the ethnic enclave from the perspective of second-generation Vietnamese. Over time, in the face of rising living costs, my goal shifted to understanding how Little Saigon could maintain its existence and space as the Vietnamese capital of America and for who.

Participant observation and qualitative research have many advantages and disadvantages. This short note explains my position in the field and details my research strategy, including entry into the field, data collection, instrumentation, relationships with gatekeepers, analysis, and ethical considerations.

DATA SOURCES AND PARTICIPANTS

Data for this book comes from multiple sources and interviews I conducted between 2008 and 2022 while working in the community as a PhD student and then as an assistant professor.

As an assistant professor, I interviewed more than fourteen residents of Green Lantern and members of tenants' rights organizations for the housing and Green Lantern chapters. I solicited perspectives from room renters and landlords between 2019 and 2022 by distributing bilingual flyers in English and Vietnamese and posting them on social media to recruit participants through community organizations, churches, and temples. My sources of data also include Vietnamese- and English-language newspapers and materials from the archives at the University of California, Irvine, as well as oral histories from the Viet Stories archives at the University of California, Irvine, and data from the US Census. Most names have been changed to protect privacy except in cases where individuals consented to share their names.

Recruitment for interviews included snowball sampling through my community connections, convenience sampling of a Vietnamese-language business directory, and sampling of individuals who identified as second-generation Vietnamese via online advertisements on Vietnamese church websites, social media groups, professional associations, and voluntary organizations in Southern California. After interviewing a few initial respondents, I asked them to recommend others they knew whom I could interview. I drew on my connections from my volunteer work in the community and with teachers, friends, community organizations, and religious groups. There is a risk of sample selection bias in snowball sampling, but the range of responses to my interview questions makes me confident that my sample did not fall prey to this bias. In addition to my snowball sampling, I also interviewed community leaders and news and magazine reporters from *Người Việt* and *Việt Báo*. I also specifically targeted Vietnamese American teachers and administrators at each of the largest Vietnamese-dominant middle and high schools in the community (Westminster High School, La Quinta High School, Bolsa Grande, and Irvine Intermediate). Many of these teachers were second generation, raised in the community, and now teaching other second- and later-generation Vietnamese. I did not compensate respondents for their time, which did not seem to influence people's willingness to speak to me. If the interview occurred at a café, I would often purchase beverages for myself and the interviewee.

Interviews were open-ended and semi-structured to cover a variety of topics. In-depth interviews focused on ten topics related to the Vietnamese experience: family history, neighborhoods, ethnic identity, social mobility, language use, peer groups/social networks, dating habits, church participation, transnationalism, and work experiences. I began each interview by asking respondents to describe how their parents first came to the United States and what they knew about their family's immigration history. I asked respondents questions about the importance of Little Saigon in their daily lives compared to their parents. My interview schedule was adapted from Tomás Jiménez's seminal work on Mexican immigration, *Replenished Ethnicity*, with additional topics that I added, including transnationalism and questions specifically directed at Little Saigon and the war.[2]

In terms of ethnic identity, I could only note those Vietnamese openly claiming Chinese-Vietnamese ancestry during interviews. This was often revealed in answers to a number of questions in the in-depth interviews: when an informant described the number of languages they spoke and to whom (grandparents or parents); customs or traditions practiced in the family; ethnic identity; and racial hierarchies.

By this determining, approximately 15 percent of my in-depth interviews included Chinese-Vietnamese (varying from one grandparent who was Chinese, one parent, to both parents).

ORGANIZATIONAL DATA

This book also draws upon my networks through a database of Vietnam-US organizations (n = 614) I created in five areas of dense concentration of Vietnamese refugees in the United States while at Princeton as a graduate student through the Center for Migration and Development. This includes the three largest Vietnamese communities, or Little Saigons, in the United States: Orange County and Santa Clara County, both in California, and Harris County in Texas. From that directory, I conducted in-depth interviews with selected groups and administered a survey to selected leaders.

In the book, I only describe cases from Orange County, but I draw upon implicit comparisons with the other communities where I did fieldwork. I conducted interviews with seventy-four organizational leaders: thirty-seven in Orange County, seven in Santa Clara, fifteen in Houston, and fifteen in other parts of the United States including Seattle, Washington, and Falls Church, Virginia. These sites were chosen because they all have Little Saigons or large concentrations of Vietnamese refugees (California and Texas have the largest concentration of Vietnamese in the United States). These interviews were invaluable in connecting me with community leaders and activities and familiarity with the organizational landscape when I returned later to reinterview organizations and community members.

NEWSPAPERS AND ONLINE ARCHIVES

This book also includes secondary analysis of interviews from newspapers, online city planning commission meetings, online city council meetings, Facebook, YouTube videos, and publications including the *Los Angeles Times*, *Orange County Register*, *Voice of OC*, *OC Weekly*, *Người Việt*, and *Việt Báo*. Any interview that is included that I did not personally conduct contains a citation to the original source. This is most relevant in chapters 1 and 2, which include several interviews with foodie entrepreneurs and analyses of the win for rent control in Santa Ana. Watching and transcribing city council and planning commission meetings that went online during COVID-19 helped document the timeline and processes of the win for rent control and the testimonials of Green Lantern residents.

Like many ethnographers, I try to emphasize the voices, stories, and perspectives of the participants' lives as an entry point for analysis. For my own analysis, I organized my findings within each chapter according to a series of themes. My interpretation cannot ignore my personal ties or the inequities I see within the community in terms of housing justice, structural violence, and suburban inequality. My father is a boat person, one of sixteen siblings who fought alongside the Americans and spent three years in reeducation prison. While growing up, foster children from Vietnam lived with us, and my parents helped support distant cousins and relatives after they arrived. I remember as a child sharing my bed with cousin Mười (literally translated "tenth child"—in larger Vietnamese families, an excess of children are often given names based on their birth order). My impetus to write the final chapter, "The Right to the Suburb," came from the experience of family members and friends living in deportation limbo. After being convicted of crimes in their youth and serving time in American prison, Southeast Asians without US citizenship can receive final orders of removal, even though these deportees have not lived in their countries of origin since they were young children and no longer have any ties to Vietnam, Cambodia, or Laos. These friends and family members in Little Saigon are not alone; they are part of nearly eight thousand Vietnamese living in deportation limbo in the United States.

My own research position was complicated. No ethnographer can exactly reproduce the results of another researcher because the information often depends on the social role held by the researcher within that environment.[3] I am both an insider and an outsider to my research community. I grew up in Little Saigon in the cities of Santa Ana and Fountain Valley until the age of eighteen, when I went away to college at UC Berkeley. My surname is Huỳnh, which is distinctly Vietnamese, but I am multiracial and have the racial privilege to pass as an ethnic chameleon—Asian, White, Latinx, or other—depending on situational contexts and cues. Strangers are often surprised to learn that I am Vietnamese since I visibly pass as other and white, but my surname is a popular Vietnamese last name. This seemed to matter less for my interviews since I was usually introduced by a mutual friend. The fact that I finished a graduate degree and am a professor distinguishes me from many of my informants. There is no value-free research. The researcher's commitments and the social and political environment in which the research occurs condition the results.[4] The social position of the researcher determines what they are likely to observe. The way the researcher interprets the field site is often conditioned by the researcher's theoretical preconceptions.[5] Observation rests on "something researchers can find constant"—that is, "their direct knowledge and their own judgment."[6] Qualitative research is thus often interpreting the interpreted. Trained as a sociologist and urban ethnographer but now teaching ethnic studies, I wrote the story of *Suburban Refugees* to link everyday experiences and voices of dissent to suburban planning and structural inequities.

The researcher needs to take social traits, such as gender, age, race, disability, class, and occupational activity, into consideration when entering a social environment.[7] When interviewing older first-generation male informants, I often brought my father with me to these events or interviews or relied on his networks with hometown associations, distant relatives, and friends since his experience of living in Orange County dates to 1980. In terms of social class, my household growing up was working class, and I'm a first-generation college graduate. As a graduate student at Princeton, I felt my class position keenly; my student stipend was more than my father's income at the time.

Much of this work owes its debt to respected Asian American researchers and authors who have documented the community throughout the years with different lenses of analysis and perspectives to share the Vietnamese experience: Karin Aguilar-San Juan, Long Bùi, Thúy Võ Đặng, Hiền Đức Đỗ, Yến Lê Espiritu, Mariam Lam, C. N. Lê, Phương Nguyễn, Marguerite Nguyễn, Kiều Linh Caroline Valverde, Linda Võ, Tường Vũ, and Min Zhou, among many others.

Telling this story is only one way of understanding the diversity of Little Saigon; I am excited for the next generation of scholars and activists to continue writing our stories. While I was writing and researching, the Critical Refugee Studies (CRS) perspective emerged on the academic landscape. In the book, I try to incorporate this way of knowing that "centers refugee lives and the creative and critical potentiality that such lives offer" and that replaces and reverses the dehumanization of refugees through "imperialist gazes and frames and savior narratives."[8] This perspective was intellectually freeing for me as most of the literature I read in graduate school and as an undergraduate used a social science assimilationist perspective and was written by nonrefugees. "CRS is a way to seize control of image and narrative, by and for refugees, centered in refugee epistemologies and experiences in ways that enable transformative interventions."[9]

NOTES

INTRODUCTION

1. Anh Đỗ, "We Will Be Adrift Again: War Veterans, Refugees Face Uncertain Future with the Sale of Their Little Saigon Mobile Home Park," *Los Angeles Times*, April 1, 2017, https://www.latimes.com/local/lanow/la-me-ln-little-saigon-eviction-20170331-story.html.

2. Scott W. Allard, *Places in Need: The Changing Geography of Poverty* (New York: Russell Sage Foundation, 2017); Elizabeth Kneebone and Emily Garr, *The Suburbanization of Poverty* (Washington, DC: Brookings Institute, 2010).

3. Roberto Suro, Jill H. Wilson, and Audrey Singer, *Immigration and Poverty in America's Suburbs* (Washington, DC: Brookings Institute, 2011).

4. Suro, Wilson, and Singer, *Immigration and Poverty*, 1.

5. Allard, *Places in Need*.

6. Linda Trinh Võ and Mary Yu Danico, "The Formation of Post-Suburban Communities: Koreatown and Little Saigon, Orange County," *International Journal of Sociology and Social Policy* 24, no. 7 (2004): 15–45.

7. Anh Đỗ, "Not Your Grandmother's Little Saigon: Entrepreneurs Expand Enclave's Horizons," *Los Angeles Times*, November 8, 2015, https://www.latimes.com/local/california/la-me-new-little-saigon-20151108-story.html.

8. The Vietnamese American community is diverse. Varying contexts for their exits from Vietnam represent a complicated story of refugees with differing levels of human capital and a broad spectrum of experiences in and memories of Vietnam. Many endured dangerous conditions while leaving Vietnam, waited for years in refugee camps in Southeast Asia and East Asia, and spent years in prison before their departure for permanent settlement abroad. Others fled to the United States more immediately and did not endure such protracted transit times; these came from the privileged rungs of Vietnamese society, including intellectuals and the exiled elite of the former South Vietnam regime. Others spent years in refugee camps in Malaysia, Indonesia, and Hong Kong and protested for repatriation. Scholars often explain migration from Vietnam to the United States through distinct periods and three waves governed by US social

policy, including government-sponsored programs such as the Orderly Departure Program and the Humanitarian Operation Program that facilitated immigration and resettlement. The first wave of 1975 consisted of an estimated 125,000 Vietnamese elite. Then came a wave of boat people, ethnic Chinese, ex-political detainees under the Humanitarian Operation Program, and mixed-race children of Vietnamese women and American soldiers under the Amerasian Homecoming Act. The third wave has been primarily immigrant students, spouses, and family reunification from the 2000s onward. For further studies that explain migration periods in detail, see Nhi T. Lieu, *The American Dream in Vietnamese* (Minneapolis: University of Minnesota Press, 2011); Phương Trần Nguyễn, *Becoming Refugee American: The Politics of Rescue in Little Saigon* (Champaign: University of Illinois Press, 2017); Karin Aguilar-San Juan, *Little Saigons: Staying Vietnamese in America* (Minneapolis: University of Minnesota Press, 2009); Nghia Võ, *The Vietnamese Boat People, 1954 and 1975–1992* (Jefferson, NC: McFarland, 2005); Kiều Linh Caroline Valverde, *Transnationalizing Viet Nam: Community, Culture, and Politics in the Diaspora* (Philadelphia: Temple University Press, 2012); Min Zhou and Carl Bankston, *Growing up American: How Vietnamese Children Adapt to Life in the United States* (New York: Russell Sage Foundation, 1998); Irene Bloemraad, *Becoming a Citizen: Incorporating Immigrants and Refugees in the United States and Canada* (Berkeley: University of California Press, 2006); Hiền Đức Đỗ, *The Vietnamese Americans* (London: Bloomsbury Publishing, 1999).

9. RJ Rummel, *Statistics of Democide: Genocide and Mass Murder Since 1900* (Munster, Germany: LIT Verlag, 1998).

10. Numbers are contested and vary, including the length of the war, etc. Please see the following: Scott Sigmund Gartner and Gary M. Segura, "Race, Casualties, and Opinion in the Vietnam War," *Journal of Politics* 62, no. 1 (2000): 115–46; Robert McMahon, ed., *Major Problems in the History of the Vietnam War: Documents and Essays* (Lexington, MA: DC Health and Company, 1990); Matthew Adam Kocher, Thomas B. Pepinsky, and Stathis N. Kalyvas, "Aerial Bombing and Counterinsurgency in the Vietnam War," *American Journal of Political Science* 55, no. 2 (2011): 201–18.

11. Yến Lê Espiritu, "The 'We-Win-Even-When-We-Lose' Syndrome: US Press Coverage of the Twenty-Fifth Anniversary of the 'Fall of Saigon,'" *American Quarterly* 58, no. 2 (2006): 329.

12. Yến Lê Espiritu, "The 'We-Win-Even-When-We-Lose' Syndrome," 329.

13. Rakesh Kochhar and Anthony Cilluffo, "Income Inequality in the US Is Rising Most Rapidly among Asians," Pew Research Center, July 12, 2018; Aujean Lee et al., "Asian American and Pacific Islander Wealth Inequality and Developing Paths to Financial Security," *AAPI Nexus: Policy, Practice and Community* 13, no. 1–2 (2015): vii–xiv; Victor Nee and Jimy Sanders, "The Road to Parity: Determinants of the Socioeconomic Achievements of Asian Americans," in *Asian American Issues Relating to Labor, Economics, and Socioeconomic Status*, ed. Franklin Ng (New York: Routledge, 2014): 157–75.

14. Peter Hepburn, Devin Q. Rutan, and Matthew Desmond, "Beyond Urban Displacement: Suburban Poverty and Eviction," *Urban Affairs Review* (2022): 759–92; Allard, *Places in Need*.

15. Hepburn, Rutan, and Desmond, "Beyond Urban Displacement."

16. Andrew Wiese, *Places of Their Own* (Chicago: University of Chicago Press, 2009); Orly Clerge, *The New Noir: Race, Identity, and Diaspora in Black Suburbia* (Berkeley: University of California Press, 2019); Christopher Niedt, ed., *Social Justice in Diverse Suburbs: History, Politics, and Prospects* (Philadelphia: Temple University Press, 2013); Dylan Gottlieb, "'Closer to Heaven': Race and Diversity in Suburban America," *Journal of Urban History* 41, no. 5 (2015): 927–35.

17. William H. Frey, *Melting Pot Cities and Suburbs: Racial and Ethnic Change in Metro America in the 2000s* (Washington, DC: Brookings Institute).

18. US Census Bureau; American Community Survey, 2022 American Community Survey 1-Year Estimates, generated by author using data.census.gov.

19. Wei Li, *Ethnoburb: The New Ethnic Community in Urban America* (Mānoa: University of Hawaii Press, 2008).

20. Willow Lung-Amam, *Trespassers?: Asian Americans and the Battle for Suburbia* (Berkeley: University of California Press, 2017).

21. Wendy Cheng, *The Changs Next Door to the Díazes: Remapping Race in Suburban California* (Minneapolis: University of Minnesota Press, 2013).

22. Henri Lefebvre, "From the Production of Space," in *Theatre and Performance Design* (New York: Routledge, 2012), 81–84; Henri Lefebvre, Eleonore Kofman, and Elizabeth Lebas, *Writings on Cities* (Oxford: Blackwell, 1996), 63; Genevieve Carpio, Clara Irazábal, and Laura Pulido, "Right to the Suburb? Rethinking Lefebvre and Immigrant Activism," *Journal of Urban Affairs* 33, no. 2 (2011): 185–208.

23. "Our Story," Right to the City, 2022, https://www.righttothecity.org/our-story; Margit Mayer, "The 'Right to the City' in the Context of Shifting Mottos of Urban Social Movements," *City* 13, no. 2–3 (2009): 362–74.

24. David Harvey, "The Right to the City," in *The Urban Sociology Reader*, eds. Jan Lin and Christopher Mele (New York: Routledge, 2012), 443.

25. Susan Fainstein, *The Just City* (Ithaca, NY: Cornell University Press, 2014), 3.

26. Hao Ding and Anastasia Loukaitou-Sideris, "Racism by Design? Asian Immigration and the Adoption of Planning and Design Regulations in Three Los Angeles Suburbs," *Journal of the American Planning Association* 89, no. 1 (2022): 1–14.

27. Carpio, Irazábal, and Pulido, "Right to the Suburb?" 189.

28. Brenna Bhandar, *Colonial Lives of Property: Law, Land, and Racial Regimes of Ownership* (Durham, NC: Duke University Press, 2018).

29. Ananya Roy and Hilary Malson, eds., *Housing Justice in Unequal Cities* (Los Angeles: UCLA Institute on Inequality and Democracy, 2019), 16.

30. Desiree Fields and Elora Lee Raymond, "Racialized Geographies of Housing Financialization," *Progress in Human Geography* 45, no. 6 (2021): 1625–45.

31. Tracy Jeanne Rosenthal, "101 Notes on the LA Tenants Union (You Can't Do Politics Alone)," *Housing Justice in Unequal Cities* (2019): 51–59.

32. David Harvey, *Rebel Cities: From the Right to the City to the Urban Revolution* (London: Verso, 2012), 14.

33. Thank you to the anonymous reviewer of this book for urging me to reimagine the rights of the suburb beyond the Right to the City framework in a broader framework of imperialism, colonialism, ecological destruction, and climate change. These are their words.

34. "Protracted Refugee Situations Explained," United Nations High Commissioner for Refugees, January 28, 2020, https://www.unrefugees.org/news /protracted-refugee-situations-explained/.

35. Liisa H. Malkki, "Speechless Emissaries: Refugees, Humanitarianism, and Dehistoricization," *Cultural Anthropology* 11, no. 3 (1996): 402.

36. Yến Lê Espiritu, *Body Counts: The Vietnam War and Militarized Refugees* (Berkeley: University of California Press, 2014), 2.

37. Yến Lê Espiritu et al., *Departures: An Introduction to Critical Refugee Studies* (Berkeley: University of California Press), 3.

38. Linda Trinh Võ, *Mobilizing an Asian American Community* (Philadelphia: Temple University Press, 2004); Long T. Bùi, *Returns of War: South Vietnam and the Price of Refugee Memory* (New York: New York University Press, 2018); Thi Bùi, *The Best We Could Do: An Illustrated Memoir* (New York: Abrams, 2017); Kieu-Linh Caroline Valverde, *Transnationalizing Viet Nam: Community, Culture, and Politics in the Diaspora* (Philadelphia: Temple University Press, 2012); Lê Espiritu, *Body Counts*; Ocean Vương, *On Earth We're Briefly Gorgeous: A Novel* (New York: Penguin, 2021); Việt Thanh Nguyễn, *The Sympathizer* (New York: Grove Atlantic, 2015); Mai-Linh K. Hồng, "Reframing the Archive: Vietnamese Refugee Narratives in the Post-9/11 Period," *Melus* 41, no. 3 (2016): 18–41.

39. Lisbeth Haas, *Conquests and Historical Identities in California, 1769–1936* (Berkeley: University of California Press, 1995).

40. Elaine Lewinnek, Gustavo Arellano, and Thúy Võ Dang, *A People's Guide to Orange County* (Oakland: University of California Press, 2022).

41. "A Brief History of Orange County," Orange County Historical Society, accessed November 11, 2023, https://www.orangecountyhistory.org/wp/?page_id=38.

42. Karin Aguilar-San Juan, *Little Saigons: Staying Vietnamese in America* (Minneapolis: University of Minnesota Press, 2009): xv.

43. Rob Kling, Spencer C. Olin, and Mark Poster, eds., *Postsuburban California: The Transformation of Orange County Since World War II* (Berkeley: University of California Press, 1995).

44. Michael Wayne Williams, "From Orange Groves to High-Tech in San Fernando Valley: Boosterism, Rezoning, and the Emergence of a R&D Regional Economy," *Southern California Quarterly* 80, no. 3 (1998): 315–48.

45. Mark Baldassare, *California in the New Millennium: The Changing Social and Political Landscape* (Berkeley: University of California Press, 2002), 146.

46. US Census Bureau, "QuickFacts, Orange County, California, Population Estimates," 2022, https://www.census.gov/quickfacts/orangecountycalifornia.

47. US Census Bureau, "Annual Business Survey, Characteristics of Business Owners," 2021 tables, https://www.census.gov/data/tables/2021/econ/abs/2021-abs -characteristics-of-owners.html.

48. Abraham F. Lowenthal, *Global California: Rising to the Cosmopolitan Challenge* (Redwood City, CA: Stanford University Press, 2009).

49. Lowenthal, *Global California*, 73.

50. Lê Espiritu et al., *Departures: An Introduction*.

51. Kling, Olin, and Poster, *Postsuburban California*; Võ and Danico, "The Formation"; Kristen Hill Maher, "Borders and Social Distinction in the Global Suburb," *American Quarterly* 56, no. 3 (2004): 781–806.

52. Maher, "Borders and Social," 783.

53. US Census Bureau, "American Community Survey, 2022" and "American Community Survey 1-Year Estimates," generated by author using data.census.gov.

54. Gabriel San Roman, "Santa Ana Prepares Formal Apology for 1906 Chinatown Burning, Past Anti-Chinese Racism," *Los Angeles Times*, May 4, 2022, https://www.latimes.com/socal/daily-pilot/entertainment/story/2022-05-04/santa-ana-prepares-formal-apology-for-1906-chinatown-burning-past-anti-chinese-racism.

55. Dana Nakano, *Japanese Americans and the Racial Uniform: Citizenship, Belonging, and the Limits of Assimilation* (New York: New York University Press, 2023).

56. Võ and Danico, "The Formation," 19.

57. Jeffrey Passel and D'Vera Cohn, "20 Metro Areas Are Home to Six-in-Ten Unauthorized Immigrants in US," PEW Research Center, June 12, 2019; Audrey Singer, Susan Hardwick, and Caroline Brettell, "Twenty-First Century Gateways: Immigrants in Suburban America," Migration Policy Institute, April 30, 2008.

58. Evin Millet, "A Demographic Profile of Undocumented Immigrants from Asia and the Pacific Islands," Center for Migration Studies, June 14, 2022, https://cmsny.org/undocumented-aapi-millet; Soo Mee Kim and Aggie J. Yellow Horse, "Undocumented Asians, Left in the Shadows," *Contexts* 17, no. 4 (2018): 70–71.

59. Karthick Ramakrishnan and Sono Shah, "One Out of Every 7 Asian Immigrants Is Undocumented," AAPI Data, September 8, 2017, http://aapidata.com/blog/asian-undoc-1in7/.

60. Kim and Yellow Horse, "Undocumented Asians."

61. Afsaneh Najmabadi, *Familial Undercurrents: Untold Stories of Love and Marriage in Modern Iran* (Durham, NC: Duke University Press, 2022), 1.

62. Nancy K. Miller, *What They Saved: Pieces of a Jewish Past* (Lincoln: University of Nebraska Press, 2011): 207.

63. Lê Espiritu et al., *Departures: An Introduction*, 89.

CHAPTER 1

1. Andy Nguyễn, "Andy Nguyễn: Creating the World's First NFT Restaurant Set to Change the Industry Forever," interview by Jazzy Cho on June 15, 2022, YouTube video, https://www.youtube.com/watch?v=Gjrm_HKuATo.

2. Mikki Kendall, *Hood Feminism: Notes from the Women That a Movement Forgot* (New York: Penguin Press, 2021).

3. Sarah Bohn, Dean Bonner, Julien LaFortune, and Tess Thorman, *Income Inequality and Economic Opportunity in California* (San Francisco: Public Policy Institute of California, 2020).

4. Jonathan Lansner, "It Takes $349,200 Income to Buy an Orange County Home, 3.5 Times the US Salary," *Orange County Register*, May 11, 2024.

5. Holly Hagler and Claudia Bonilla Keller, "Empowering Older Adults in Orange County through Nutrition," *Daily Pilot*, April 18, 2024; Orange County Strategic Plan for Aging, "Food Insecurity," 2024, https://data.ocagingplan.org/food-insecurity.

6. Hosam Elattar, "Many Orange County Residents Still Struggle Putting Food on Table," *Voice of OC*, November 22, 2023; California Department of Education, "Free or Reduced Meal (Student Poverty Data)," https://www.cde.ca.gov/ds/ad/filessp.asp, accessed on May 13, 2024.

7. Katherine Alaimo, "Food Insecurity in the United States: An Overview," *Topics in Clinical Nutrition* 20, no. 4 (2005): 281–98; Mecca Burris, Laura Kihlstrom, Karen Serrano Arce, Kim Prendergast, Jessica Dobbins, Emily McGrath, Andrew Renda et al., "Food Insecurity, Loneliness, and Social Support among Older Adults," *Journal of Hunger & Environmental Nutrition* 16, no. 1 (2021): 29–44; Sarah Bowen, Sinikka Elliott, and Annie Hardison-Moody, "The Structural Roots of Food Insecurity: How Racism Is a Fundamental Cause of Food Insecurity," *Sociology Compass* 15, no. 7 (2021): 1–23.

8. *Little Saigon Blueprint for Investment* (City of Westminster report commissioned by Streetsense, Washington, DC, 2021), 10.

9. Bourdieu's theorizing of status and class helps us understand how such groups use social practices to distinguish themselves from others and reinforce class hierarchies. He employs the concept of cultural capital to denote symbolic and hidden aspects of status displayed in the lifestyles of elites to reinforce their position over others. Other scholars have since reformulated Bourdieu's theory of cultural capital to identify a shift from the exclusive endowment of cultural capital through highbrow genres to the consumption of multiple cultural forms. See Pierre Bourdieu, *Distinction: A Social Critique of the Judgement of Taste* (Oxford: Routledge, 2010); Nathan McClintock, "Cultivating (a) Sustainability Capital: Urban Agriculture, Ecogentrification, and the Uneven Valorization of Social Reproduction," *Annals of the American Association of Geographers* 108, no. 2 (2018): 579–90; Merin Oleschuk, "Foodies of Color: Authenticity and Exoticism in Omnivorous Food Culture," *Cultural Sociology* 11, no. 2 (2017): 217–33.

10. Michelle Boyd, "Defensive Development: The Role of Racial Conflict in Gentrification," *Urban Affairs Review* 43, no. 6 (2008): 751–56.

11. Emmanuel Delgado and Kate Swanson, "Gentefication in the Barrio: Displacement and Urban Change in Southern California," *Journal of Urban Affairs* 43, no. 7 (2021): 928–29.

12. Mahesh Somashekhar, "Racial Inequality between Gentrifiers: How the Race of Gentrifiers Affects Retail Development in Gentrifying Neighborhoods," *City & Community* 19, no. 4 (2020): 811–44; Lance Freeman, *There Goes the Hood:*

Views of Gentrification from the Ground Up (Philadelphia: Temple University Press, 2006).

13. Matthew B. Anderson and Carolina Sternberg, "'Non-white' Gentrification in Chicago's Bronzeville and Pilsen: Racial Economy and the Intraurban Contingency of Urban Redevelopment," *Urban Affairs Review* 49, no. 3 (2013): 435–67.

14. Brittany Woolsey, "An Update on the Vietnamese Dining Experience," *Los Angeles Times*, December 11, 2015.

15. Woolsey, "An Update."

16. Anh Do, "Not Your Grandmother's Little Saigon: Entrepreneurs Expand the Enclave's Horizons," *Los Angeles Times*, November 8, 2015.

17. Do, "Not Your Grandmother's Little Saigon."

18. Caitlin Kandil Yoshiko, "Little Saigon's Restaurant Scene Revives as Second-Generation Vietnamese Americans Mix It Up," *Los Angeles Times*, November 29, 2017, https://www.latimes.com/socal/daily-pilot/news/tn-wknd-et-little-saigon-201711-story.html.

19. Kandil Yoshiko, "Little Saigon's Restaurant."

20. Ian Hathaway, *Almost Half of Fortune 500 Companies Were Founded by American Immigrants or Their Children* (Washington, DC: Brookings Institute, 2017).

21. Alejandro Portes and Jessica Yiu, "Entrepreneurship, Transnationalism, and Development," *Migration Studies* 1, no. 1 (2013): 75–95.

22. Linus Yamane, "Labor Market Discrimination: Vietnamese Immigrants," *Journal of Southeast Asian American Education and Advancement* 7, no. 1 (2012).

23. Samia Chreim, Martine Spence, David Crick, and Xiaolu Liao, "Review of Female Immigrant Entrepreneurship Research: Past Findings, Gaps and Ways Forward," *European Management Journal* 36, no. 2 (2018): 210–22.

24. Alejandro Portes and Brandon P. Martinez, "They Are Not All the Same: Immigrant Enterprises, Transnationalism, and Development," *Journal of Ethnic and Migration Studies* 46, no. 10 (2020): 1991–2007; Randall Akee and Maggie R. Jones, "Immigrants' Earnings Growth and Return Migration from the US: Examining Their Determinants Using Linked Survey and Administrative Data" (NBER Working Paper Series 25639, National Bureau of Economic Research, Cambridge, MA, 2019); Alejandro Portes and Min Zhou, "Self-Employment and the Earnings of Immigrants," *American Sociological Review* (1996): 219–30.

25. Steven Tuttle and Alfredo Huante, "Taking Race Seriously in Gentrification Research," in *A Research Agenda for Gentrification*, eds. Winifred Curran and Leslie Kern (Northampton, MAs: Edward Elgar Publishing, 2023).

26. When the term gentrification was first coined in 1964, scholarship analyzed it primarily in terms of class; gentrification is still often understood as the "process of neighborhood change that includes economic changes in a historically disinvested neighborhood by means of real estate investment and new higher-income residents, as well as demographic change, not only in terms of income level but also in terms of changes in education level." In other words, "higher income people typically move to these areas to capitalize on low property values and rents." In doing so, they inflate property values, displacing low-income people and changing the

neighborhood's character. See "What Are Gentrification and Displacement," Urban Displacement Project, University of California, Berkeley, 2021, https://www .urbandisplacement.org/about/what-are-gentrification-and-displacement/, and Stacey Sutton, "What We Don't Understand about Gentrification," TEDx Talks, filmed January 15, 2015 in New York, https://noureanthology.wordpress .com/2015/04/24/what-we-dont-understand-about-gentrification/.

27. Alfredo Huante, "A Lighter Shade of Brown? Racial Formation and Gentrification in Latino Los Angeles," *Social Problems* 68, no. 1 (2021): 63–79.

28. Thus, both ethnic gentrifier and gente-fication refer to "a distinct process in which new, wealthier arrivals share existing residents' racial or ethnic background" while displacing vulnerable working-class and immigrant residents' right to remain in the neighborhood. See Tuttle and Huante, "Taking Race Seriously in Gentrification Research."

29. Zawadi Rucks-Ahidiana, "Theorizing Gentrification as a Process of Racial Capitalism," *City & Community* 21, no. 3 (2022): 183.

30. Rucks-Ahidiana, "Theorizing Gentrification."

31. Delgado and Swanson, "Gentefication in the Barrio."

32. Michelle Boyd, "The Downside of Racial Uplift: Meaning of Gentrification in an African American Neighborhood," *City & Society* 17, no. 2 (2005): 265–88.

33. Theories of gentrification usually assume that the gentrifying residents are white and middle-class, settling the "frontiers" of working-class, immigrant communities of color. I want to disentangle if it's appropriate to refer to this pattern of neighborhood change as gentrification when the gentrifiers are Vietnamese. How does this mode of community redevelopment differ from earlier models of gentrification? New scholarship is showing how race and ethnicity shape gentrification processes in more complex ways than relegating people into "dichotomous roles of victims of gentrification or emulators of white gentrifiers." See Kesha S. Moore, "Gentrification in Black Face?: The Return of the Black Middle Class to Urban Neighborhoods," *Urban Geography* 30, no. 2 (2009): 118–42; Delgado and Swanson, "Gentefication in the Barrio."

34. Anderson and Sternberg, "'Non-white' Gentrification in Chicago's Bronzeville and Pilsen"; Moore, "Gentrification in Black Face?"

35. Delgado and Swanson, "Gentefication in the Barrio."

36. Boyd, "Defensive Development," 752.

37. Kandil Yoshiko, "Little Saigon's Restaurant."

38. Winifred Curran, "'Mexicans Love Red' and Other Gentrification Myths: Displacements and Contestations in the Gentrification of Pilsen, Chicago, USA," *Urban Studies* 55, no. 8 (2018): 1711–28.

39. Expressive entrepreneurship is a term coined by Patricia Fernández-Kelly to designate the propensity of second-generation immigrants to engage in creative and artistic ventures to circumvent formal labor markets, including working-class immigrants who face limited job opportunities: "When desirable jobs require high levels of education and formal skills that many do not have or cannot afford, immigrant youth turn to the arts as a path to success." See Patricia Fernández-Kelly, "A Howl

to the Heavens," in *Art in the Lives of Immigrant Communities in the United States*, eds. Paul DiMaggio and Patricia Fernández-Kelly (New Brunswick, NJ: Rutgers University Press, 2010), 52–71.

40. Mareike Ahrens, "'Gentrify? No! Gentefy? Sí!': Urban Redevelopment and Ethnic Gentrification in Boyle Heights, Los Angeles," *Aspeers* 8 (2015).

41. Boyd, "The Downside of Racial Uplift."

42. Robyn Moran and Lisbeth A. Berbary, "Placemaking as Unmaking: Settler Colonialism, Gentrification, and the Myth of 'Revitalized' Urban Spaces," in *Leisure Myths and Mythmaking* (New York: Routledge, 2022), 106–20.

43. Philip Kasinitz, John Mollenkopf, Mary Waters, and Jennifer Holdaway, *Inheriting the City: The Children of Immigrants Come of Age* (Cambridge, MA: Harvard University Press, 2009); Jessica Yiu, "Calibrated Ambitions: Low Educational Ambition as a Form of Strategic Adaptation among Chinese Youth in Spain," *International Migration Review* 47, no. 3 (2013): 573–611; Zuelma Valdez, "Segmented Assimilation among Mexicans in the Southwest," *Sociological Quarterly* 47, no 3 (2006): 397–424.

44. Pascale Joassart-Marcelli, *The $16 Taco: Contested Geographies of Food, Ethnicity, and Gentrification* (Seattle: University of Washington Press, 2021), 7.

45. Alec R. Levenson, "Millennials and the World of Work: An Economist's Perspective," *Journal of Business and Psychology* 25, no. 2 (2010): 257–64; Brandon Rigoni and Amy Adkins, "What Millennials Want from a New Job," *Harvard Business Review* 11 (2016).

46. Robert W. Fairlie, "Entrepreneurship, Economic Conditions, and the Great Recession," *Journal of Economics and Management Strategy* 22, no. 2 (2013): 207–31.

47. Lawrence F. Katz and Alan B. Krueger, "The Rise and Nature of Alternative Work Arrangements in the US, 1995–2015," *Industrial and Labor Relations Review* 72, no. 2 (2019): 382–416.

48. Fairlie, "Entrepreneurship, Economic Conditions, and the Great Recession."

49. Josée Johnston and Shyon Baumann, *Foodies: Democracy and Distinction in the Gourmet Foodscape* (New York: Routledge, 2014).

50. Johnston and Baumann, *Foodies*.

51. Curran, "'Mexicans Love Red.'"

52. Huante, "A Lighter Shade of Brown?"

53. Daniel Cueto-Villalobos, "A New Face of Gentrification: Gente-fication in Boyle Heights," *Discoveries Magazine*, March 3, 2022.

54. Sharon Zukin, "Urban Lifestyles: Diversity and Standardisation in Spaces of Consumption," *Urban Studies* 35, no. 5–6 (1998): 825–39; Steven Tuttle, "Place Attachment and Alienation from Place: Cultural Displacement in Gentrifying Ethnic Enclaves," *Critical Sociology* 48, no. 3 (2022): 517–31.

55. Delgado and Swanson, "Gentefication in the Barrio," 931.

56. Moran and Berbary, "Placemaking as Unmaking."

57. Samantha Dunn, "Sonny Nguyễn, 'Change Agent' at 7 Leaves Café Company," *Orange County Register*, October 1, 2019, https://www.ocregister.com/2019/10/01/coast-game-changer-sonny-nguyen-change-agent-at-7-leaves-cafe-company/.

58. Michelle Paragan, "Sonny Nguyễn, Co-Founder of 7 Leaves Café, on the Company's Rapid Growth," *Orange Coast Magazine*, April 8, 2019.

59. Oleschuk, "Foodies of Color."

60. Paragan, "Sonny Nguyễn."

61. Yael Shmaryahu-Yeshurun, "Gentrifiers of Color: Class Inequalities in Ethnic/Racial Neighborhood Displacement," *American Planning Association* 90 (2023): 434–51.

62. Kandil Yoshiko, "Little Saigon's Restaurant."

63. Lok Siu, "Twenty-First-Century Food Trucks: Mobility, Social Media, and Urban Hipness," in *Eating Asian America: A Food Studies Reader*, eds. Robert Ji-Song Ku, Martin F. Manalansan, and Anita Mannur (New York: NYU Press, 2013), 231–44.

64. Kandil Yoshiko, "Little Saigon's Restaurant."

65. Kandil Yoshiko, "Little Saigon's Restaurant."

66. "About Dos Chinos," Dos Chinos Latin Asian Grub, November 20, 2022, http:doschinos.com/about-dos-chinos/.

67. "About Dos Chinos."

68. Anita Mannur, "Culinary Nostalgia: Authenticity, Nationalism, and Diaspora," *Melus* 32, no. 4 (2007): 11–31.

69. Lisa Lowe, *Immigrant Acts: On Asian American Cultural Politics* (Durham, NC: Duke University Press, 1996), 86.

70. Graeme Turner, "The Cosmopolitan City and Its Other: The Ethnicizing of the Australian Suburb," *Inter-Asia Cultural Studies* 9, no. 4 (2008): 568–82.

71. Jennie Germann Molz, *Travel Connections: Tourism, Technology and Togetherness in a Mobile World* (New York: Routledge, 2012), 77.

72. Molz, *Travel Connections*, 77.

73. Joassart-Marcelli, *The $16 Taco*, 37.

74. Kandil Yoshiko, "Little Saigon's Restaurant."

75. Chris Haire, "The Next Big Thing in Tourism Could Be Little Saigon," *Orange County Register*, April 13, 2017, https://www.ocregister.com/2017/04/13/little-saigon-story/; Kandil Yoshiko, "Little Saigon's Restaurant."

76. Millennial usually refers to persons born between 1981 and 1996; Gen Z often refers to persons born between 1997 and 2012. Gen Alpha or Gen A refers to the generation or cohort of people born after 2010. See Michael Dimock, "Defining Generations: Where Millennials End and Generation Z Begins," PEW Research Center, January 17, 2019, https://www.pewresearch.org/short-reads/2019/01/17/where-millennials-end-and-generation-z-begins/; Marius Drugas, "Screenagers or 'Screamagers'? Current Perspectives on Generation Alpha," *Psychological Thought* 15, no. 1 (2022): 1.

77. Thorstein Veblen and C. Wright Mills, *The Theory of the Leisure Class* (New York: Routledge, 2017).

78. Brooke Erin Duffy, *(Not) Getting Paid to Do What You Love: Gender, Social Media, and Aspirational Work* (New Haven, CT: Yale University Press, 2017).

79. Angela Woo, "Understanding the Research on Millennial Shopping Behaviors," *Forbes*, June 4, 2018.

80. Nguyễn, "Andy Nguyễn."

81. Nguyễn, "Andy Nguyễn."

82. Siu, "Twenty-First-Century," 236.

83. Lok Siu, "Chino Latino Restaurants: Converging Communities, Identities, and Cultures," *Afro-Hispanic Review* 27, no. 1 (2008): 161–71.

84. Irene Bronsvoort and Justus Uitermark, "Seeing the Street through Instagram: Digital Platforms and the Amplification of Gentrification," *Urban Studies* 59, no. 14 (2022): 2857–74.

85. John Logan and Harvey Luskin Molotch, *Urban Fortunes: The Political Economy of Place* (Oakland: University of California Press, 2007: 144–45).

86. Logan and Luskin Molotch, *Urban Fortunes*, 145; Kevin Cox, "Social Change, Turf Politics, and Concepts of Turf Politics," in *Public Service Provision and Urban Development*, eds. Andrew Kirby, Paul Knox, and Steven Pinch (New York: St. Martin's Press, 1981), 438; Boyd, "The Downside of Racial Uplift."

87. David Harvey, *A Brief History of Neoliberalism* (Oxford: Oxford University Press, 2007); Milton Friedman and Anna Jacobson Schwartz, *A Monetary History of the US, 1867–1960* (Princeton, NJ: Princeton University Press, 2008), 16; Michael Hardt and Antonio Negri, *Multitude: War and Democracy in the Age of Empire* (London: Penguin Books, 2005); Ulrich Beck, "The Terrorist Threat: World Risk Society Revisited," *Theory, Culture and Society* 19, no. 4 (2002): 39–55.

88. Alejandra Marchevsky and Jeanne Theoharis, "Welfare Reform, Globalization, and the Racialization of Entitlement," *American Studies* 41, no. 2/3 (2000): 235–65.

89. Duffy, *(Not) Getting Paid*.

90. Duffy, *(Not) Getting Paid*, 17.

91. Duffy, *(Not) Getting Paid*, 7.

92. Jonathon Woetzel et al., *Closing California's Housing Gap* (New York: McKinsey Global Institute, 2016).

93. Karen A. Warner, *City of Yorba Linda 2021–2029 Housing Element Draft* (Yorba Linda, CA: City of Yorba Linda Community Development Department, 2021).

94. Andrew Aurand and Matthew Clarke, *Out of Reach: The High Cost of Housing* (Washington, DC: National Low Income Housing Coalition, 2022).

95. Warner, *City of Yorba Linda 2021–2029 Housing Element Draft*.

96. Warner, *City of Yorba Linda 2021–2029 Housing Element Draft*.

97. Mark Baldassare et al., *PPIC Statewide Survey: Californians and Their Government* (San Francisco: Public Policy Institute of California, 2021).

98. Woetzel et al., *Closing California's Housing Gap*.

99. Richard Fry, "Millennials Overtake Baby Boomers as America's Largest Generation," (Washington, DC: Pew Research Center, 2020).

100. Burhan Kılıç, Aydan Bekar, and Nisan Yozukmaz, "The New Foodie Generation: Gen Z," in *Generation Z Marketing and Management in Tourism and Hospitality* (New York: Palgrave Macmillan, 2021), 223–47; Elmira Djafarova and Tamar Bowes, "'Instagram Made Me Buy It': Generation Z Impulse Purchases in Fashion Industry," *Journal of Retailing and Consumer Services* 59 (2021).

101. Erkan Sezgin and Beyza Uyanik, "Priorities of Consumers for Restaurant Preferences: A Conjoint Analysis Study on Generation Z," *Journal of Tourism Leisure and Hospitality* 4, no. 2 (2021); "Taking Stock with Teens," Piper Jaffray, Inc., 2019, http://www.piperjaffray.com/2col.aspx?id=5752. 2019; Edmund Goh and Ferry Jie, "To Waste or Not to Waste: Exploring Motivational Factors of Generation Z Hospitality Employees towards Food Wastage in the Hospitality Industry," *International Journal of Hospitality Management* 80 (2019): 126–35.

102. Anthony Turner, "Generation Z: Technology and Social Interest," *Journal of Individual Psychology* 71, no. 2 (2015): 103–13; Ryan Faughnder, "Gen Z Spends Half of Its Waking Hours on Screen Time. Here's the Good and Bad News for Hollywood," *Los Angeles Times*, April 12, 2022.

103. Vivian S. Louie, *Compelled to Excel: Immigration, Education, and Opportunity among Chinese Americans* (Redwood City, CA: Stanford University Press, 2004); Pyong Gap Min, *Ethnic Solidarity for Economic Survival: Korean Greengrocers in New York City* (New York: Russell Sage Foundation, 2008); Lisa Sun-Hee Park, *Consuming Citizenship: Children of Asian Immigrant Entrepreneurs* (Redwood City, CA: Stanford University Press, 2005).

104. Patricia Fernández-Kelly and Lisa Konczal, "'Murdering the Alphabet' Identity and Entrepreneurship among Second-Generation Cubans, West Indians, and Central Americans," *Ethnic and Racial Studies* 28, no. 6 (2005).

105. Fernández-Kelly and Konczal, "'Murdering the Alphabet.'"

106. Fernández-Kelly and Konczal, "'Murdering the Alphabet'": 1155.

107. Hanna-Mari Ikonen and Minna Nikunen, "Young Adults and the Tuning of the Entrepreneurial Mindset in Neoliberal Capitalism," *Journal of Youth Studies* 22, no. 6 (2019): 824–38.

108. Ikonen and Nikunen, "Young Adults," 825.

109. Laura Gurney and Vittoria Grossi, "Exploring Contours of the Entrepreneurial Self in the Contemporary University: Developing Learning and Teaching under Neoliberal Conditions," *International Journal for Academic Development* (2021): 1–12.

110. Portes and Zhou, "Self-Employment"; Steve Gold, "Chinese-Vietnamese Entrepreneurs in California," in *The New Asian Immigration in Los Angeles and Global Restructuring*, eds. Paul M. Ong, Edna Bonacich, and Lucie Cheng (Philadelphia: Temple University Press, 1994), 196–226; Marta Tienda and Rebeca Raijman, "Promoting Hispanic Immigrant Entrepreneurship in Chicago," *Journal of Developmental Entrepreneurship* 9, no. 1 (2004): 1–22; Pyong Gap Min and Mehdi Bozorgmehr, "Immigrant Entrepreneurship and Business Patterns: A Comparison of Koreans and Iranians in Los Angeles," *International Migration Review* 34, no. 3 (2000): 707–38.

111. Min Zhou, "Revisiting Ethnic Entrepreneurship: Convergencies, Controversies, and Conceptual Advancements 1," *International Migration Review* 38, no. 3 (2004): 1040–74; Portes and Martinez, "They Are Not All the Same; Min, *Ethnic Solidarity*; Steven J. Gold, *The Israeli Diaspora* (New York: Routledge, 2005); Hasia R. Diner, *Hungering for America: Italian, Irish, and Jewish Foodways in the Age of Migration* (Cambridge, MA: Harvard University Press, 2003); Pawan Dhingra, *Life behind the Lobby: Indian America Motel Owners and the American Dream* (Redwood City, CA: Stanford University Press, 2012).

112. Ivan Light, "Immigrant and Ethnic Enterprise in North America," *Ethnic and Racial Studies* 7, no. 2 (1984): 195–216; Zhou, "Revisiting Ethnic Entrepreneurship"; George J. Borjas, "Making It in America: Social Mobility in the Immigrant Population" (NBER Working Paper Series 12088, National Bureau of Economic Research, Cambridge, MA, 2006); Pawan Dhingra and Robyn Magalit Rodriguez, *Asian America: Sociological and Interdisciplinary Perspectives* (Hoboken, NJ: John Wiley and Sons, 2014).

113. Padma Rangaswamy, "South Asians in Dunkin' Donuts: Niche Development in the Franchise Industry," *Journal of Ethnic and Migration Studies* 33, no. 4 (2007): 671–86; Philip Kasinitz et al., *Inheriting the City: The Children of Immigrants Come of Age* (Cambridge, MA: Harvard University Press, 2009).

114. Dhingra, *Life Behind the Lobby*.

115. Sadegh Iranmanesh, "Oral History of Tâm Thanh Nguyễn," Viet Stories: Vietnamese American Oral History Project, University of California, Irvine, February 19, 2012, https://calisphere.org/item/ark:/81235/d82k25/.

116. Dhingra, *Life Behind the Lobby*.

117. Kasinitz et al., *Inheriting the City*.

118. Hoa Phát, "Home," https://www.hoaphatusa.com/.

119. Tom Berg, "Little Saigon Snapshot: How Phu Nguyễn's Family Spent 28 Days at Sea to Escape Vietnam and Now Runs Money Transfer Company," *Orange County Register*, April 30, 2015, https://www.ocregister.com/2015/04/30/little-saigon-snapshot-how-phu-nguyens-family-spent-28-days-at-sea-to-escape-vietnam-and-now-runs-money-transfer-company/.

120. Thúy Võ Đặng, "Oral History of Nguyễn Trong Phat," Viet Stories: Vietnamese American Oral History Project, University of California, Irvine, May 15, 2012; Berg, "Little Saigon Snapshot."

121. Sharon Zukin et al., "New Retail Capital and Neighborhood Change: Boutiques and Gentrification in New York City," *City & Community* 8, no. 1 (2009): 47–64.

122. Zukin et al., "New Retail Capital."

123. Joassart-Marcelli, *The $16 Taco*.

124. Nancy Burns, *The Formation of American Local Governments: Private Values in Public Institutions* (Oxford: Oxford University Press, 1994).

125. Mark Boyle, "Civic Boosterism in the Politics of Local Economic Development—'Institutional Positions'; and 'Strategic Orientations' in the Consumption of Hallmark Events," *Environment and Planning A* 29, no. 11 (1997): 1975–97.

126. "American Frontiers: California as Western Destination/Mediterranean Boosterism," Special Collections and College Archives, Occidental College, February 12, 2013, https://sites.oxy.edu/special-collections/amer-frontier /americanfrontiersgroup-boosterism.htm; Tom Zimmerman, "Paradise Promoted: Boosterism and the Los Angeles Chamber of Commerce," *California History* 64, no. 1 (1985): 22–33.

127. *Little Saigon Blueprint*, 10.

128. *Little Saigon Blueprint*, 50.

129. Salla Jokela, "Transformative City Branding and the Evolution of the Entrepreneurial City: The Case of 'Brand New Helsinki,'" *Urban Studies* 57, no. 10 (2020): 2031.

130. Marcus Andersson and Per Ekman, "Ambassador Networks and Place Branding," *Journal of Place Management and Development*, 2, no. 1 (2009): 41–51.

131. Kovačić et al., "Shaping City Brand Strategies Based on the Tourists' Brand Perception: Report on Banja Luka Main Target Groups," *International Journal of Tourism Cities* (2019): 22.

132. Senay Oguztimur and Ulun Akturan, "Synthesis of City Branding Literature (1988–2014) as a Research Domain," *International Journal of Tourism Research* 18, no. 4 (2016): 357–72.

133. *Little Saigon Blueprint*, 25.

134. Claire Colomb, *Staging the New Berlin: Place Marketing and the Politics of Urban Reinvention Post-1989* (New York: Routledge, 2013).

135. Colomb, *Staging the New Berlin*, 11.

136. Miriam Greenberg, *Branding New York: How a City in Crisis Was Sold to the World* (New York: Routledge, 2009), 220.

137. David Reyes, "250,000 Expected for Little Saigon's 3 Day Tet Festival," *Los Angeles Times*, January 29, 1989, https://www.latimes.com/archives/la-xpm-1989 -01-29-me-2037-story.html.

138. Richard Chang, "Dueling Tet Parades in Little Saigon Still Lead to Happiness," *Voice of OC Magazine*, January 27, 2020, https://voiceofoc.org/2020/01 /dueling-tet-parades-in-little-saigon-still-lead-to-happiness/.

139. Roxana Kopetman, "Two Tet Parades in Orange County? Garden Grove Says Yes," *Orange County Register*, November 13, 2019, https://www.ocregister .com/2019/11/13/two-tet-parades-in-orange-county-garden-grove-says-yes/.

140. Kopetman, "Two Tet Parades in Orange County?"

141. David Harvey, "The Right to the City," in *The City Reader* (New York: Routledge, 2015), 314–22; David Harvey, "From Managerialism to Entrepreneurialism: The Transformation in Urban Governance in Late Capitalism," *Geografiska Annaler: Series B, Human Geography* 71, no. 1 (1989): 3–17; Tim Hall and Phil Hubbard, "The Entrepreneurial City: New Urban Politics, New Urban Geographies?" *Progress in Human Geography* 20, no. 2 (1996): 153–74.

142. Steven Tötösy de Zepetnek and I-Chun Wang, eds., *Mapping the World, Culture, and Border-Crossing* (Kaohsiung: National Sun Yat-Sen University Press, 2010), 140.

143. Claire Colomb, "Place Marketing and Branding in (Anglophone) Urban Studies and Urban Political Economy: A Critical Review," Γεωγραφίες/*Geographies*, 30 (2017): 8.

144. Lily Dizon, "Acrimony over Project Called Harmony," *Los Angeles Times*, June 25, 1996, https://www.latimes.com/archives/la-xpm-1996-06-25-mn-18336 -story.html; Lily Dizon, "Bridge Brings Discord Instead of Harmony into Little Saigon," *Los Angeles Times*, June 25, 1996.

145. Nam Ha, "Business and Politics in Little Saigon, California" (PhD diss., Rice University, 2002), 28.

146. Phương Trần Nguyễn, *Becoming Refugee American* (Champaign: University of Illinois Press, 2017).

147. Dizon, "Bridge Brings Discord."

148. Karin Aguilar-San Juan, "Staying Vietnamese: Community and Place in Orange County and Boston," *City & Community* 4, no. 1 (2005): 37–65.

149. Nhi T. Lieu, *The American Dream in Vietnamese* (Minneapolis: University of Minnesota Press, 2011).

150. HaeRan Shin, *The Cultural Politics of Urban Development in South Korea: Art, Memory and Urban Boosterism in Gwangju* (New York: Routledge, 2020).

151. Charles Lee, "Improvising Nonexistent Rights: Immigrants, Ethnic Restaurants, and Corporeal Citizenship in Suburban California," *Social Inclusion* 7, no. 4 (2019): 82.

152. Tuttle and Huante, "Taking Race Seriously in Gentrification Research," 67.

153. Jimenez, Carlos, and Alfredo Huante. "Home in *Vida* and *Gentefied*: The Politics of Representation in Gente-fication Narratives," *Aztlan* 48, no. 1 (2023): 21–52; George Sánchez, *Boyle Heights: How a Los Angeles Neighborhood Became the Future of American Democracy* (Berkeley: University of California Press, 2021).

154. Rucks-Ahidiana, "Theorizing Gentrification."

155. Sánchez, *Boyle Heights*, 61.

156. Sánchez, *Boyle Heights*.

157. Geoffrey DeVerteuil, "Immigration and Gentrification," in *Handbook of Gentrification Studies*, ed. Loretta Lees (Northampton, MA: Edward Elgar Publishing, 2018).

158. Moran and Berbary, "Placemaking as Unmaking."

159. Dan Walters, *High Living Costs Solidify California's Two-Tier Economy* (Sacramento: CALMatters, 2023).

160. "Out of Reach: How Much Do You Need to Earn to Afford a Modest Apartment in Your State?" (Washington, DC: National Low Income Housing Coalition, 2023).

161. Andrew Khouri, "Some Sanity Is Finally Returning to SoCal's Brutal Apartment Market: A Rental Guide," *Los Angeles Times*, May 3, 2023, https://www .latimes.com/california/story/2023-05-03/apartment-rent-guide-southern-california -los-angeles-orange-county.

CHAPTER 2

1. Dan Immergluck, "A Look Back: What We Now Know about the Causes of the US Mortgage Crisis," *International Journal of Urban Sciences* 19, no. 3 (2015): 269–85; Dan Immergluck and Geoff Smith, "Measuring the Effect of Subprime Lending on Neighborhood Foreclosures: Evidence from Chicago," *Urban Affairs Review* 40, no. 3 (2005): 362–89.

2. Rachel G. Bratt and Dan Immergluck, "The Mortgage Crisis: Historical Context and Recent Responses," *Journal of Urban Affairs* 37, no. 1 (2015): 32–37; Benjamin Keys and Susan Watchter, "The Real Causes and Casualties of the Housing Crisis," *Knowledge at Wharton Podcast*, podcast audio, September 13, 2018, https://knowledge.wharton.upenn.edu/podcast/knowledge-at-wharton-podcast/housing-bubble-real-causes/.

3. Noelle Stout, *Dispossessed: How Predatory Bureaucracy Foreclosed on the American Middle Class* (Oakland: University of California Press, 2019).

4. Sarah Burd-Sharps and Rebecca Rasch, *Impact of the US Housing Crisis on the Racial Wealth Gap across Generations*, Social Science Research Council, 2015, 11.

5. Burd-Sharps and Rasch, *Impact of the US*.

6. Anh Đỗ, "Behind Little Saigon's Riches, the Poor Pack into Small Rooms to Survive," *Los Angeles Times*, March 13, 2017, https://www.latimes.com/local/lanow/la-me-rooms-for-rent-20170228-story.html.

7. Ingrid Gould Ellen, Jeffrey Lubell, and Mark A. Willis, *Through the Roof What Communities Can Do About the High Cost of Rental Housing in America*, Lincoln Institute of Land Policy, March 15, 2021, 22.

8. Ellen et al., *Through the Roof*.

9. Jenny Schuetz, *Fixer-Upper: How to Repair America's Broken Housing Systems* (Washington, DC: Brookings Institution Press, 2022); Jean Conway and Pete Alcock, *Housing Policy in The United States: An Introduction* (New York: Routledge, 2003).

10. City of Westminster, *City of Westminster Consolidated Plan 2020/21–2024/25*, 2021, https://www.westminster-ca.gov/home/showpublisheddocument?id=982.

11. Matthew Desmond, "Heavy Is the House: Rent Burden among the American Urban Poor," *International Journal of Urban and Regional Research* 42, no. 1 (2018): 160–70; Whitney Airgood-Obrycki, Alexander Hermann, and Sophia Wedeen, "'The Rent Eats First': Rental Housing Unaffordability in the United States," *Housing Policy Debate* (2022): 1–21; Stuart Gabriel and Gary Painter, "Why Affordability Matters," *Regional Science and Urban Economics* 80 (2020): 1–6.

12. Tobias Armborst, Daniel D'Oca, Georgeen Theodore, and Riley Gold, *The Arsenal of Exclusion & Inclusion* (New York: Actar Publishers, 2017).

13. Robert C. Ellickson, "The Zoning Straitjacket: The Freezing of American Neighborhoods of Single-Family Houses," *Indiana Law Journal* 96, no. 2 (2020): 395–427.

14. "Greater LA Region Zoning Maps," Othering and Belonging Institute, UC Berkeley, 2023, https://belonging.berkeley.edu/greater-la-region-zoning-maps.

15. "Greater LA Region Zoning Maps."

16. M. Nolan Gray, *Arbitrary Lines: How Zoning Broke the American City and How to Fix It* (Washington, DC: Island Press, 2022).

17. Keeanga-Yamahtta Taylor, *Race for Profit: How Banks and the Real Estate Industry Undermined Black Homeownership* (Chapel Hill: University of North Carolina Press, 2019); Richard Rothstein, *The Color of Law: A Forgotten History of How Our Government Segregated America* (New York: Liveright Publishing Corporation, 2017).

18. The Federal Housing Administration also played a role in codifying the building of single-family homes. "The FHA insured single-family homes at much higher rates than multifamily homes from four to one to seven to one. Even in 1971, when FHA insured the largest number of multifamily units in its history, single-family houses were more numerous by 27 percent." See Kenneth T. Jackson, "Race, Ethnicity, and Real Estate Aappraisal: The Home Owners Loan Corporation and the Federal Housing Administration," *Journal of Urban History* 6, no. 4 (1980): 419–52.

19. Charles J. McClain, *In Search of Equality: The Chinese Struggle against Discrimination in Nineteenth-Century America* (Oakland: University of California Press, 1994); Gray, *Arbitrary Lines.*

20. McClain, *In Search of Equality.*

21. Gray, *Arbitrary Lines.*

22. Sara Zeimer, "Exclusionary Zoning, School Segregation, and Housing Segregation: An Investigation into a Modern Desegregation Case and Solutions to Housing Segregation," *Hastings Constitutional Law Quarterly* 48 (2020): 205–6.

23. Charles Abrams, "The Housing Problem and the Negro," *Daedalus* 95, no. 1 (1966): 68, quoted in Zeimer, "Exclusionary Zoning," 208.

24. See *Village of Euclid v. Ambler Realty Company*, 272 US 365 (October 12, 1926).

25. See *City of Westminster Municipal Code: Residential Single Family*, Westminster, CA, Chapter 17, Article 2.10.015 "Residential Zoning District Development Standards," https://ecode360.com/43534707.

26. Linn Elizabeth Groft, "Do Multi-Family Housing Zoning Ordinances Affect Segregation in California?" (PhD diss., Georgetown University, 2022).

27. Gerrit Knaap, Stuart Meck, Terry Moore, Robert Parker, and American Planning Association, *Zoning as a Barrier to Multifamily Housing Development* (Chicago: American Planning Association, 2007).

28. Dolores Hayden, *Redesigning the American Dream: The Future of Housing, Work, and Family Life* (New York: W. W. Norton & Company, 2002).

29. Ananya Roy and Hilary Malson, eds., *Housing Justice in Unequal Cities* (Los Angeles: Institute on Inequality and Democracy, 2019).

30. Thy Võ, "Anaheim's New Oversized Vehicle Parking Ban Leaves Dwellers Wondering Where to Live," *Voice of Orange County News*, December 8, 2020, https://voiceofoc.org/2018/06/anaheims-new-oversized-vehicle-parking-ban-leaves-rv-dwellers-wondering-where-to-live/.

31. Michele Wakin, "The Regulation-Resistance Dynamic: An Ethnographic Study of RV Living in Santa Barbara, California" (PhD diss., University of California Santa Barbara, 2005); Michele Wakin, "Not Sheltered, Not Homeless: RVs as Makeshifts," *American Behavioral Scientist* 48, no. 8 (2005): 1013–32.

32. Manuela Tobias and Jackie Botts, "California's Section 8 Renters Face a Severe Housing Shortage. Can Lawmakers Help?" *KQED News*, August 30, 2019.

33. Manuela Tobias, "Lawmakers Tackle a Severe Housing Shortage for Renters Who Have Federal Vouchers," *KQED News*, August 30, 2019.

34. Jenna Bernstein, "Section 8, Source of Income Discrimination, and Federal Preemption: Setting the Record Straight," *Cardozo Law Review* 31 (2009): 1407–36.

35. The Fair Market Rent is set by HUD and represents median rents for a particular area. Section 8 housing must also pass a building code inspection and a safety inspection. See Bernstein, "Section 8," for further details.

36. "California Legislative Information Code 12921 and 12955(d)," State of California, accessed December 15, 2023, https://leginfo.legislature.ca.gov/faces/codes _displaySection.xhtml?lawCode=GOV&sectionNum=12921.

37. Since January 2020, California is one of nineteen states with SOI protection laws. The statewide law replaces the SOI ordinances that were in place in San Jose and Los Angeles. The Poverty and Race Research Action Council has a list that is regularly updated of all SOI laws across the United States. See "State and Local Source-of-Income Nondiscrimination Laws: Protections that Expand Housing Choice and Access," Poverty and Race Research Action Council, updated March 2024, https://www.prrac.org/appendixb/; *Source of Income FAQ* (Elk Grove, CA: Department of Fair Employment and Housing, Civil Rights Department, 2023), https://calcivilrights.ca.gov/wp-content/uploads/sites/32/2020/02/Sourceof IncomeFAQ_ENG.pdf.

38. Eva Rosen, *The Voucher Promise: "Section 8" and the Fate of an American Neighborhood* (Princeton, NJ: Princeton University Press, 2020).

39. Theresa Walker, "Nonprofits Join Forces in Experimental Program to Help OC Homeless," *Orange County Register*, August 28, 2020.

40. The Section 8 acceptable rental ceiling is set; for example, the maximum allowable rental price in Westminster under the Section 8 program was $3,345 for 2021. See OC Housing Authority, "2021 Payment Standards," https://www .ochousing.org/sites/ocha/files/import/data/files/117974.pdf.

41. Rosen, *The Voucher Promise*.

42. Will Fischer, Sonya Acosta, and Erik Gartland, *More Housing Vouchers: Most Important Step to Help More People Afford Stable Homes*, Center on Budget and Policy Priorities, May 13, 2021, https://www.cbpp.org/research/housing /more-housing-vouchers-most-important-step-to-help-more-people-afford -stable-homes.

43. US Census Bureau, "QuickFacts: Orange County, California, Population Estimates," 2021, https://www.census.gov/quickfacts/orangecountycalifornia.

44. City of Westminster, "Housing Choice Voucher Program (Section 8), City of Westminster, 2022," https://www.westminster-ca.gov/departments/community

-development/grants-housing-division/housing-choice-voucher-program-section-8; Alexa Pratt, "Orange County Housing Authority Opens Their Waiting List for the Housing Choice Voucher Program," Orange County Government, September 29, 2023, https://www.ocgov.com/press/oc-housing-authority-opens-housing-choice -voucher-program-waiting-list.

45. "Waiting List for the Housing Choice Voucher Program (Formerly Section 8), Wichita Falls, Texas," accessed August 3, 2023, https://www.wichitafallstx .gov/965/Waiting-List-Housing-Choice-Voucher-Prog; "Home," Indianapolis Housing Agency, accessed October 5, 2023, https://www.indyhousing.org/.

46. City of Westminster, "Affordable Rental Units," 2022, https://www .westminster-ca.gov/home/showpublisheddocument/948/637836314326500000; City of Westminster, "Affordable Housing," https://www.westminster-ca.gov /departments/community-development/grants-housing-division/affordable -housing; US Census Bureau, "Quick Facts: Westminster, California, Population Estimates," 2021, https://www.census.gov/quickfacts/fact/table/westminstercity california/PST045221.

47. US Census Bureau, "Quick Facts: Midway City, California, Population Estimates," 2021, https://www.census.gov/quickfacts/fact/table/midwaycitycdpcal ifornia,reddingcitycalifornia,burlingamecitycalifornia,lakelosangelescdpcalifor nia/PST045221; "Jackson Aisle," A Community of Friends, accessed December 20, 2022, https://www.acof.org/consultant-projects/jackson-aisle/.

48. Courtney Cooperman, "California," National Low Income Housing Coali- tion, accessed December 30, 2022, https://nlihc.org/housing-needs-by-state /california.

49. Paul Groth, *Living Downtown: The History of Residential Hotels in the United States* (Los Angeles: University of California Press, 1994).

50. Paul Ong, Chhandara Pech, Melany De-La Cruz Viesca, and Caroline Cal- deron, *Crisis to Impact: Reflecting on a Decade of Housing Counseling Services in Asian American and Pacific Islander Communities*, UCLA Asian American Studies Center, 2021.

51. The contemporary literature on SROs associate them with criminality, drug use, and deviance. See Julie M. Krupa, Lyndsay N. Boggess, Alyssa W. Chamberlain, and Tony H. Grubesic, "Noxious Housing: The Influence of Single Room Occu- pancy (SRO) Facilities on Neighborhood Crime," *Crime & Delinquency* 67, no. 9 (2021): 1404–28; Brian J. Sullivan and Jonathan Burke, "Single-Room Occupancy Housing in New York City: The Origins and Dimensions of a Crisis," *CUNY Law Review* 17 (2013): 113–43; Kelly R. Knight, Andrea M. Lopez, Megan Comfort, Martha Shumway, Jennifer Cohen, and Elise D. Riley, "Single Room Occupancy (SRO) Hotels as Mental Health Risk Environments among Impoverished Women: The Intersection of Policy, Drug Use, Trauma, and Urban Space," *International Journal of Drug Policy* 25, no. 3 (2014): 556–68.

52. See one of the few examples that counter this narrative: Tony Robinson, "Gentrification and Grassroots Resistance in San Francisco's Tenderloin," *Urban Affairs Quarterly* 30, no. 4 (1995): 483–513.

53. *Asian and Pacific Islander Anti-Displacement Strategies*, National Coalition for Asian Pacific American Community Development and Council for Native Hawaiian Advancement, 2016, 14.

54. Xiaoxiao Bao and Hoi Leung, "Community-Based Art Projects in San Francisco Chinatown: A Survival Strategy," *Journal of Cultural Research in Art Education* 38, no. 1 (2021): 65–77.

55. See City of Santa Ana, "Business Operating in Santa Ana," https://www .santa-ana.org/business-operating-in-santa-ana/, accessed August 20, 2022. Immediate relatives are exclusively defined as "mothers and fathers, grandmothers and grandfathers, sons and daughters, grandsons and granddaughters, brothers and sisters, and husbands and wives." This does not match the reality that many extended family members, such as cousins, live in this type of housing.

56. The passage of the ADU law in 2020 was the culmination of a nearly forty-year battle that began in 1982 to encourage the legalization of ADU ordinances. However, the law still allows cities sufficient leeway to adopt excessively restrictive rules, resulting in few ADUs being built. For instance, Santa Ana setback requirements demand a minimum setback of four feet for an ADU, which makes many potential lots too small to build them. In Garden Grove and Westminster, an ADU (either as a stand-alone unit or garage conversion) requires at least one parking space per ADU. Besides setback requirements and parking restrictions, height limits also restrict the building of ADUs. In 2018, only forty-two ADU projects were approved in Santa Ana, with the city given a C+ score by the UC Berkeley Center for Innovation. See Karen Chapple, Audrey Lieberworth, Eric Hernandez, Dori Ganestosos, Alejo Alvarado and Josie Morgan, *The ADU Scorecard: Grading ADU Ordinances in California*, Center for Community Innovation, February 1, 2020, https://www .aducalifornia.org/grades/. See City of Santa Ana, Accessory Dwelling Unit Ordinance, 2020, https://www.santa-ana.org/accessory-dwelling-units/.

57. At time of writing, there is no language that refers to the number of people who can live in an ADU in the cities of Little Saigon.

58. Kriti Ramakrishnan, Elizabeth Champion, Megan Gallagher, and Keith Fudge, *Why Housing Matters for Upward Mobility: Evidence and Indicators for Practitioners and Policymakers* (Washington, DC: Urban Institute, 2021), https://www .urban.org/research/publication/why-housing-matters-upward-mobility-evidence -and-indicators-practitioners-and-policymakers.

59. Naewon Kang and Nojin Kwak, "A Multilevel Approach to Civic Participation: Individual Length of Residence, Neighborhood Residential Stability, and Their Interactive Effects with Media Use," *Communication Research* 30, no. 1 (2003): 80–106; Matthew Desmond, *Evicted: Poverty and Profit in the American City* (New York: Crown Publishers, 2016); Mary Cunningham, Sarah Gillespie, and Samantha Batko, *How Housing Matters for Families*, (Washington, DC: Urban Institute, 2019); Brett Theodos, Eric Hangen, Brady Meixell, and Prasanna Rajasekaran, *Neighborhood Disparities in Investment Flows in Chicago*, (Washington, DC: Urban Institute, 2019).

60. Matthew Desmond, "Unaffordable America: Poverty, Housing, and Eviction," in *The Affordable Housing Reader*, eds. Elizabeth Mueller and Rosie Tighe (New York: Routledge, 2022), 390.

61. Nazli Kibria, *Family Tightrope* (Princeton, NJ: Princeton University Press, 1995).

62. City of Westminster, *City of Westminster Consolidated Plan 2020/21–2024/25*, 2021, https://www.westminster-ca.gov/home/showpublisheddocument?id=982.

63. Robin Bartram, *Stacked Decks: Building Inspectors and the Reproduction of Urban Inequality* (Chicago: University of Chicago Press, 2022); Desmond, *Evicted*.

64. Robin Bartram, "The Cost of Code Violations: How Building Codes Shape Residential Sales Prices and Rents," *Housing Policy Debate* 29, no. 6 (2019): 931–46; Geoff Rose and Richard Harris, "The Three Tenures: A Case of Property Maintenance," *Urban Studies* 59, no. 9 (2022): 1926–43.

65. Hiếu Trần Phan, "Subletting Is Dream Down Payment," *Orange County Register*, May 31, 2001.

66. Ellen Pader, "Housing Occupancy Standards: Inscribing Ethnicity and Family Relations on the Land," *Journal of Architectural and Planning Research* 19, no. 4 (2002): 300–18.

67. Geneva Collins, "Zoning and Public Housing Rules Dictate Who May Live with Whom," *Los Angeles Times*, March 19, 1989, https://www.latimes.com/archives/la-xpm-1989-03-19-mn-274-story.html.

68. Peter Hong, "Council Weighs Definition of 'Family,'" *Los Angeles Times*, September 21, 1997, https://www.latimes.com/archives/la-xpm-1997-sep-21-me-34681-story.html.

69. Lawsuits have relied on a functionalist definition of family, including *McMinn v. Town of Oyster Bay*, in Long Island, New York, where four childhood friends wanted to live together after graduating college. One of the issues was whether the young men ate dinner together, and the fact that they did not contributed to them losing the case. In Santa Barbara, the Supreme Court of California took note that a household group provided "emotional support" to one another while taking a trip to Mexico together. See Rigel Oliveri. "Single-Family Zoning, Intimate Association, and the Right to Choose Household Companions," *Florida Law Review* 67 (2015): 1401–53.

70. "Arlington County, Zoning Ordinance," adopted April 17, 2021, accessed December 14, 2023, https://arlingtonva.s3.amazonaws.com/wp-content/uploads/sites/38/2019/10/ACZO.pdf.

71. See "City of Garden Grove, CA: Code of Ordinances" and its definition of single-family residential requirements, "9.08.040.010 Single-family residential: General requirements," https://ecode360.com/GA4928.

72. Sara Bronin, "Zoning for Families," *Indiana Law Journal* 95, no. 1 (2020).

73. See Santa Ana City Code 1952, 9210.3; Ord. No. NS-455, 1, 6–20–60, https://www.santa-ana.org/charter-and-municipal-code?pagename=charter-and-municipal-code.

74. See Westminster, California Municipal Code 2069 1, 1987 under "Title 9 Public Peace Morals and Welfare" for the definition of family https://library.qcode.us/lib/westminster_ca/pub/municipal_code/item/title_9-chapter_9_04-9_04_025.

75. "Sacramento County Educators Meet with Legislators on State Budget Crisis," Sacramento Country Office of Education, April 25, 2008, https://www.scoe.net/news/library/2008/april/25budget_hearing/.

76. Pader, "Housing Occupancy," 302.

77. Executive Order No. 11365, 3 C.F.R. 675 (1966–1970); Melissa Lee, Jessica Levin, Robert Chang, and Lorraine Bannai, "Brief of Fred T. Korematsu Center for Law and Equality as Amicus Curiae in Support of Petitioner" (2018), Fred T. Korematsu Center for Law and Equality, https://digitalcommons.law.seattleu.edu/korematsu_center/112/.

78. Jane G. Greene and Glenda P. Blake, *A Study of How Restrictive Rental Practices Affect Families with Children*, Office of Policy Development and Research, 1980.

79. Robert W. Marans and Mary Ellen Colten, *A Report on Measuring Restrictive Rental Practices Affecting Families with Children: A National Survey*, Office of Policy Development and Research, 1980, 73.

80. Claudia Maria López, R. Varisa Patraporn, and Suzie Weng, "The Impact of Housing Experience on the Well-Being of 1.5-Generation Immigrants: The Case of Millennial and Gen-Z Renters in Southern California," *Housing Policy Debate* 33, no. 1 (2022): 1–27; Manuela Tobias, "Are Immigrants Getting Left Out of California's Rent Relief?" Cal Matters, October 13, 2021, https://calmatters.org/housing/2021/10/california-rent-relief-immigrants-barriers/.

81. Dulce Gonzalez, Michael Karpman, and Clara Alvarez Caraveo, *Immigrant Families in California Faced Barriers Accessing Safety Net Programs in 2021, but Community Organizations Helped Many Enroll* (Washington, DC: Urban Institute, 2022).

82. Tobias, "Are Immigrants Getting Left Out."

83. Tiffany Hickey, Charles Evans, and Jenna Miara, "Attachment to Intake Form and Request to Investigate Discrimination by Department of Housing and Community Development," Asian Americans Advancing Justice, June 25, 2021, https://www.advancingjustice-alc.org/wp-content/uploads/2021/06/DFEH-Complaint-HCD_FINAL.pdf.

84. Scott A. Bollens, "Municipal Decline and Inequality in American Suburban Rings, 1960–1980," *Regional Studies* 22, no. 4 (1988): 277–85; John M. Quigley and Steven Raphael, "Is Housing Unaffordable? Why Isn't It More Affordable?" *Journal of Economic Perspectives* 18, no. 1 (2004): 191–214; David Schleicher, "Stuck! The Law and Economics of Residential Stagnation," *Yale Law Journal* (2017): 78–154; Corianne Payton Scally and J. Rosie Tighe, "Democracy in Action? NIMBY as Impediment to Equitable Affordable Housing Siting: Housing Studies, 2015," in *The Affordable Housing Reader*, eds. Elizabeth Mueller and J. Rosie Tighe (New York: Routledge, 2022), 337–54; Georgina McNee and Dorina Pojani, "NIMBYism as a

Barrier to Housing and Social Mix in San Francisco," *Journal of Housing and the Built Environment* 37, no. 1 (2022): 553–73.

85. Gray, *Arbitrary Lines*.

86. City of Oakland, "Understanding Evictions in Oakland," 2023, https://www.oaklandca.gov/topics/understanding-evictions-in-oakland.

87. See Georgia House Bill 346 (HB 346) signed into law on May 8, 2019, https://gov.georgia.gov/document/signed-legislation/hb-346pdf/download.

88. "Home Repair," City of Westminster Housing Division, https://www.westminster-ca.gov/departments/community-development/grants-housing-division.

89. "Home Repair Program," City of Garden Grove, 2022, https://ggcity.org/home-repair-program; City of Garden Grove, "Pre-certified Local Housing Data for the City of Garden Grove," Southern California Association of Governments, updated April 2021.

90. US Census Bureau, "Quick Facts: Population Estimates, July 1, 2022 (V2022)- Santa Ana, CA," accessed December 10, 2023, https://www.census.gov/quickfacts/fact/table/santaanacitycalifornia/PST045222.

91. Rebecca Diamond, Tim McQuade, and Franklin Qian, "The Effects of Rent Control Expansion on Tenants, Landlords, and Inequality: Evidence from San Francisco," *American Economic Review* 109, no. 9 (2019): 3365–94; Matthew Desmond and Monica Bell, "Housing, Poverty, and the Law," *Annual Review of Law and Social Science* 11 (2015): 15–35; Blair Jenkins, "Rent Control: Do Economists Agree?" *Econ Journal Watch* 6, no. 1 (2009): 73; William Smith and Michael Teitz, *Rent Control in North America and Four European Countries: Regulation and the Rental Housing Market* (New York: Routledge, 2020); Benjamin F. Teresa, "New Dynamics of Rent Gap Formation in New York City Rent-Regulated Housing: Privatization, Financialization, and Uneven Development," *Urban Geography* 40, no. 10 (2019): 1399–1421.

92. Rent stabilization and rent control are terms often used interchangeably. Rent control can cover a broad spectrum of rent regulations: "These regulations can vary from hard caps on maximum rents (often associated with traditional rent control) to limits on the amount that rent can increase over time (a method that is often referred to as rent stabilization which is popular currently)" (Stacy et al., 3). Rent stabilization policies typically refer to regulations that limit how much rent can increase at one time and the frequency of increases. Early rent control policies "imposed strict price ceilings," often referred to as first-generation rent control, while today, "most local regulations are rent-stabilization efforts that target particular types of property within a city and allow for periodic increases," often referred to as second-generation rent control (Rajasekaran et al., 1). See Christina Plerhoples Stacy, Owen Noble, Jorge Morales-Burnett, Timothy Hodge, and Timothy Komarek, *Rent Control: Key Policy Components and Their Equity Implications*, (Washington, DC: Urban Institute, 2021), 3; Nicole Montojo, Stephen Barton, and Eli Moore, "Opening the Door for Rent Control: Toward a Comprehensive Approach to Protecting California's Renters," Othering and Belonging Institute,

UC Berkeley, 2018; Prasanna Rajasekaran, Mark Treskon, and Solomon Greene, *Rent Control: What Does the Research Tell Us about the Effectiveness of Local Action?* (Washington, DC: Urban Institute, 2019).

93. Smith and Teitz, *Rent Control.*

94. Smith and Teitz, *Rent Control.*

95. Smith and Teitz, *Rent Control.*

96. Daniel K. Fetter, "The Home Front: Rent Control and the Rapid Wartime Increase in Home Ownership," *Journal of Economic History* 76, no. 4 (2016): 1001–43.

97. Smith and Teitz, *Rent Control*, 4.

98. Dennis W. Keating, "Rent Control: Its Origins, History, and Controversies," in *Rent Control in North America and Four European Countries*, eds. William Teitz and Michael Smith (New York: Routledge, 2020): 1–14.

99. Katrin B. Anacker, "Inclusionary Zoning and Inclusionary Housing in the United States: Measuring Inputs and Outcomes," in *Research Handbook on Community Development*, eds. Rhonda Phillips, Eric Trevan, and Patsy Kraeger (Northampton: Edward Elgar Publishing, 2020).

100. James Burling, "Property Rights and the Modern Resurgence of Rent Control," *Brigham-Kanner Property Rights Conference Journal*, 10 (2021): 111–46.

101. Brian J. Asquith and Shane M. Reed, *Rent Control in California*, Upjohn Institute for Employment Research, September 3, 2021.

102. "Repeal the Costa-Hawkins Rental Housing Act," Tenants United, 2023, https://www.tenantstogether.org/campaigns/repeal-costa-hawkins-rental -housing-act.

103. "AB 1482: The California Tenant Protection Act of 2019," Berkeley Rent Board, accessed December 23, 2023. https://rentboard.berkeleyca.gov.

104. Abby Boshart, *Local Policies to Strengthen the Renter Safety Net* (Washington, DC: Urban Institute, 2023).

105. Isabella Rhee, "Santa Ana's Mobile Home Communities Deserve Rent Control," *Voice of OC*, January 12, 2022, https://voiceofoc.org/2022/01/rhee-santa -anas-mobile-home-communities-deserve-rent-control/?amp=.

106. Corianne Scally and Dulce Gonzalez, *Homeowner and Renter Experiences of Material Hardship* (Washington, DC: Urban Institute, 2018), 10.

107. Roxana Kopetman, "Santa Ana Approves Rent Control, Other Tenant Protections, after Emotional Debate," *Orange County Register*, September 22, 2021.

108. VietRISE, 2023, "Home," accessed December 20, 2023, https://vietrise.org.

109. Nancy Foner and Joanna Dreby, "Relations between the Generations in Immigrant Families," *Annual Review of Sociology* 37 (2011): 545–64; John Connolly, "Generational Conflict and the Sociology of Generations: Mannheim and Elias Reconsidered," *Theory, Culture and Society* 36, no. 7–8 (2019): 153–72.

110. Hugo Vásquez, Laia Palència, Ingrid Magna, Carlos Mena, Jaime Neira, and Carme Borrell, "The Threat of Home Eviction and Its Effects on Health through the Equity Lens: a Systematic Review," *Social Science and Medicine* 175 (2017): 199–208.

III. See the Supreme Court case *Buchanan v. Warley* (1917), which removed explicit race-based government zoning policies. Thereafter, a new system of economic and colorblind zoning was created. For more on this case, see Richard Chused, "Strategic Thinking about Racism in American Zoning," *New York Law School Law Review* 66, no. 2 (2022): 307–37; Michael Kim, "Exclusionary Economic Zoning: How the United States Government Circumvented Prohibitions on Racial Zoning through the Standard State Zoning Enabling Act," *Journal of Legislation* 48 (2022): 124–44.

CHAPTER 3

1. Sơn Đỗ, written testimonial to the author, November 2020.

2. I use the terms *mobile home* and *manufactured home* interchangeably. According to the HUD 2021 government definition, "A manufactured home (formerly known as a mobile home) is built to the Manufactured Home Construction and Safety Standards (HUD Code) and displays a red certification label on the exterior of each transportable section. Manufactured homes are built in the controlled environment of a manufacturing plant and are transported in one or more sections on a permanent chassis." The American Planning Association differentiates a mobile home as any manufactured home built before June 15, 1976, before HUD policy changes. Manufactured homes are now "built in conformity with the provisions of the federal HUD Code. Mobile Homes are those built before the adoption of the HUD Code." All the homes in Green Lantern Village are formally manufactured homes built after 1976. For these definitions, see US Department of Housing and Urban Development, "Frequently Asked Questions," https://www.hud.gov /program_offices/housing/rmra/mhs/faqs, and the American Planning Association, *APA Policy Guide on Factory Built Housing*, https://www.planning.org/policy /guides/adopted/factoryhousing.htm.

3. Esther Sullivan, "Moving Out: Mapping Mobile Home Park Closures to Analyze Spatial Patterns of Low–Income Residential Displacement," *City & Community* 16, no. 3 (2017): 304–29.

4. "California Mobile Home Park Statistics," Mobile Home Park Home Owners Allegiance, June 1, 2023, https://mhphoa.com/ca/mhp/statistics.

5. Esther Sullivan, "Displaced in Place: Manufactured Housing, Mass Eviction, and the Paradox of State Intervention," *American Sociological Review* 82, no. 2 (2017): 243–69.

6. Sullivan, "Moving Out."

7. Anna Jane Lund, "Tenant Protections in Mobile Home Park Closures," *UC Berkeley Law Review* 53 (2020): 759–841; Esther Sullivan, "Becoming Visible in the Public Sphere: Mobile Home Park Residents' Political Engagement in City Council Hearings," *Qualitative Sociology* 44, no. 3 (2021): 349–66.

8. Allison Formanack, "This Land Is My Land: Absence and Ruination in the American Dream of (Mobile) Homeownership," *City & Society* 30, no. 3 (2018): 293–317; Dick Bryan and Mike Rafferty, "Political Economy and Housing in the

Twenty-First Century–From Mobile Homes to Liquid Housing?" *Housing, Theory and Society* 31, no. 4 (2014): 404–12.

9. Jim Baker, Liz Voigt, and Linda Jun, "Private Equity Giants Converge on Manufactured Homes: How Private Equity Is Manufacturing Homelessness & Communities Are Fighting Back," MHAction, February 2019.

10. Parris Mayhood, "A Threatened Species of Homeowner: Mobile Home Owner-Tenants and Their Shocking Lack of Legal Safeguards," *University of Missouri-Kansas Law Review* 90 (2021): 481–92.

11. Michael Casey and Carolyn Thompson, "Rent Spike as Big-Pocketed Investors Buy Mobile Home Parks," Associated Press, July 25, 2022; "Duty to Serve Underserved Markets Plan 2022–2024," Freddie Mac, accessed August 12, 2023, https://www.fhfa.gov/.

12. Adam Travis, "The Organization of Neglect: Limited Liability Companies and Housing Disinvestment," *American Sociological Review* 84, no. 1 (2019): 142–70; Joshua Akers and Eric Seymour, "Instrumental Exploitation: Predatory Property Relations at City's End," *Geoforum* 91 (2018): 127–40.

13. Manuel Aalbers, *The Financialization of Housing: A Political Economy Approach* (New York: Routledge, 2019); Martine August, "Financialization of Housing from Cradle to Grave: COVID-19, Seniors' Housing, and Multifamily Rental Housing in Canada," *Studies in Political Economy* 102, no. 3 (2021): 289–308; Desiree Fields and Elora Raymond, "Housing Financialization and Racial Capitalism after the Global Financial Crisis," in *Housing Justice in Unequal Cities*, eds. Ananya Roy and Hilary Malson (Los Angeles: Institute on Inequality and Democracy at UCLA, 2019), https://challengeinequality.luskin.ucla.edu/wp-content /uploads/sites/16/2019/10/Housing-Justice-in-Unequal-Cities.pdf.

14. Andrew Crosby, "Financialized Gentrification, Demoviction, and Landlord Tactics to Demobilize Tenant Organizing," *Geoforum* 108 (2020): 184–93.

15. Loretta Lees (2016) argues in *Planetary Gentrification* that gentrification research has moved beyond the binaries of city and suburb, urban and rural. Eric Clark's (2005: 258) definition, via Lees (2016, 9), is expansive: "Gentrification is a process involving a change in the population of land-users such that the new users are of a higher socio-economic status than the previous users, together with an associated change in the built environment through a reinvestment in fixed capital" that results in the displacement process for low-income groups. See Loretta Lees, Hyun Bang Shin, and Ernesto López-Morales, *Planetary Gentrification* (New York: John Wiley and Sons, 2016), 8. See also Suzanne Lanyi Charles, *Suburban Gentrification: Understanding the Determinants of Single-Family Residential Redevelopment, a Case Study of the Inner-Ring Suburbs of Chicago, IL, 2000–2010* (Cambridge, MA: Joint Center for Housing Studies of Harvard University, 2011); Delik Hudalah and Nabilla Dina Adharina, "Toward a Global View on Suburban Gentrification: From Redevelopment to Development," *Indonesian Journal of Geography* 51, no. 1 (2019): 97–105.

16. Suburban gentrification includes physical and socioeconomic changes to a neighborhood with potential to displace vulnerable populations such as low-income

residents, renters, and working-class residents. This displacement of low-income groups is often orchestrated and initiated by the private sector and facilitated by the government. Suburban gentrification is most visible through capital reinvestment in the built environment. See Lees et al., *Planetary Gentrification*; Charles, *Suburban Gentrification*; Hudalah and Adharina, "Toward a Global View on Suburban Gentrification"; Scott Markley, "Suburban Gentrification? Examining the Geographies of New Urbanism in Atlanta's Inner Suburbs," *Urban Geography* 39, no. 4 (2018): 606–30; Craig E. Jones, "Transit-Oriented Development and Suburban Gentrification: A 'Natural Reality' of Refugee Displacement in Metro Vancouver," *Housing Policy Debate* 33, no. 3 (2023): 533–52; John D. Landis, "Tracking and Explaining Neighborhood Socioeconomic Change in US Metropolitan Areas between 1990 and 2010," *Housing Policy Debate* 26, no. 1 (2016): 2–52; Weishan Huang, "Immigration and Gentrification—A Case Study of Cultural Restructuring in Flushing, Queens," *Diversities* 12, no. 1 (2010): 59–72; Christopher Niedt, "Gentrification and the Grassroots: Popular Support in the Revanchist Suburb," *Journal of Urban Affairs* 28, no. 2 (2006): 99–120.

17. Alex Ramiller, "Displacement through Development? Property Turnover and Eviction Risk in Seattle," *Urban Studies* 59, no. 6 (2021): 1148–66.

18. Ramiller, "Displacement through Development?"

19. "Financialization of Housing," United Nations, accessed December 19, 2023, https://www.ohchr.org/en/special-procedures/sr-housing/financialization -housing.

20. Raquel Rolnik, *Special Rapporteur on Adequate Housing as a Component of the Right to an Adequate Standard of Living and on the Right to Nondiscrimination in this Context*, A/67/286, New York: United Nations Human Rights Council, 2012.

21. Rolnik, *Special Rapporteur*.

22. Esther Sullivan, *Manufactured Insecurity: Mobile Home Parks and Americans' Tenuous Right to Place* (Berkeley: University of California Press, 2018); Mark Kear, Dugan Meyer, and Margaret Wilder, "Real Property Supremacy: Manufactured Housing and the Limits of Inclusion through Finance," *Annals of the American Association of Geographers* 113, no. 8 (2023): 1900–17.

23. Esther Sullivan, "Personal, Not Real: Manufactured Housing Insecurity, Real Property, and the Law," *Annual Review of Law and Social Science* 18 (2022): 119–38.

24. Sullivan, "Personal, Not Real."

25. Anh Đỗ, "'We Will Be Adrift Again': War Veterans, Refugees Face Uncertain Future with Sale of Their Little Saigon Mobile Home Park," *Los Angeles Times*, April 1, 2017, https://www.latimes.com/local/lanow/la-me-ln-little-saigon-eviction -20170331-story.html.

26. Jess Bravin, "Center Pieces: Design of Civic Structures in County Reveals Character of Cities' Time, Place," *Los Angeles Times*, December 1, 1988.

27. Bravin, "Center Pieces."

28. Scott Lazenby, "How Room Arrangement Encourages or Discourages Civility," *Public Management Magazine*, March 2019.

29. Westminster City Council meetings and planning commission meetings can be viewed live on the city's YouTube Channel, website, or cable TV stations. The city's website includes an archive of meeting notes and recordings from 2009 to the present. Residents can even email comments, which will be provided to the city council. See City of Westminster online archives, https://westminsterca.granicus.com/ViewPublisher.php?view_id=2.

30. Sullivan, "Displaced in Place," 248.

31. Michael Liu and Kim Geron, "Changing Neighborhood: Ethnic Enclaves and the Struggle for Social Justice," *Social Justice* 35, no. 2 (2008): 18–35.

32. Liu and Geron, "Changing Neighborhood," 25.

33. Linda Trinh Võ, "Constructing a Vietnamese American Community: Economic and Political Transformation in Little Saigon, Orange County," *Amerasia Journal* 34, no. 3 (2008): 86.

34. Laura Harjanto and Jeanne Batalova, "Vietnamese Immigrants in the United States," Migration Policy Institute Spotlight, October 15, 2021, https://www.migrationpolicy.org/.

35. Võ, "Constructing a Vietnamese American Community," 84–109.

36. Pyong Gap Min, "The Advantages of Suburban Enclaves over Urban Enclaves for Community Empowerment: Korean Immigrants in Greater New York," *Ethnic and Racial Studies* 46, no. 7 (2023): 1357–77.

37. Min, "The Advantages of Suburban Enclaves," 1357–77.

38. Sookhee Oh and Angie Chung, "A Study on the Sociospatial Context of Ethnic Politics and Entrepreneurial Growth in Koreatown and Monterey Park," *GeoJournal* 79 (2014): 59–71.

39. Võ, "Constructing a Vietnamese American Community," 84–109.

40. Janelle Wong argues that it is critical to recognize variation within groups when studying immigrant political incorporation and that to develop or generalize a model of political incorporation for a certain immigrant or Asian population is a mistake, given the multiple categories of identity. Janelle Wong, "Immigrant Political Incorporation: Beyond the Foreign-Born versus Native-Born Distinction," in *Outsiders No More? Models of Immigrant Political Incorporation*, eds. Jennifer Hochschild, Jacqueline Chattopadhyay, Claudine Gay, and Michael Jones-Correa (Oxford: Oxford University Press, 2013).

41. Thy Võ, "Seniors, Refugees Protest Closure of Westminster Mobile Home Park," *Voice of OC Magazine*, March 7, 2018, https://voiceofoc.org/2018/03/seniors-refugees-protest-closure-of-westminster-mobile-home-park/.

42. Võ, "Seniors, Refugees Protest."

43. Nadia Y. Kim, *Refusing Death: Immigrant Women and the Fight for Environmental Justice in LA* (Palo Alto, CA: Stanford University Press, 2021); Alvaro Huerta, "Looking beyond 'Mow, Blow and Go': A Case Study of Mexican Immigrant Gardeners in Los Angeles," *Berkeley Planning Journal* 20, no. 1 (2007): 1–25.

44. The California Senate passed the bill, with fifty-one in favor and twenty opposed. The California State Assembly followed suit, and within two months, the governor signed it into law. See Zarina Khairzada, "Mobile Home Park Closure

Brings Development, Displacement Fears for Seniors," *Spectrum News* 1, October 28, 2020, https://spectrumnews1.com/ca/la-west/housing/2020/10/28/mobile-home-park-closure-brings-development—displacement-fears-for-seniors.

45. Peter Marcuse, "To Control Gentrification: Anti-Displacement Zoning and Planning for Stable Residential Districts," *NYU Review of Law and Social Change* 13 (1984): 931.

46. Sonya Salamon and Katherine MacTavish, "Quasi-Homelessness among Rural Trailer-Park Households in the United States," in *International Perspectives on Rural Homelessness*, eds. Paul Cloke and Paul Milbourne (London: Routledge, 2006), 45–62.

47. Salamon and MacTavish, "Quasi-Homelessness"; Matthew Furman, *Eradicating Substandard Manufactured Homes: Replacement Programs as a Strategy* (Boston, MA: Harvard Joint Center for Housing Studies and NeighborWorks America, 2014); California State Board of Equalization, *Assessment of Manufactured Homes and Parks* (Sacramento: California State Board of Equalization, 2001, reprinted 2015), https://www.boe.ca.gov/proptaxes/pdf/ah511final.pdf.

48. Kenneth K. Baar, "The Right to Sell the 'Im'mobile Manufactured Home in Its Rent Controlled Space in the 'Im'mobile Home Park: Valid Regulation or Unconstitutional Taking?" *Urban Lawyer* 24, no. 1 (1992): 157–221.

49. Mayhood, "A Threatened Species of Homeowner," 481.

50. Baar, "The Right to Sell the 'Im'mobile Manufactured Home."

51. Reggie James, Director Jane Briesemeister, Kathy Mitchell, and Kevin Jewell, "Manufactured Homeowners Who Rent Lots Lack Security of Basic Tenants Rights," Consumers Union, accessed August 12, 2023, https://inspectapedia.com/Manufactured_Homes/Manufactured-Home-Tenants-Rights.pdf.

52. "Data Spotlight: Older Adults Living in Mobile Homes," Consumer Financial Protection Bureau, May 10, 2022.

53. "California MHP Rent Stabilization Ordinances (RSO aka SRSO)," Mobile Home Park Owners Allegiance, accessed August 16, 2023, https://mhphoa.com/ca/rso/.

54. Matthew Desmond and Rachel Tolbert Kimbro, "Eviction's Fallout: Housing, Hardship, and Health," *Social Forces* 94, no. 1 (2015): 295–324.

55. Daniel Baker, Kelly Hamshaw, and Corey Beach, "A Window into Park Life: Findings from a Resident Survey of Nine Mobile Home Park Communities in Vermont," *Journal of Rural and Community Development* 6, no. 2 (2011): 62.

56. Reina Ehrenfeucht, "Moving beyond the Mobile Myth: Preserving Manufactured Housing Communities," Grounded Solutions Network, 2018, https://groundedsolutions.org.

57. "About Us," Caritas Corporation, accessed August 22, 2023, https://www.caritascorp.org.

58. Nemoy Lewis, *The Uneven Racialized Impacts of Financialization* (Ottawa: Canadian Human Rights Commission, 2022), 21.

59. Mayhood, "A Threatened Species of Homeowner."

60. Mayhood, "A Threatened Species of Homeowner," 482.

61. Frank Rolfe, "Why Invest in Mobile Home Parks," Mobile Home University, accessed August 17, 2023, https://www.mobilehomeuniversity.com/.

62. Gina Silva, "Paramount Families Fear Homelessness after New Owners Raise Rent," FOX 11 News Los Angeles, June 12, 2023; Ian Richardson, "Iowa Mobile Home Owners Get Extra 30 Days before Steep Rent Increases Begin," *Des Moines Register*, April 18, 2019; Catherine Reagor, Juliette Rihl, and Kunle Falayi, "'We Are Going to Be Homeless': How Mobile Homeowners Are Being Forced Out in Metro Phoenix," *Arizona Republic*, October 22, 2022.

63. "Chapter 5: Which Assets Are Most Important?" in *Wealth Gaps Rise to Record Highs Between Whites, Blacks, Hispanics*, PEW Research Center, July 26, 2011.

64. Mary Childs, "Mobile Home Parked," August 6, 2021, in *Planet Money*, produced by Dave Blanchard, podcast, MP3 audio, https://www.npr.org/transcripts/1025557463.

65. Childs, "Mobile Home Parked."

66. Childs, "Mobile Home Parked."

67. Jennifer Molinsky, "Older Adults Increasingly Face Housing Affordability Challenges," Housing Perspectives, Joint Center for Housing Studies of Harvard University, September 21, 2018; Lorie Konish, "Less than 5% of the US Housing Supply Is Accessible to Older, Disabled Americans. These Changes May Help," CNBC, July 31, 2023, https://www.cnbc.com/2023/07/21/less-than-5percent-of-housing-is-accessible-to-older-disabled-americans.html.

68. Lou Ponsi, "Rent Increases Will Be Limited at One OC Mobile Home Park," *Orange County Register*, October 29, 2021, https://www.ocregister.com/2021/10/29/in-january-one-oc-mobile-home-park-will-have-limits-on-rent-increases/.

69. Zachary Lamb, Linda Shi, Stephanie Silva, and Jason Spicer, "Resident-Owned Resilience: Can Cooperative Land Ownership Enable Transformative Climate Adaptation for Manufactured Housing Communities?" *Housing Policy Debate* 33, no. 5 (2023): 1055–77.

70. Ehrenfeucht, "Moving beyond the Mobile Myth."

71. Lamb et al., "Resident-Owned Resilience."

CHAPTER 4

1. "Vietnamese and Asian American Organizations across the Country Denounce Upcoming March 15 Deportation Flight to Vietnam, Say Deporting Refugees Is Anti-Asian Violence," VietRISE, March 12, 2021, https://vietrise.org/vietnamese-and-asian-american-organizations-across-the-country-denounce-upcoming-march-15-deportation-flight-to-viet-nam-say-deporting-refugees-is-anti-asian-violence/.

2. Name is changed to protect the privacy of the interviewee. Personal interview with author on September 21, 2022. Given that many of the interviewees in this chapter have uncertain legal status, I changed names for everyone except secondary

personal stories from Asian American social justice organizations and legal cases, which are cited in the notes.

3. Kony Kim, *From Prison to ICE to Freedom: A Handbook for Immigrants Inside* (Oakland, CA: Asian Americans Advancing Justice and Asian Prisoner Support Committee, 2020).

4. The remaining fifteen thousand Southeast Asians live in the United States undocumented, in a state of limbo, waiting with uncertainty for if and when ICE will deport them. See Cody Uyeda, "Addressing Gendered Trauma, Identity, and the Crime-to-Deportation Pipeline among Southeast Asian Men," *UCLA Asian Pacific American Law Journal* 25, no. 1 (2021).

5. Southeast Asia Resource Action Center, "The Devastating Impact of Deportation on Southeast Asian Americans," SEARAC Fact Sheet, https://www.searac .org/wp-content/uploads/2018/04/The-Devastating-Impact-of-Deportation-on -Southeast-Asian-Americans-1.pdf.

6. Việt Thành Nguyễn, ed., *The Displaced: Refugee Writers on Refugee Lives* (New York: Abrams, 2018).

7. Vinh Nguyễn, *Lived Refuge: Gratitude, Resentment, Resilience* (Oakland: University of California Press, 2023).

8. Vinh Nguyễn, "Refugeetude: When Does a Refugee Stop Being a Refugee," *Social Text* 37, no. 2 (2019): 109–31.

9. Tanya Maria Golash-Boza, *Deported: Immigrant Policing, Disposable Labor and Global Capitalism* (New York: New York University Press, 2015).

10. Kevin D. Lâm, *Youth Gangs, Racism, and Schooling: Vietnamese American Youth in a Postcolonial Context* (New York: Palgrave Macmillan, 2015): 7.

11. Lâm, *Youth Gangs.*

12. Angela E. Oh and Karen Umemoto, "Asian Americans and Pacific Islanders: From Incarceration to Re-Entry," *Amerasia Journal* 31, no. 3 (2005): 43–59.

13. Lâm, *Youth Gangs.*

14. Lâm, *Youth Gangs.*

15. Ruth Wilson Gilmore, *Golden Gulag: Prisons, Surplus, Crisis, and Opposition in Globalizing California* (Berkeley: University of California Press, 2007); Grace Deng, "Immigrants and Refugees Are Spending Decades in Prison Only to Be Released into ICE Custody," *Prism*, March 10, 2022, https://prismreports .org/2022/03/10/immigrants-released-into-ice-custody/.

16. Heba Gowayed, *Refuge: How the State Shapes Human Potential* (Princeton, NJ: Princeton University Press, 2022).

17. Gowayed, *Refuge,* 8.

18. Gowayed, *Refuge.*

19. Magnus Lofstrom, Mia Bird, and Brandon Martin, *California's Historic Corrections Reforms* (San Francisco: Public Policy Institute of California, 2016).

20. Michelle Harris, "California Law Gives Youth Sentenced to Life without Parole Another Chance," National Center for Youth Law, January 1, 2013, https:// youthlaw.org/news/california-law-gives-youth-sentenced-life-without-parole-an other-chance.

21. "Resources on Deportation of Vietnamese Immigrants Who Entered the US before 1995," Advancing Justice, Asian Law Caucus, 2023, https://www.advancingjustice-aajc.org.

22. Kim, *From Prison to ICE to Freedom*.

23. Lý Thị Hải Trân, "Outsiders No More?: The Discourse of Political Incorporation of Vietnamese Refugees in the United States (1975–2020)," *Journal of Asian American Studies* 23, no. 2 (2020): 229–64.

24. Bill Ong Hing, "Deporting Cambodian Refugees: Justice Denied?" *Crime & Delinquency* 51, no. 2 (2005): 265–90.

25. Rebecca L. Naser and Nancy G. La Vigne, "Family Support in the Prisoner Reentry Process: Expectations and Realities," *Journal of Offender Rehabilitation* 43, no. 1 (2006): 93–106.

26. Angela S. García, *Legal Passing: Navigating Undocumented Life and Local Immigration Law* (Berkeley: University of California Press, 2019), 134.

27. API Rise, "Van's Story," May 11, 2020.

28. Richard Menel, *Why Youth Incarceration Fails: An Updated Review of the Evidence*, The Sentencing Project, March 1, 2023, https://www.sentencingproject.org/reports/why-youth-incarceration-fails-an-updated-review-of-the-evidence/.

29. Kristen Bell, "A Stone of Hope: Legal and Empirical Analysis of California Juvenile Lifer Parole Decisions," *Harvard Civil Rights-Civil Liberties Law Review* 54, no. 2 (2019): 455–548; James Garbarino, *Miller's Children: Why Giving Teenage Killers a Second Chance Matters for All of Us* (Berkeley: University of California Press, 2018).

30. API Rise, "Van's Story."

31. Jamie Longazel, Jake Berman, and Benjamin Fleury-Steiner, "The Pains of Immigrant Imprisonment," *Sociology Compass* 10, no. 11 (2016): 989–98; Maya Manian, "Immigration Detention and Coerced Sterilization History Tragically Repeats Itself," ACLU, September 29, 2020.

32. Manian, "Immigration Detention."

33. Emily Durkin, Margaret Brown Vega, Nathan Craig, Neil Harvey, Daniela Navarro Verdugo, Brennan Ramsey, Fernanda Reyes, and Avigail Turima Romo, *The Pains and Profits of Immigrant Imprisonment: Migrant Testimonies from ICE Detention Centers in the El Paso ICE Field Office* (Las Cruces: New Mexico State University, 2020); "Conditions in Migrant Detention Centers," American Oversight, May 23, 2023.

34. Merill Smith, ed., *Warehousing Refugees: A Denial of Rights, a Waste of Humanity* (Arlington, VA: US Committee for Refugees and Immigrants, 2005).

35. Nancy Morawetz, "Understanding the Impact of the 1996 Deportation Laws and the Limited Scope of Proposed Reforms," *In Defense of the Alien* 23 (2000): 1–30.; Jacqueline Hagan, Brianna Castro, and Nestor Rodriguez, "The Effects of US Deportation Policies on Immigrant Families and Communities: Cross-Border Perspectives," *North Carolina Law Review* 88 (2009): 1799–1824.

36. Longazel, Berman, and Fleury-Steiner, "The Pains."

37. Trịnh Trường, "Trinh v. Homan: The Indefinite Detention of Vietnamese Refugees in the 21st Century," *Southern California Review of Law and Social Justice* 30 (2021): 415–47.

38. *Trinh v. Homan*, 466 F. Supp. 3d 1077 (C. D. Cal. 2020).

39. Golash-Boza, *Deported: Immigrant Policing*, 8–9.

40. David K. Hausman, "The Unexamined Law of Deportation," *Georgetown Law Journal* 110 (2021): 973–1020.

41. Hausman, "The Unexamined Law," 973.

42. *Trinh v. Homan*, 466 F. Supp. 3d 1077 (C. D. Cal. 2020).

43. Yến Lê Espiritu, Lan Duong, Ma Vang, Victor Bascara, Khatharya Um, Lila Sharif, and Nigel Hatton, *Departures: An Introduction to Critical Refugee Studies* (Berkeley: University of California Press), 54–55.

44. Sarah Pierce and Andrew Selee, *Immigration under Trump: A Review of Policy Shifts in the Year since the Election* (Washington DC: Migration Policy Institute, 2017).

45. Daniel J. Van Lehman and Estelle M. McKee, "Removals to Somalia in Light of the Convention against Torture: Recent Evidence from Somali Bantu Deportees," *Georgetown Immigration Law Journal* 33 (2018): 357–61; Bill Ong Hing, "Deporting Our Souls and Defending Our Immigrants," *Amerasia Journal* 31, no. 3 (2005): x–xxii.

46. Bill Ong Hing, "Deporting Cambodian Refugees: Justice Denied?" *Crime & Delinquency* 51, no. 2 (2005): 265–90.

47. Lindsay Daniels, "The End of Special Treatment for Cubans in the US Immigration System: Consequences and Solutions for Cubans with Final Orders of Removal," *Dickinson Law Review* 122 (2017): 707–39. Daniels also notes that there were removals of nearly two thousand refugees who came from Cuba in the Mariel boatlift in 1980 and removals of Cubans in 2014 who had criminal convictions of murder.

48. Cecilia Menjívar, "Liminal Legality: Salvadoran and Guatemalan Immigrants' Lives in the United States," *American Journal of Sociology* 111, no. 4 (2006): 1000.

49. Menjívar, "Liminal Legality."

50. Cecilia Menjívar, Andrea Gómez Cervantes, and Daniel Alvord, "The Expansion of 'Crimmigration,' Mass Detention, and Deportation," *Sociology Compass* 12, no. 4 (2018): 1–15.

51. Jillian Beck, "Formerly Incarcerated Students from Cal State LA's Groundbreaking Prison Education Program Walk at Commencement," *Newsroom Cal State LA*, July 30, 2021, https://news.calstatela.edu/2021/07/30/formerly-incarcerated-students-cal-state-la-groundbreaking-prison-education-program-walk-at-commencement/.

52. VietRISE, "HOME Act Press Conference at Santa Ana and Announcement of the Pardon Vietnamese Refugee Tin Nguyen Campaign," video posted on Facebook, August 29, 2023, https://www.facebook.com/watch/live/?ref=watch_permalink&v=1323969844918711.

53. VietRISE, "HOME Act Press."

54. VietRISE, "HOME Act Press."

55. Uyeda, "Addressing Gendered Trauma"; Jaclyn Dean, ed., *Dreams Detained, in Her Words: The Effects of Detention and Deportation on Southeast Asian American Women and Families* (Washington DC: Southeast Asia Resource Action Center, 2018).

56. Southeast Asia Resource Action Center, "SEADRA 118th Reintroduction Press Conference," Facebook, August 22, 2013, https://www.searac.org.

57. Beth C. Caldwell, *Deported Americans: Life after Deportation to Mexico* (Durham, NC: Duke University Press, 2019): 2.

58. Golash-Boza, *Deported: Immigrant Policing*, 15.

59. "Immigration Reform Can Keep Millions of Mixed-Status Families Together," FWD.us, September 9, 2021, https://www.fwd.us/news/mixed-status -families/; Diana Guelespe, Paola Echave, and Dulce Gonzalez, *Mixed-Status Immigrant Families Disproportionately Experienced Material Hardships in 2021* (Washington DC: Urban Institute, 2023).

60. Joanna Dreby, *Everyday Illegal: When Policies Undermine Immigrant Families* (Oakland: University of California Press, 2015); Abigail Andrews, *Banished Men: How Migrants Endure the Violence of Deportation* (Oakland: University of California Press, 2023).

61. Andrews, *Banished Men.*

62. Andrews, *Banished Men.*

63. Golash-Boza, *Deported: Immigrant Policing.*

64. Southeast Asia Resource Action Center, "SEADRA 118th Reintroduction."

65. Uyeda, "Addressing Gendered Trauma."

66. Cát Bảo Lê, private correspondence with the author, August 8, 2023.

67. Daniela Domínguez, "Abolitionist Feminism, Liberation Psychology, and Latinx Migrant Womxn," *Women & Therapy* 45, no. 2–3 (2022): 207–25.

68. Cát Bảo Lê, interview with the author, August 8, 2023.

69. Simon Denver, "Thousands of Vietnamese, Including Offspring of US Troops, Could Be Deported under Trump Policy," *Washington Post*, September 1, 2018.

70. They also work with at-risk populations within the Vietnamese community, including Amerasians (the children of American soldiers), Vietnamese women, Montagnards, and Indigenous people from the Central Highlands of Vietnam who were recruited and trained by the US government to fight in the war and face marked racism and discrimination.

71. Yuki Noguchi, "Unequal Outcomes: Most ICE Detainees Held in Rural Areas Where Deportation Risks Soar," NPR, August 15, 2019, https://www.npr .org/2019/08/15/748764322/; Ingrid Eagly and Steven Shafer, "A National Study of Access to Counsel in Immigration Court," *University of Pennsylvania Law Review* 164 (2015): 1–91.

72. Jeremy Slack, *Deported to Death: How Drug Violence Is Changing Migration on the US–Mexico Border* (Berkeley: University of California Press, 2019).

73. Golash-Boza, *Deported: Immigrant Policing.*

74. Golash-Boza, *Deported: Immigrant Policing*, 229.

75. Caldwell, *Deported Americans*, 13.

76. "Critical Vocabularies," Critical Refugee Studies Collective, https://criticalrefugeestudies.com./resources/critical-vocabularies. There is also a history of protracted displacement for Vietnamese refugees in Thailand and the Philippines. See the documentaries *Stateless* (2013) and *Nothing Left to Lose* (2017) directed by Duc Nguyễn with Trinh Hội.

77. Adam Goodman, *The Deportation Machine: America's Long History of Expelling Immigrants* (Princeton, NJ: Princeton University Press, 2020), 1.

78. Mavelli, "Citizenship for Sale," 482.

79. Lê Espiritu et al., *Departures: An Introduction*, 71.

80. Soo Ah Kwon, "Deporting Cambodian Refugees: Youth Activism, State Reform, and Imperial Statecraft," *Positions: East Asia Cultures Critique* 20, no. 3 (2012): 737–62.

81. Lê Espiritu et al., *Departures: An Introduction*, 25.

CONCLUSION

1. Donald Trump (@realDonaldTrump), "I am happy to inform all people . . ." Twitter, July 29, 2020, 11:19 a.m., https://x.com/realDonaldTrump/status/1288509568578777088?s=20 via National Low Income Housing Coalition, "The Myth of the White Suburb and 'Suburban Invasion,'" February 22, 2021, https://nlihc.org/resource/myth-white-suburb-and-suburban-invasion.

2. Donald Trump (@realDonaldTrump), "The Suburban Housewives of America . . ." Twitter, July 23, 1:46 p.m., https://x.com/realDonaldTrump/status/1286372175117791236; Kevin Liptak, "Trump Pitches White Suburban Voters in Blatantly Political White House Event," CNN News, July 17, 2020, https://www.cnn.com/2020/07/16/politics/donald-trump-white-suburbs/index.html; Tamara Keith, "Down in the Polls, Trump Pitches Fear: 'They Want to Destroy Our Suburbs,'" NPR, July 22, 2020, https://www.npr.org/2020/07/22/893899254/down-in-the-polls-trump-pitches-fear-they-want-to-destroy-our-suburbs.

3. Annie Karni, Maggie Haberman, and Sydney Ember, "Trump Plays on Racist Fears of Terrorized Suburbs to Court White Voters," *New York Times*, July 29, 2020.

4. Scott Markley, "Suburban Gentrification? Examining the Geographies of New Urbanism in Atlanta's Inner Suburbs," *Urban Geography* 39, no. 4 (2018): 606–30; Katharine N. Rankin and Heather McLean, "Governing the City's Commercial Streets: New Terrains of Disinvestment and Gentrification in Toronto's Inner Suburbs," *Antipode* 47, no. 1 (2015): 216–39.

5. Willow S. Lung-Amam, "Surviving Suburban Redevelopment: Resisting the Displacement of Immigrant-Owned Small Businesses in Wheaton, Maryland," *Journal of Urban Affairs* 43, no. 3 (2021): 449–66.

6. Alex Schafran, *The Road to Resegregation: Northern California and the Failure of Politics* (Oakland: University of California Press, 2018).

7. Schafran, *Road to Resegregation*, 23.

8. George J. Sanchez, *Boyle Heights: How a Los Angeles Neighborhood Became the Future of American Democracy* (Oakland: University of California Press, 2021).

9. Scott W. Allard, *Places in Need: The Changing Geography of Poverty* (New York: Russell Sage Foundation, 2017), 180–81.

10. Jan Nijman and Yehua Dennis Wei, "Urban Inequalities in the 21st Century Economy," *Applied Geography* 117 (2020): 1–8; Cody Hochstenbach and Sako Musterd, "Gentrification and the Suburbanization of Poverty: Changing Urban Geographies through Boom and Bust Periods," *Urban Geography* 39, no. 1 (2018): 26–53; Alexandra Murphy and Scott W. Allard, "The Changing Geography of Poverty," *Focus* 32, no. 1 (2015): 19–23.

11. Ananya Roy, "Dis/possessive Collectivism: Property and Personhood at City's End," *Geoforum* 80 (2017): 1–11.

12. Ananya Roy, "Racial Banishment," in *Keywords in Radical Geography: Antipode at 50,* (Hoboken, NJ: John Wiley and Sons, Inc, 2019), 227–30.

13. Ananya Roy and Emma Shaw Crane, eds., *Territories of Poverty: Rethinking North and South* (Athens: University of Georgia Press, 2015), 2.

14. Tanya Maria Golash-Boza, *Deported: Immigrant Policing, Disposable Labor and Global Capitalism* (New York: New York University Press, 2015).

15. Gianpaolo Baiocchi and H. Jacob Carlson, *The Case for a Social Housing Development Authority* (New York: NYU Urban Democracy Lab, 2020), 3.

16. Adam Travis, "The Organization of Neglect: Limited Liability Companies and Housing Disinvestment," *American Sociological Review* 84, no. 1 (2019): 142–70; Fay Walker and Eleanor Noble, "Ensuring Safe and Affordable Housing Starts with Understanding Who Owns Rental Units," Urban Institute, September 6, 2022, https://www.urban.org/urban-wire/ensuring-safe-and-affordable-housing-stock -starts-understanding-who-owns-rental-units.

17. Travis, "Organization of Neglect."

18. Ingrid Gould and Laurie Goodman, *Single-family Rentals: Trends and Policy Recommendations* (Washington, DC: The Hamilton Project, Brookings Institute, 2023); Edward Goetz, Anthony Damiano, Peter Brown, Patrick Alcorn, and Jeff Matson, *Minneapolis, Rent Stabilization Study* (Minneapolis: University of Minnesota Center for Urban and Regional Affairs, 2021).

19. Jenny Schuetz, *Fixer-Upper: How to Repair America's Broken Housing Systems* (Washington, DC: Brookings Institution Press, 2022), 61.

20. Philippe Van Parijs, "The Universal Basic Income: Why Utopian Thinking Matters, and How Sociologists Can Contribute to It," *Politics and Society* 41, no. 2 (2013): 171–82; Jenny Schuetz, *Fixer-Upper*; Louise Haagh, *The Case for Universal Basic Income* (Cambridge, UK: Polity Press, 2019).

21. Jennifer Gilbert, "Making Affordable Housing Easier to Find," Shelterforce, April 21, 2022, https://shelterforce.org/2022/04/21/making-affordable-housing -easier-to-find/.

22. Karan Kaul and Daniel Pang, "Research Report: The Role of Manufactured Housing in Increasing the Supply of Affordable Housing," Urban Institute, July

2022; Aaron Shroyer, "How Manufactured Housing Can Fill Affordable Housing Gaps," Urban Institute, July 8, 2020; Erika Bolstad, "Factory-Built Homes Could Help Solve Housing Crisis," PEW Charitable Trusts, August 15, 2022.

23. High-opportunity neighborhoods are often defined by access to high-quality schools, healthy food retailers, and green spaces. These neighborhoods are often measured as census tracts with poverty rates below 15 percent; labor force participation rates above 60 percent; and more than two hundred thousand low-wage jobs located within five miles of the tract center, among other characteristics. See Margery Turner, Austin Nichols, and Jennifer Comey, *Benefits of Living in High-Opportunity Neighborhoods: Insights from the Moving to Opportunity Demonstration* (Washington, DC: Urban Institute, 2012); *Community Health and Economic Prosperity: Engaging Businesses as Stewards and Stakeholders—a Report of the Surgeon General* (Washington, DC: US Department of Health and Human Services, Centers for Disease Control and Prevention, Office of the Associate Director for Policy and Strategy, 2021).

24. Andrew Ross, *Sunbelt Blues: The Failure of American Housing* (New York: Metropolitan Books, 2021).

25. Désirée Bender, Tina Hollstein, and Cornelia Schweppe, "International Retirement Migration Revisited: From Amenity Seeking to Precarity Migration?" *Transnational Social Review* 8, no. 1 (2018): 98–102.

26. Alejandro Portes and Ariel C. Armony, *The Global Edge: Miami in the Twenty-First Century* (Berkeley: University of California Press, 2018); Susan Eckstein, *The Immigrant Divide: How Cuban Americans Changed the US and Their Homeland* (New York: Routledge, 2009); Ahmed Ismail Yusuf, *Somalis in Minnesota* (St. Paul: Minnesota Historical Society Press, 2012); Cindy Horst, *Connected Lives: Somalis in Minneapolis, Family Responsibilities and the Migration Dreams of Relatives* (Oslo: United Nations High Commissioner for Refugees, Policy Development and Evaluation Service, 2006); Nabeel Abraham and Andrew Shryock, eds., *Arab Detroit: From Margin to Mainstream* (Detroit, MI: Wayne State University Press, 2000).

27. Linda Trinh Võ and Mary Yu Danico, "The Formation of Post-Suburban Communities: Koreatown and Little Saigon, Orange County," *International Journal of Sociology and Social Policy* 24, no. 7/8 (2004): 15–45.

28. Jennifer Huynh, "Female Vietnamese Entrepreneurs," in *Toward a Framework for Vietnamese American Studies*, eds. Linda Ho Peche and Tuong Vu (Philadelphia, PA: Temple University Press, 2023).

29. Blair Sackett and Annette Lareau, *We Thought It Would Be Heaven: Refugees in an Unequal America* (Berkeley: University of California Press, 2023).

30. Nazli Kibria, *Family Tightrope: The Changing Lives of Vietnamese Americans* (Princeton, NJ: Princeton University Press, 1995).

31. Kibria, *Family Tightrope*.

32. Jeremy Hein, "Refugees, Immigrants, and the State," *Annual Review of Sociology* 19, no. 1 (1993): 43–59.

33. Suong Elwing Gonzalez, "Building a Place in Los Angeles: Mutual Assistance Association, Government Funding, and Vietnamese Refugee Community

Development," in *Toward a Framework for Vietnamese American Studies*, eds. Linda Ho Peche and Tuong Vu (Philadelphia, PA: Temple University Press, 2023); Karin Aguilar-San Juan, *Little Saigons: Staying Vietnamese in America* (Minneapolis: University of Minnesota Press, 2009).

34. Linda Trinh Võ, "Constructing a Vietnamese American Community: Economic and Political Transformation in Little Saigon, Orange County," *Amerasia Journal* 34 (2008): 84–109.

35. "Protracted Refugee Situations Explained," United Nations High Commissioner for Refugees, January 28, 2020, https://www.unrefugees.org/news /protracted-refugee-situations-explained/.

36. Albert Kraler, Benjamin Etzold, and Nuno Ferreira, "Understanding the Dynamics of Protracted Displacement," *Forced Migration Review* 68 (2021): 49–52.

37. Yến Lê Espiritu, "Critical Refugee Studies and Native Pacific Studies: A Transpacific Critique," *American Quarterly* 69, no. 3 (2017): 483–90.

38. Yến Lê Espiritu, "Critical Refugee Studies and Native Pacific Studies," 487.

39. Yến Lê Espiritu et al., *Departures: An Introduction to Critical Refugee Studies* (Berkeley: University of California Press, 2022).

40. Yến Lê Espiritu et al., *Departures: An Introduction*, 100.

41. "Operation Allies Welcome," Department of Homeland Security, accessed November 1, 2023, https://www.dhs.gov/allieswelcome; "Humanitarian Parole," US Citizenship and Immigration Services, accessed November 2, 2023, https://www .dhs.gov/allieswelcome.

42. Elinor R. Jordan, "What We Know and Need to Know about Immigrant Access to Justice," *South Carolina Law Review* 67, no. 2 (Winter 2016): 295–328.

43. Ananya Roy, "Housing Justice: Towards a Field of Inquiry," in *Housing Justice in Unequal Cities*, eds. Ananya Roy and Hilary Malson (Los Angeles: Institute on Inequality and Democracy at UCLA, 2019), https://challengeinequality. luskin.ucla.edu/wp-content/uploads/sites/16/2019/10/Housing-Justice-in-Unequal -Cities.pdf.

44. "Tenant Power Toolkit," Debt Collective, accessed December 23, 2023, https://tools.debtcollective.org/run/eviction/#/1.

45. Roy, "Housing Justice: Towards a Field of Inquiry."

46. Vinh Nguyen, "Refugeetude: When Does a Refugee Stop Being a Refugee," *Social Text* 37 (2019): 109–31.

APPENDIX

1. Douglas Massey and Jonathan Tannen, "Suburbanization and Segregation in the United States: 1970–2010," *Ethnic and Racial Studies* 41, no. 9 (2018): 1594–1611; Alexandra Murphy, "The Suburban Ghetto: The Legacy of Herbert Gans in Understanding the Experience of Poverty in Recently Impoverished American Suburbs," *City & Community* 6, no. 1 (2007): 21–37; Willow Lung–Amam, "Out of the Urban

Shadows: Uneven Development and Spatial Politics in Immigrant Suburbs," *City & Community* 19, no. 2 (2020): 303–9.

2. Tomás Jiménez, *Replenished Ethnicity: Mexican Americans, Immigration, and Identity* (Berkeley: University of California Press, 2010).

3. David M. Fetterman, *Ethnography: Step-by-Step* (Thousand Oaks, CA: Sage Publications, 2019).

4. Norman Denzin and Yvonna Lincoln, "Introduction: The Discipline and Practice of Qualitative Research," in *Strategies of Qualitative Inquiry*, eds. Norman Denzin and Yvonna Lincoln (Thousand Oaks, CA: Sage Publications, 2008), 13.

5. Margaret LeCompte and Judith Preissle Goetz, "Ethnographic Data Collection in Evaluation Research," *Educational Evaluation and Policy Analysis* 4, no. 3 (1982): 387–400.

6. Norman Denzin, *Collecting and Interpreting Qualitative Materials* (Thousand Oaks, CA: Sage Publications, 2013), 162.

7. Fetterman, *Ethnography*.

8. Yến Lê Espiritu et al., *Departures: An Introduction to Critical Refugee Studies* (Berkeley: University of California Press), 11–12.

9. Lê Espiritu et al., *Departures: An Introduction*, 14.

REFERENCES

Aalbers, Manuel. *The Financialization of Housing: A Political Economy Approach.* New York: Routledge, 2019.

Abraham, Nabeel, and Andrew Shryock, eds. *Arab Detroit: From Margin to Mainstream.* Detroit, MI: Wayne State University Press, 2000.

Abrams, Charles. "The Housing Problem and the Negro." *Daedalus* 95, no. 1 (1966): 64–76.

Ahrens, Mareike. "'Gentrify? No! Gentefy? Sí!': Urban Redevelopment and Ethnic Gentrification in Boyle Heights, Los Angeles." *Aspeers* 8 (2015): 9–26.

Airgood-Obrycki, Whitney, Alexander Hermann, and Sophia Wedeen. "'The Rent Eats First': Rental Housing Unaffordability in the United States." *Housing Policy Debate* (2022): 1–21.

Akee, Randall, and Maggie R. Jones. "Immigrants' Earnings Growth and Return Migration from the US: Examining Their Determinants Using Linked Survey and Administrative Data." Working paper, NBER Working Paper Series 25639, National Bureau of Economic Research, Cambridge, MA, 2019.

Akers, Joshua, and Eric Seymour. "Instrumental Exploitation: Predatory Property Relations at City's End." *Geoforum* 91 (2018): 127–40.

Allard, Scott W. *Places in Need: The Changing Geography of Poverty.* New York: Russell Sage Foundation, 2017.

American Venture Solutions Regional Center. "Trung Tâm Vùng EB5 Việt Nam." Facebook, https://www.facebook.com/photo/?fbid=818717469894940& set=a.525566992543324&__tn__=%2CO*F, July 17, 2023.

Anacker, Katrin B., "Inclusionary Zoning and Inclusionary Housing in the United States: Measuring Inputs and Outcomes." In *Research Handbook on Community Development.* Northampton: Edward Elgar Publishing, 2020.

Andersson, Marcus, and Per Ekman. "Ambassador Networks and Place Branding." *Journal of Place Management and Development* 2, no. 1 (2009): 41–51.

Andrews, Abigail. *Banished Men: How Migrants Endure the Violence of Deportation.* Oakland: University of California Press, 2023.

APRI Rise. "Van's Story." Facebook, May 11, 2020. https://www.api-rise.org.

Asian Americans Advancing Justice. "Resources on Deportation of Vietnamese Immigrants Who Entered the US Before 1995." Last updated September 19, 2023. https://www.advancingjustice-alc.org/news-resources/guides-reports/trinh -reports.

August, Martine. "Financialization of Housing from Cradle to Grave: COVID-19, Seniors' Housing, and Multifamily Rental Housing in Canada." *Studies in Political Economy* 102, no. 3 (2021): 289–308.

Aurand, Andrew, and Matthew Clarke. *Out of Reach: The High Cost of Housing.* Washington, DC: National Low Income Housing Coalition, 2022.

Baar, Kenneth K. "The Right to Sell the 'Im'mobile Manufactured Home in Its Rent Controlled Space in the 'Im'mobile Home Park: Valid Regulation or Unconstitutional Taking?" *Urban Lawyer* 24, no. 1 (1992): 157–221.

Baker, Daniel, Kelly Hamshaw, and Corey Beach. "A Window into Park Life: Findings from a Resident Survey of Nine Mobile Home Park Communities in Vermont." *Journal of Rural and Community Development* 6, no. 2 (2011).

Baker, Jim, Liz Voigt, and Linda Jun. "Private Equity Giants Converge on Manufactured Homes: How Private Equity Is Manufacturing Homelessness and Communities Are Fighting Back." MHAction. February 2019. https://pestakeholder .org/wp-content/uploads/2019/02/Private-Equity-GIants-Converge-on -Manufactured-Homes-PESP-MHAction-AFR-021419.pdf.

Baldassare, Mark. *California in the New Millennium: The Changing Social and Political Landscape.* Oakland: University of California Press, 2002.

Baldassare, Mark, Dean Bonner, Rachel Lawler, and Deja Thomas. *PPIC Statewide Survey: Californians and Their Government.* San Francisco: Public Policy Institute of California, 2021.

Bao, Xiaoxiao, and Hoi Leung. "Community-Based Art Projects in San Francisco Chinatown: A Survival Strategy." *Journal of Cultural Research in Art Education* 38, no. 1 (2021): 65–77.

Bartram, Robin. "Cost of Code Violations: How Building Codes Shape Residential Sales Prices and Rents." *Housing Policy Debate* 29, no. 6 (2019): 931–46.

———. *Stacked Decks: Building Inspectors and the Reproduction of Urban Inequality.* Chicago: University of Chicago Press, 2022.

Becher, Debbie. *Private Property and Public Power: Eminent Domain in Philadelphia.* Oxford: Oxford University Press, 2014.

Beck, Jillian. "Formerly Incarcerated Students from Cal State LA's Groundbreaking Prison Education Program Walk at Commencement." Newsroom Cal State LA, July 30, 2021. https://news.calstatela.edu/2021/07/30/formerly-incarcerated- students-cal-state-la-groundbreaking-prison-education-program-walk-at -commencement/.

Beck, Ulrich. "The Terrorist Threat: World Risk Society Revisited." *Theory, Culture & Society* 19, no. 4 (2002): 39–55.

Bell, Kristen. "A Stone of Hope: Legal and Empirical Analysis of California Juvenile Lifer Parole Decisions." *Harvard Civil Rights-Civil Liberties Law Review* 54, no. 2 (2019): 455–558.

Berg, Tom. "Little Saigon Snapshot: How Phu Nguyễn's Family Spent 28 Days at Sea to Escape Vietnam and Now Runs Money Transfer Company." *Orange County Register*, April 30, 2015. https://www.ocregister.com/2015/04/30/little-saigon -snapshot-how-phu-s-family-spent-28-days-at-sea-to-escape-vietnam-and-now-runs -money-transfer-company/.

Bernstein, Jenna. "Section 8, Source of Income Discrimination, and Federal Preemption: Setting the Record Straight." *Cardozo Law Review* 31 (2009): 1407–36.

Bharath, Deepa. "Garden Grove RV Park Residents Sue City." *Orange County Register*, August 11, 2009. https://www.ocregister.com/2009/08/11/garden-grove-rv -park-residents-sue-city/.

Bollens, Scott A. "Municipal Decline and Inequality in American Suburban Rings, 1960–1980." *Regional Studies* 22, no. 4 (1988): 277–85.

Bolstad, Erika. "Factory-Built Homes Could Help Solve Housing Crisis." Governing, August 15, 2022. https://www.governing.com/community/factory-built -homes-could-help-solve-housing-crisis.

Borjas, George J. "Making It in America: Social Mobility in the Immigrant Population." Working paper, NBER Working Paper Series 12088, National Bureau of Economic Research, Cambridge, MA, 2006.

Boshart, Abby. *Local Policies to Strengthen the Renter Safety Net*. Washington, DC: Urban Institute, 2023.

Boston, Amanda T. "Manufacturing Distress: Race, Redevelopment, and the EB-5 Program in Central Brooklyn." *Critical Sociology* 47, no. 6 (2021): 961–76.

Boyle, Mark. "Civic Boosterism in the Politics of Local Economic Development— 'Institutional Positions'; and 'Strategic Orientations' in the Consumption of Hallmark Events." *Environment and Planning A* 29, no. 11 (1997): 1975–97.

Brand, Anna Livia, Kate Lowe, and Em Hall. "Colorblind Transit Planning: Modern Streetcars in Washington, DC, and New Orleans." *Journal of Race, Ethnicity and the City* 1, no. 1–2 (2020): 87–108.

Bratt, Rachel G., and Dan Immergluck. "The Mortgage Crisis: Historical Context and Recent Responses." *Journal of Urban Affairs* 37, no. 1 (2015): 32–37.

Bravin, Jess. "Center Pieces: Design of Civic Structures in County Reveals Character of Cities' Time, Place." *Los Angeles Times*, December 1, 1988. https://www .latimes.com/archives/la-xpm-1988-12-01-li-900-story.html.

"A Brief History of Orange County." Orange County Historical Society. Accessed November 11, 2023. https://www.orangecountyhistory.org/wp/?page _id=38.

Bronin, Sara. "Zoning for Families." *Indiana Law Journal* 95, no. 1 (2020).

Bronsvoort, Irene, and Justus L. Uitermark. "Seeing the Street through Instagram. Digital Platforms and the Amplification of Gentrification." *Urban Studies* 59, no. 14 (2022): 2857–74.

Bryan, Dick, and Mike Rafferty. "Political Economy and Housing in the Twenty-First Century—From Mobile Homes to Liquid Housing?" *Housing, Theory and Society* 31, no. 4 (2014): 404–12.

Bùi, Long. *Returns of War: South Vietnam and the Price of Refugee Memory*. New York: New York University Press, 2018.

Bùi, Thi. *The Best We Could Do: An Illustrated Memoir*. New York: Abrams, 2017.

Burd-Sharps, Sarah, and Rebecca Rasch. *Impact of the US Housing Crisis on the Racial Wealth Gap across Generations*. Social Science Research Council, 2015. https://www.ssrc.org/publications/impact-of-the-us-housing-crisis-on-the-racial -wealth-gap-across-generations/.

Burling, James. "Property Rights and the Modern Resurgence of Rent Control." *Brigham-Kanner Property Rights Conference Journal*, 10 (2021): 111–46.

Burns, Nancy. *The Formation of American Local Governments: Private Values in Public Institutions*. Oxford, UK: Oxford University Press, 1994.

Byrley, Taylor C. "Selling Citizenship to the Highest Bidder: A Proposal to Reform the United States EB-5 Investor Visa Program." *Indiana International & Comparative Law Review* 27 (2017): 79–116.

Caldwell, Beth C. *Deported Americans: Life after Deportation to Mexico*. Durham, NC: Duke University Press, 2019.

California Real Estate Regional Center. "News." Accessed December 3, 2023. https://eb5socal.com/.

California State Board of Equalization. *Assessment of Manufactured Homes and Parks*. Sacramento: California State Board of Equalization, 2001, reprinted 2015. https://www.boe.ca.gov/proptaxes/pdf/ah511final.pdf.

Carpio, Genevieve, Clara Irazábal, and Laura Pulido. "Right to the Suburb? Rethinking Lefebvre and Immigrant Activism." *Journal of Urban Affairs* 33, no. 2 (2011): 185–208.

Casey, Michael, and Carolyn Thompson. "Rent Spike as Big-Pocketed Investors Buy Mobile Home Parks." Associated Press, July 25, 2022. https://apnews.com /article/mobile-home-parks-rent-investors-8dbadf3f9a33faddb06abc980b046176.

Chang, Richard. "Dueling Tet Parades in Little Saigon Still Lead to Happiness." *Voice of OC*, January 27, 2020. https://voiceofoc.org/2020/01/dueling-Tet-parades -in-little-saigon-still-lead-to-happiness/.

Cheng, Wendy. *The Changs Next Door to the Díazes: Remapping Race in Suburban California*. Minneapolis: University of Minnesota Press, 2013.

Chishti, Muzaffar, and Faye Hipsman. "Controversial Eb-5 Immigrant Investor Program Faces Possibility of Overhaul." Migration Policy Institute, May 25, 2016. https://www.migrationpolicy.org/article/controversial-eb-5-immigrant-investor -program-faces-possibility-overhaul.

Chreim, Samia, Martine Spence, David Crick, and Xiaolu Liao. "Review of Female Immigrant Entrepreneurship Research: Past Findings, Gaps and Ways Forward." *European Management Journal* 36, no. 2 (2018): 210–22.

Chung, Angie Park, and Jay Lin. *Immigrant Growth Machines: Urban Growth Politics in Koreatown and Monterey Park*. New York: Russell Sage Foundation, forthcoming.

City News Service. "After Rent Hikes Up to 300%, LA Considers Buying Chinatown Building." *Los Angeles Daily News*, May 26, 2022. https://www.dailynews.com.

City of Garden Grove. "Home Repair Program." Accessed November 1, 2022. https://ggcity.org/home-repair-program.

City of Garden Grove. "Pre-certified Local Housing Data for the City of Garden Grove." Southern California Association of Governments (SCAG). Updated April 2021. https://ggcity.org/housing-element.

City of Oakland. "Understanding Evictions in Oakland." Last updated 2023. https://www.oaklandca.gov/topics/understanding-evictions-in-oakland.

City of Westminster. *City of Westminster Consolidated Plan 2020/21–2024/25*. Westminster, CA: 2021. https://www.westminster-ca.gov/home/showpublished document?id=982.

———. "Housing Choice Voucher Program (Section 8)." Accessed December 20, 2023. https://www.westminster-ca.gov/departments/community-development /grants-housing-division/housing-choice-voucher-program-section-8.

City of Westminster, Community Development Housing Division. "Affordable Housing." Accessed November 12, 2023. https://www.westminster-ca.gov/departments /community-development/grants-housing-division/affordable-housing.

Clark, Eric. "The Order and Simplicity of Gentrification: A Political Challenge." In *Gentrification in a Global Context*, edited by Rowland Atkinson and Gary Bridge. London: Routledge, 2005.

Clerge, Orly. *The New Noir: Race, Identity, and Diaspora in Black Suburbia*. Oakland: University of California Press, 2019.

Collins, Geneva. "Zoning and Public Housing Rules Dictate Who May Live with Whom." *Los Angeles Times*, March 19, 1989. https://www.latimes.com/archives /la-xpm-1989-03-19-mn-274-story.html.

Colomb, Claire. "Place Marketing and Branding in (Anglophone) Urban Studies and Urban Political Economy: A Critical Review." Γεωγραφίες/*Geographies*, 30 (2017): 41–52.

———. *Staging the New Berlin: Place Marketing and the Politics of Urban Reinvention Post-1989*. New York: Routledge, 2013.

Connolly, John. "Generational Conflict and the Sociology of Generations: Mannheim and Elias Reconsidered." *Theory, Culture & Society* 36, no. 7–8 (2019): 153–72.

Conway, Jean, and Pete Alcock. *Housing Policy in the United States: An Introduction*. New York: Routledge, 2003.

Cooperman, Courtney. "California." National Low Income Housing Coalition. Accessed December 30, 2022. https://nlihc.org/housing-needs-by-state/california.

Critical Refugee Studies Collective. "Critical Vocabularies." Accessed December 12, 2023. https://criticalrefugeestudies.com./resources/critical-vocabularies.

Crosby, Andrew. "Financialized Gentrification, Demoviction, and Landlord Tactics to Demobilize Tenant Organizing." *Geoforum* 108 (2020): 184–93.

Cueto-Villalobos, Daniel. "A New Face of Gentrification: Gente-fication in Boyle Heights." *Discoveries Magazine*, March 3, 2022. https://thesocietypages.org /discoveries/2022/03/03/a-new-face-of-gentrification-gente-fication-in-boyle -heights/.

Cunningham, Mary, Sarah Gillespie, and Samantha Batko. *How Housing Matters for Families*. Washington, DC: Urban Institute, 2019.

Curran, Winifred. "Mexicans Love Red and Other Gentrification Myths: Displacements and Contestations in the Gentrification of Pilsen, Chicago, USA." *Urban Studies* 55, no. 8 (2018): 1711–28.

Đặng, Thúy Võ. "Oral History of Nguyễn Trong Phat." Viet Stories: Vietnamese American Oral History Project. University of California, Irvine. May 15, 2012.

———. "Cultural Work of Anticommunism in the San Diego Vietnamese Community." *Amerasia* 31, no 2. (2005): 64–86.

Daniels, Lindsay. "The End of Special Treatment for Cubans in the US Immigration System: Consequences and Solutions for Cubans with Final Orders of Removal." *Dickinson Law Review* 122 (2017): 707–39.

Dean, Jaclyn, ed. *Dreams Detained, in Her Words: The Effects of Detention and Deportation on Southeast Asian American Women and Families*. Washington, DC: Southeast Asia Resource Action Center, 2018.

Deng, Grace. "Immigrants and Refugees Are Spending Decades in Prison Only to Be Released into ICE Custody." *Prism*, March 10, 2022.

Denver, Simon. "Thousands of Vietnamese, Including Offspring of US Troops Could Be Deported under Trump Policy." *Washington Post*, September 1, 2018. https://www.washingtonpost.com/world/asia_pacific/thousands-of-vietnamese -including-offspring-of-us-troops-could-be-deported-under-tough-trump-policy /2018/08/30/8de80848-a6d0-11e8-b76b-d513a40042f6_story.html.

Denzin, Norman K. *Collecting and Interpreting Qualitative Materials*. Vol. 3. Thousand Oaks, CA: Sage Publications, 2013.

Denzin, Norman K., and Yvonna S. Lincoln. "Introduction: The Discipline and Practice of Qualitative Research." In *Strategies of Qualitative Inquiry*, edited by Norman K. Denzin and Yvonna S. Lincoln, 1–32. Thousand Oaks, CA: Sage Publications, 2008.

Department of Homeland Security. "Operation Allies Welcome." Accessed November 1, 2023. https://www.dhs.gov/allieswelcome.

Desmond, Matthew. *Evicted: Poverty and Profit in the American City*. New York: Crown Publishers, 2016.

———. "Heavy Is the House: Rent Burden among the American Urban Poor." *International Journal of Urban and Regional Research* 42, no. 1 (2018): 160–70.

———. "Unaffordable America: Poverty, Housing, and Eviction." In *The Affordable Housing Reader*, edited by Elizabeth Mueller and Rosie Tighe, 389–95. New York: Routledge, 2022.

Desmond, Matthew, and Monica Bell. "Housing, Poverty, and the Law." *Annual Review of Law and Social Science* 11 (2015): 15–35.

Desmond, Matthew, and Rachel Tolbert Kimbro. "Eviction's Fallout: Housing, Hardship, and Health." *Social Forces* 94, no. 1 (2015): 295–324.

Dhingra, Pawan. *Life behind the Lobby: Indian American Motel Owners and the American Dream*. Palo Alto, CA: Stanford University Press, 2012.

Dhingra, Pawan, and Robyn Magalit Rodriguez. *Asian America: Sociological and Interdisciplinary Perspectives*. Hoboken, NJ: John Wiley and Sons, 2014.

Diamond, Rebecca, Tim McQuade, and Franklin Qian. "The Effects of Rent Control Expansion on Tenants, Landlords, and Inequality: Evidence from San Francisco." *American Economic Review* 109, no. 9 (2019): 3365–94.

Diggs, Surayya, Yingqing He, Xuelong Li, Xinmei Wu, Yilu Xu, Keying Yan, Yan Yuan, and Sihan Zhao. *What Is the Most Cost-Effective Way to Finance Affordable Rental Housing?* New York: Columbia University School of International and Public Affairs, 2019.

Diner, Hasia R. *Hungering for America: Italian, Irish, and Jewish Foodways in the Age of Migration*. Cambridge, MA: Harvard University Press, 2003.

Ding, Hao, and Anastasia Loukaitou-Sideris. "Racism by Design? Asian Immigration and the Adoption of Planning and Design Regulations in Three Los Angeles Suburbs." *Journal of the American Planning Association* 89, no. 1 (2022): 1–14.

Dizon, Lily. "Acrimony over Project Called Harmony." *Los Angeles Times*, June 25, 1996. https://www.latimes.com/archives/la-xpm-1996-06-25-mn-18336-story.html.

———. "Bridge Brings Discord Instead of Harmony into Little Saigon." *Los Angeles Times*, June 25, 1996. https://www.latimes.com/archives/la-xpm-1996-06-25-mn-18226-story.html.

Djafarova, Elmira, and Tamar Bowes. "'Instagram Made Me Buy It': Generation Z Impulse Purchases in Fashion Industry." *Journal of Retailing and Consumer Services* 59 (2021): 102345.

Đỗ, Anh. "Behind Little Saigon's Riches, the Poor Pack into Small Rooms to Survive." *Los Angeles Times*, March 13, 2017. https://www.latimes.com/local/lanow/la-me-rooms-for-rent-20170228-story.html.

———. "Not Your Grandmother's Little Saigon: Entrepreneurs Expand Enclave's Horizons." *Los Angeles Times*, November 8, 2015. https://www.latimes.com/local/california/la-me-new-little-saigon-20151108-story.html.

———. "'We Will Be Adrift Again': War Veterans, Refugees Face Uncertain Future with Sale of Their Little Saigon Mobile Home Park." *Los Angeles Times*, April 1, 2017. https://www.latimes.com/local/lanow/la-me-ln-little-saigon-eviction-20170331-story.html.

Đỗ, Hiến. *The Vietnamese Americans*. London, UK: Bloomsbury Publishing, 1999.

Domínguez, Daniela. "Abolitionist Feminism, Liberation Psychology, and Latinx Migrant Women." *Women & Therapy* 45, no. 2–3 (2022): 207–25.

Douglis, Sylvie. "Mobile Home Parked." August 6, 2021. In *This is Planet Money*, produced by Dave Blanchard. NPR podcast, MP3 audio. https://www.npr.org/transcripts/1025557463.

Dreby, Joanna. *Everyday Illegal: When Policies Undermine Immigrant Families*. Oakland: University of California Press, 2015.

Duffy, Brooke Erin. *(Not) Getting Paid to Do What You Love: Gender, Social Media, and Aspirational Work*. New Haven, CT: Yale University Press, 2017.

Dunn, Samantha. "Sonny Nguyễn, 'Change Agent' at 7 Leaves Café Company." *Orange County Register*, October 1, 2019.

Durkin, Emily, Margaret Brown, Nathan Craig, Neil Harvey, Daniela Navarro Verdugo, Brennan Ramsey, Fernanda Reyes, and Avigail Turima Romo. *The Pains and Profits of Immigrant Imprisonment: Migrant Testimonies from ICE Detention Centers in the El Paso ICE Field Office.* Las Cruces: New Mexico State University, 2020.

Eagly, Ingrid V., and Steven Shafer. "A National Study of Access to Counsel in Immigration Court." *University of Pennsylvania Law Review* 164 (2015).

Eb-5 Investors. "What Is an EB-5 Project?" Accessed December 27, 2023. https://www.eb5investors.com/eb5-basics/what-is-a-project.

Eckstein, Susan. *The Immigrant Divide: How Cuban Americans Changed the US and Their Homeland.* New York: Routledge, 2009.

Ehrenfeucht, Reina. "Moving beyond the Mobile Myth: Preserving Manufactured Housing Communities." Grounded Solutions Network, 2018. https://issuu.com/groundedsolutionsnetwork/docs/moving_beyond_the_mobile_myth.

Ellen, Ingrid Gould, Jeffrey Lubell, and Mark A. Willis. *Through the Roof: What Communities Can Do about the High Cost of Rental Housing in America.* Lincoln Institute of Land Policy, March 15, 2021.

Ellickson, Robert C. "The Zoning Straitjacket: The Freezing of American Neighborhoods of Single-Family Houses." *Indiana Law Journal* 96, no. 2 (2020): 395–427.

Fainstein, Susan. *The Just City.* Vol. 3. Ithaca, NY: Cornell University Press, 2014.

Fairlie, Robert W. "Entrepreneurship, Economic Conditions, and the Great Recession." *Journal of Economics & Management Strategy* 22, no. 2 (2013): 207–31.

Faughnder, Ryan. "Gen Z Spends Half of Its Waking Hours on Screen Time. Here's the Good and Bad News for Hollywood." *Los Angeles Times*, April 12, 2022. https://www.latimes.com/entertainment-arts/business/newsletter/2022-04-12/gen-z-spends-half-its-waking-hours-on-screen-time-heres-the-good-and-bad-news-for-hollywood-the-wide-shot.

Fernandez, Rodrigo, Annelore Hofman, and Manuel B. Aalbers. "London and New York as a Safe Deposit Box for the Transnational Wealth Elite." *Environment and Planning A: Economy and Space* 48, no. 12 (2016): 2443–61.

Fernández-Kelly, Patricia, and Lisa Konczal. "'Murdering the Alphabet': Identity and Entrepreneurship among Second-Generation Cubans, West Indians, and Central Americans." *Ethnic and Racial Studies* 28, no. 6 (2005): 1153–81.

Fetter, Daniel K. "The Home Front: Rent Control and the Rapid Wartime Increase in Home Ownership." *Journal of Economic History* 76, no. 4 (2016): 1001–43.

Fetterman, David M. *Ethnography: Step-by-Step.* Thousand Oaks, CA: Sage Publications, 2019.

Fields, Desiree, and Elora Lee Raymond. "Housing Financialization and Racial Capitalism after the Global Financial Crisis." In *Housing Justice in Unequal Cities*, edited by Ananya Roy and Hilary Malson. Los Angeles: UCLA Institute on Inequality and Democracy, 2019. https://challengeinequality.luskin.ucla.edu/wp-content/uploads/sites/16/2019/10/Housing-Justice-in-Unequal-Cities.pdf.

————. "Racialized Geographies of Housing Financialization." *Progress in Human Geography* 45, no. 6 (2021): 1625–45.

Fischer, Will, Sonya Acosta, and Erik Gartland. *More Housing Vouchers: Most Important Step to Help More People Afford Stable Homes.* Center on Budget and Policy Priorities, May 13, 2021. https://www.cbpp.org/research/housing /more-housing-vouchers-most-important-step-to-help-more-people-afford-stable -homes.

Foner, Nancy, and Joanna Dreby. "Relations between the Generations in Immigrant Families." *Annual Review of Sociology* 37 (2011): 545–64.

Formanack, Allison. "This Land Is My Land: Absence and Ruination in the American Dream of (Mobile) Homeownership." *City & Society* 30, no. 3 (2018): 293–317.

Frank, Knight. "Where Do the Ultra Wealthy Live in the World?" The Intelligence Lab. March 3, 2020. https://www.knightfrank.com/research/article/2020-03-03 -where-do-the-ultra-wealthy-live-in-the-world.

Friedman, Milton, and Anna Jacobson Schwartz. *A Monetary History of the US, 1867–1960.* Vol. 16. Princeton, NJ: Princeton University Press, 2008.

Fry, Richard. "Millennials Overtake Baby Boomers as America's Largest Generation." Washington, DC: Pew Research Center, 2020.

Furman, Matthew. *Eradicating Substandard Manufactured Homes: Replacement Programs as a Strategy.* Boston, MA: Harvard Joint Center for Housing Studies and NeighborWorks America, 2014.

Gabriel, Stuart, and Gary Painter. "Why Affordability Matters." *Regional Science and Urban Economics* 80 (2020): 1–6.

Garbarino, James. *Miller's Children: Why Giving Teenage Killers a Second Chance Matters for All of Us.* Oakland: University of California Press, 2018.

García, Angela S. *Legal Passing: Navigating Undocumented Life and Local Immigration Law.* Oakland: University of California Press, 2019.

Gilbert, Jennifer. "Making Affordable Housing Easier to Find." Shelterforce, April 21, 2022. https://shelterforce.org/2022/04/21/making-affordable-housing -easier-to-find/.

Gilmore, Ruth Wilson. *Golden Gulag: Prisons, Surplus, Crisis, and Opposition in Globalizing California.* Oakland: University of California Press, 2007.

Goh, Edmund, and Ferry Jie. "To Waste or Not to Waste: Exploring Motivational Factors of Generation Z Hospitality Employees Towards Food Wastage in the Hospitality Industry." *International Journal of Hospitality Management* 80 (2019): 126–35.

Golash-Boza, Tanya Maria. *Deported: Immigrant Policing, Disposable Labor and Global Capitalism.* New York: New York University Press, 2015.

Gold, Steve. "Chinese-Vietnamese Entrepreneurs in California." In *The New Asian Immigration in Los Angeles and Global Restructuring*, edited by Paul M. Ong, Edna Bonacich, and Lucie Cheng, 196–226. Philadelphia, PA: Temple University Press, 1994.

Gold, Steven J. *The Israeli Diaspora.* New York: Routledge, 2005.

Gonzalez, Dulce, Michael Karpman, and Clara Alvarez Caraveo. *Immigrant Families in California Faced Barriers Accessing Safety Net Programs in 2021, but Community Organizations Helped Many Enroll.* Washington, DC: Urban Institute, 2022.

Gonzalez, Suong Elwing. "Building a Place in Los Angeles: Mutual Assistance Association, Government Funding, and Vietnamese Refugee Community Development." In *Toward a Framework for Vietnamese American Studies*, edited by Linda Ho Peche and Tuong Vu. Philadelphia, PA: Temple University Press, 2023.

Goodman, Adam. *The Deportation Machine: America's Long History of Expelling Immigrants.* Princeton, NJ: Princeton University Press, 2020.

Gottlieb, Dylan. "'Closer to Heaven': Race and Diversity in Suburban America." *Journal of Urban History* 41, no. 5 (2015): 927–35.

Gowayed, Heba. *Refuge: How the State Shapes Human Potential.* Princeton, NJ: Princeton University Press, 2022.

Gray, M. Nolan. *Arbitrary Lines: How Zoning Broke the American City and How to Fix It.* Washington, DC: Island Press, 2022.

Greenberg, Miriam. *Branding New York: How a City in Crisis Was Sold to the World.* New York: Routledge, 2009.

Greene, Jane G., and Glenda P. Blake. *A Study of How Restrictive Rental Practices Affect Families with Children.* Washington, DC: The Office of Policy Development and Research, 1980.

Groft, Linn Elizabeth. "Do Multi-Family Housing Zoning Ordinances Affect Segregation in California?" PhD diss., Georgetown University, 2022.

Groth, Paul. *Living Downtown: The History of Residential Hotels in the United States.* Oakland: University of California Press, 1994.

Guelespe, Diana, Paola Echave, and Dulce Gonzalez. *Mixed-Status Immigrant Families Disproportionately Experienced Material Hardships in 2021.* Washington, DC: Urban Institute, 2023.

Gurney, Laura, and Vittoria Grossi. "Exploring Contours of the Entrepreneurial Self in the Contemporary University: Developing Learning and Teaching under Neoliberal Conditions." *International Journal for Academic Development* (2021): 1–12.

Ha, Nam. "Business and Politics in Little Saigon, California." PhD diss., Rice University, 2002.

Haas, Lisbeth. *Conquests and Historical Identities in California, 1769–1936.* Oakland: University of California Press, 1995.

Hackworth, Jason. *Manufacturing Decline: How Racism and the Conservative Movement Crush the American Rust Belt.* New York: Columbia University Press, 2019.

Hagan, Jacqueline, Brianna Castro, and Nestor Rodriguez. "The Effects of US Deportation Policies on Immigrant Families and Communities: Cross-Border Perspectives." *North Carolina Law Review* 88 (2009): 1799–1824.

Haire, Chris. "Garden Grove Residents Sue State over Relocation Costs." *Orange County Register,* January 1, 2015. https://www.ocregister.com/2015/01/01/garden-grove-residents-sue-state-over-relocation-costs/.

————. "The Next Big Thing in Tourism Could Be Little Saigon" *Orange County Register*, April 13, 2017. https://www.ocregister.com/2017/04/13/little-saigon -story/.

Hall, Tim, and Phil Hubbard. "The Entrepreneurial City: New Urban Politics, New Urban Geographies?" *Progress in Human Geography* 20, no. 2 (1996): 153–74.

Hamel, Jacob. "Teeming Shore to Golden Door: A Comparative Analysis of Investment and Demand in Investment Immigration." *Eleven* (2018): 42–62.

Hardt, Michael, and Antonio Negri. *Multitude: War and Democracy in the Age of Empire*. London: Penguin Books, 2005.

Harjanto, Laura, and Jeanne Batalova. "Vietnamese Immigrants in the United States." Migration Policy Institute Spotlight, October 15, 2021. https://www .migrationpolicy.org.

Harris, Michelle. "California Law Gives Youth Sentenced to Life without Parole Another Chance." National Center for Youth Law, January 1, 2013. https:// youthlaw.org/news/california-law-gives-youth-sentenced-life-without-parole -another-chance.

Harvey, David. *A Brief History of Neoliberalism*. Oxford, UK: Oxford University Press, 2007.

————. "From Managerialism to Entrepreneurialism: The Transformation in Urban Governance in Late Capitalism." *Geografiska Annaler: Series B, Human Geography* 71, no. 1 (1989): 3–17.

————. *Rebel Cities: From the Right to the City to the Urban Revolution*. London: Verso, 2012.

————. "The Right to the City." In *The Urban Sociology Reader*, edited by Jan Lin and Christopher Mele. New York: Routledge, 2012.

Hathaway, Ian. *Almost Half of Fortune 500 Companies Were Founded by American Immigrants or Their Children*. Washington, DC: Brookings Institution, 2017.

Hausman, David K. "The Unexamined Law of Deportation." *Georgetown Law Journal* 110 (2021): 973–1020.

Hayden, Dolores. *Redesigning the American Dream: The Future of Housing, Work, and Family Life*. New York: W. W. Norton & Company, 2002.

Hayes, Matthew, and Hila Zaban. "Transnational Gentrification: The Crossroads of Transnational Mobility and Urban Research." *Urban Studies* 57, no. 15 (2020): 3009–24.

Hepburn, Peter, Devin Q. Rutan, and Matthew Desmond. "Beyond Urban Displacement: Suburban Poverty and Eviction." *Urban Affairs Review* (2022): 759–92.

Hersh, Barry. "Megaprojects." In *Urban Redevelopment*, edited by Barry Hersh, 136–48. New York: Routledge, 2017.

Hickey, Tiffany, Charles Evans, and Jenna Miara. "Attachment to Intake Form and Request to Investigate Discrimination by Department of Housing and Community Development." Asian Americans Advancing Justice, June 25, 2021. https://www.advancingjustice-alc.org/wp-content/uploads/2021/06/DFEH -Complaint-HCD_FINAL.pdf.

Hing, Bill Ong. "Deporting Cambodian Refugees: Justice Denied?" *Crime & Delinquency* 51, no. 2 (2005): 265–90.

Hong, Mai-Linh K. "Reframing the Archive: Vietnamese Refugee Narratives in the Post-9/11 Period." *Melus* 41, no. 3 (2016): 18–41.

Hong, Peter. "Council Weighs Definition of 'Family.'" *Los Angeles Times*, September 21, 1997. https://www.latimes.com/archives/la-xpm-1997-sep-21-me-34681-story.html.

Horst, Cindy. *Connected Lives: Somalis in Minneapolis, Family Responsibilities and the Migration Dreams of Relatives*. Oslo: Policy Development and Evaluation Service, United Nations High Commissioner for Refugees, 2006.

Hsu, Madeline Y. *The Good Immigrants: How the Yellow Peril Became the Model Minority*. Princeton, NJ: Princeton University Press, 2015.

Huante, Alfredo. "A Lighter Shade of Brown? Racial Formation and Gentrification in Latino Los Angeles." *Social Problems* 68, no. 1 (2021): 63–79.

Huerta, Alvaro. "Looking beyond 'Mow, Blow and Go': A Case Study of Mexican Immigrant Gardeners in Los Angeles." *Berkeley Planning Journal* 20, no. 1 (2007): 1–23.

Huston, Malo André. *The Urban Struggle for Economic, Environmental, and Social Justice: Deepening Their Roots*. New York: Routledge, 2015.

Huynh, Jennifer. "Female Vietnamese Entrepreneurs." In *Toward a Framework for Vietnamese American Studies*, edited by Linda Ho Peche and Tuong Vu. Philadelphia, PA: Temple University Press, 2023.

Ikonen, Hanna-Mari, and Minna Nikunen. "Young Adults and the Tuning of the Entrepreneurial Mindset in Neoliberal Capitalism." *Journal of Youth Studies* 22, no. 6 (2019): 824–38.

Immergluck, Dan. "A Look Back: What We Now Know about the Causes of the US Mortgage Crisis." *International Journal of Urban Sciences* 19, no. 3 (2015): 269–85.

Immergluck, Dan, and Geoff Smith. "Measuring the Effect of Subprime Lending on Neighborhood Foreclosures: Evidence from Chicago." *Urban Affairs Review* 40, no. 3 (2005): 362–89.

Indianapolis Housing Agency. "Home." Accessed October 5, 2023. https://www.indyhousing.org/.

Iranmanesh, Sadegh. "Oral History of Tam Thanh Nugyen." Viet Stories: Vietnamese American Oral History Project. University of California, Irvine. February 19, 2012.

James, Reggie, Jane Briesemeister, Kathy Mitchell, and Kevin Jewell. "Manufactured Homeowners Who Rent Lots Lack Security of Basic Tenants Rights." Consumers Union. Accessed August 12, 2023.

Jenkins, Blair. "Rent Control: Do Economists Agree?" *Econ Journal Watch* 6, no. 1 (2009): 73–112.

Jimenez, Carlos, and Alfredo Huante. "Home in Vida and Gentefied: The Politics of Representation in Gente-fication Narratives." *Aztlan: A Journal of Chicano Studies* 48, no. 1 (2023): 21–52.

Jiménez, Thomás. *Replenished Ethnicity: Mexican Americans, Immigration, and Identity*. Oakland: University of California Press, 2010.

Joassart-Marcelli, Pascale. *The $16 Taco: Contested Geographies of Food, Ethnicity, and Gentrification*. Seattle: University of Washington Press, 2021.

Johnston, Josée, and Shyon Baumann. *Foodies: Democracy and Distinction in the Gourmet Foodscape*. New York: Routledge, 2014.

Jokela, Salla. "Transformative City Branding and the Evolution of the Entrepreneurial City: The Case of 'Brand New Helsinki.'" *Urban Studies* 57, no. 10 (2020): 2031–46.

Juan, Karin Aguilar-San. *Little Saigons: Staying Vietnamese in America*. Minneapolis: University of Minnesota Press, 2009.

———. "Staying Vietnamese: Community and Place in Orange County and Boston." *City & Community* 4, no. 1 (2005): 37–65.

Kandil Yoshiko, Caitlin. "Little Saigon's Restaurant Scene Revives as Second-Generation Vietnamese Americans Mix It Up." *Los Angeles Times*, November 29, 2017. https://www.latimes.com/socal/daily-pilot/news/tn-wknd-et-little-saigon-201711-story.html.

Kang, Naewon, and Nojin Kwak. "A Multilevel Approach to Civic Participation: Individual Length of Residence, Neighborhood Residential Stability, and Their Interactive Effects with Media Use." *Communication Research* 30, no. 1 (2003): 80–106.

Karni, Annie, Maggie Haberman, and Sydney Ember. "Trump Plays on Racist Fears of Terrorized Suburbs to Court White Voters." *New York Times*, July 29, 2020. https://www.nytimes.com/2020/07/29/us/politics/trump-suburbs-housing-white-voters.html.

Kasinitz, Philip, Mary C. Waters, John H. Mollenkopf, and Jennifer Holdaway. *Inheriting the City: The Children of Immigrants Come of Age*. Cambridge, MA: Harvard University Press, 2009.

Katz, Lawrence F., and Alan B. Krueger. "The Rise and Nature of Alternative Work Arrangements in the US, 1995–2015." *ILR review* 72, no. 2 (2019): 382–416.

Kaul, Karan, and Daniel Pang. *The Role of Manufactured Housing in Increasing the Supply of Affordable Housing*. Washington, DC: Urban Institute, 2022.

Kear, Mark, Dugan Meyer, and Margaret Wilder. "Real Property Supremacy: Manufactured Housing and the Limits of Inclusion through Finance." *Annals of the American Association of Geographers* 113, no. 8 (2023): 1900–17.

Keating, W. Dennis. "Rent Control: Its Origins, History, and Controversies." In *Rent Control in North America and Four European Countries: Regulation and the Rental Housing Market*, edited by W. Dennis Keating, William Smith, and Michael Teitz, 1–14. New York: Routledge, 2020.

Kendall, Mikki. *Hood Feminism: Notes from the Women That a Movement Forgot*. New York: Penguin Press, 2021.

Keys, Benjamin, and Susan Wachter. "The Real Causes and Casualties of the Housing Crisis." September 13, 2018. Knowledge at Wharton Podcast, audio. https://knowledge.wharton.upenn.edu/podcast/knowledge-at-wharton-podcast/housing-bubble-real-causes/.

Khouri, Andrew. "Some Sanity Is Finally Returning to SoCal's Brutal Apartment Market: A Rental Guide." *Los Angeles Times*, May 3, 2023.

Kibria, Nazli. *Family Tightrope: The Changing Lives of Vietnamese Americans*. Princeton, NJ: Princeton University Press, 1995.

Kılıç, Burham, Aydan Bekar, and Nisan Yozukmaz. "The New Foodie Generation: Gen Z." In *Generation Z Marketing and Management in Tourism and Hospitality*, edited by Nikolaos Stylos, Roya Rahimi, Bendegul Okumus, Sarah Williams, 223–47. New York: Palgrave Macmillan, 2021.

Kim, Kony. *From Prison to ICE to Freedom: A Handbook for Immigrants Inside*. Oakland, CA: Asian Americans Advancing Justice and Asian Prisoner Support Committee, 2020.

Kim, Nadia Y. *Refusing Death: Immigrant Women and the Fight for Environmental Justice in LA*. Palo Alto, CA: Stanford University Press, 2021.

Kim, Soo Mee, and Aggie J. Yellow Horse. "Undocumented Asians, Left in the Shadows." *Contexts* 17, no. 4 (2018): 70–71.

Kling, Rob, Spencer C. Olin, and Mark Poster, eds. *Postsuburban California: The Transformation of Orange County since World War II*. Oakland: University of California Press, 1995.

Knaap, Gerrit, Stuart Meck, Terry Moore, Robert Parker, and American Planning Association. *Zoning as a Barrier to Multifamily Housing Development*. Chicago: American Planning Association, 2007.

Kneebone, Elizabeth, and Emily Garr. *The Suburbanization of Poverty*. Washington, DC: Brookings Institution, 2010.

Kochhar, Rakesh, and Anthony Cilluffo. "Income Inequality in the US Is Rising Most Rapidly among Asians." Pew Research Center, July 12, 2018. https://www.pewresearch.org/social-trends/2018/07/12/income-inequality-in-the-u-s-is-rising-most-rapidly-among-asians/.

Konish, Lorie. "Less than 5% of the US Housing Supply Is Accessible to Older, Disabled Americans. These Changes May Help." CNBC, July 31, 2023. https://www.cnbc.com/2023/07/21/less-than-5percent-of-housing-is-accessible-to-older-disabled-americans.html.

Kopetman, Roxana. "Santa Ana Approves Rent Control, Other Tenant Protections, after Emotional Debate." *Orange County Register*, September 22, 2021.

———. "Two Tet Parades in Orange County? Garden Grove Says Yes." *Orange County Register*, November 13, 2019. https://www.ocregister.com/2019/11/13/two-tet-parades-in-orange-county-garden-grove-says-yes/.

Kovačić, Sanja, Nemanja Milenković, Iva Slivar, and Milica Rancic. "Shaping City Brand Strategies Based on the Tourists' Brand Perception: Report on Banja Luka Main Target Groups." *International Journal of Tourism Cities* (2019): 371–96.

Kraler, Albert, Benjamin Etzold, and Nuno Ferreira. "Understanding the Dynamics of Protracted Displacement." *Forced Migration Review* 68 (2021): 49–52.

Kwansa, Francis A., and Xiangmei Yang. "The Impact of the EB-5 Program in the Hospitality Industry: Now and the Future." *Journal of Hospitality Financial Management* 29, no. 2 (2021): 82–89.

Kwon, Soo Ah. "Deporting Cambodian Refugees: Youth Activism, State Reform, and Imperial Statecraft." *Positions: East Asia Cultures Critique* 20, no. 3 (2012): 737–62.

Lam, Kevin D. *Youth Gangs, Racism, and Schooling: Vietnamese American Youth in a Postcolonial Context.* New York: Palgrave Macmillan, 2015.

Lazenby, Scott. "How Room Arrangement Encourages or Discourages Civility." *Public Management Magazine*, March 2019.

Lê Espiritu, Yến. *Body Counts: The Vietnam War and Militarized Refugees.* Oakland: University of California Press, 2014.

———. "Critical Refugee Studies and Native Pacific Studies: A Transpacific Critique." *American Quarterly* 69, no. 3 (2017): 483–90.

———. "The 'We-Win-Even-When-We-Lose' Syndrome: US Press Coverage of the Twenty-Fifth Anniversary of the 'Fall of Saigon.'" *American Quarterly* 58, no. 2 (2006): 329–52.

Lê Espiritu, Yến, Lan Duong, Ma Vang, Victor Bascara, Khatharya Um, Lila Sharif, and Nigel Hatton. *Departures: An Introduction to Critical Refugee Studies.* Oakland: University of California Press, 2022.

LeCompte, Margaret, D., and Judith Preissle Goetz. "Ethnographic Data Collection in Evaluation Research." *Educational Evaluation and Policy Analysis* 4, no. 3 (1982): 387–400.

Lee, C. Aujean, Lisa Hasegawa, Melany De La Cruz-Viesca, and Paul M. Ong. "Asian American and Pacific Islander Wealth Inequality and Developing Paths to Financial Security." *AAPI Nexus: Policy, Practice and Community* 13, no. 1–2 (2015): vii–xiv.

Lee, Charles. "Improvising Nonexistent Rights: Immigrants, Ethnic Restaurants, and Corporeal Citizenship in Suburban California." *Social Inclusion* 7, no. 4 (2019): 79–89.

Lees, Loretta, Hyun Bang Shin, and Ernesto López-Morales. "Introduction: 'Gentrification'—A Global Urban Process?" In *Global Gentrifications*, edited by Loretta Lees, Hyun Bang Shin, and Ernesto López-Morales, 1–18. Bristol: Policy Press, 2015.

———. *Planetary Gentrification.* Hoboken, NJ: John Wiley and Sons, 2016.

Lefebvre, Henri. "From the Production of Space." In *Theatre and Performance Design*, 81–84. New York: Routledge, 2012.

Lefebvre, Henri, Eleonore Kofman, and Elizabeth Lebas. *Writings on Cities.* Oxford: Blackwell, 1996.

Lehman, Daniel J. Van, and Estelle M. McKee. "Removals to Somalia in Light of the Convention against Torture: Recent Evidence from Somali Bantu Deportees." *Georgetown Immigration Law Journal* 33 (2018): 357–98.

Levenson, Alec R. "Millennials and the World of Work: An Economist's Perspective." *Journal of Business and Psychology* 25, no. 2 (2010): 257–64.

Lewinnek, Elaine, Gustavo Arellano, and Thuy Võ Đặng. *A People's Guide to Orange County.* Oakland: University of California Press, 2022.

Li, Wei. *Ethnoburb: The New Ethnic Community in Urban America.* Mānoa: University of Hawaii Press, 2008.

Lieu, Nhi T. *The American Dream in Vietnamese*. Minneapolis: University of Minnesota Press, 2011.

Light, Ivan. "Immigrant and Ethnic Enterprise in North America." *Ethnic and Racial Studies* 7, no. 2 (1984): 195–216.

Little Saigon Blueprint for Development. Washington, DC: Streetsense, 2021.

Liu, Michael, and Kim Geron. "Changing Neighborhood: Ethnic Enclaves and the Struggle for Social Justice." *Social Justice* 35, no. 2 (2008): 18–35.

Liu-Farrer, Gracia. "Migration as Class-Based Consumption: The Emigration of the Rich in Contemporary China." *China Quarterly* 226 (2016): 499–518.

Lofstrom, Magnus, Mia Bird, and Brandon Martin. *California's Historic Corrections Reforms*. San Francisco: Public Policy Institute of California, 2016.

Longazel, Jamie, Jake Berman, and Benjamin Fleury-Steiner. "The Pains of Immigrant Imprisonment." *Sociology Compass* 10, no. 11 (2016): 989–98.

López, Claudia Maria, R. Varisa Patraporn, and Suzie Weng. "The Impact of Housing Experience on the Well-Being of 1.5-Generation Immigrants: The Case of Millennial and Gen-Z Renters in Southern California." *Housing Policy Debate* 33, no. 1 (2022): 1–27.

Louie, Vivian S. *Compelled to Excel: Immigration, Education, and Opportunity among Chinese Americans*. Redwood City, CA: Stanford University Press, 2004.

Lowe, Lisa. *Immigrant Acts: On Asian American Cultural Politics*. Durham, NC: Duke University Press, 1996.

Lowenthal, Abraham F. *Global California: Rising to the Cosmopolitan Challenge*. Redwood City, CA: Stanford University Press, 2009.

Lund, Anna Jane. "Tenant Protections in Mobile Home Park Closures." *UC Berkeley Law Review* 53 (2020): 759–830.

Lung-Amam, Willow S. "Surviving Suburban Redevelopment: Resisting the Displacement of Immigrant-Owned Small Businesses in Wheaton, Maryland." *Journal of Urban Affairs* 43, no. 3 (2021): 449–66.

Maher, Kristen Hill. "Borders and Social Distinction in the Global Suburb." *American Quarterly* 56, no. 3 (2004): 781–806.

Malkki, Liisa H. "Speechless Emissaries: Refugees, Humanitarianism, and Dehistoricization." *Cultural Anthropology* 11, no. 3 (1996): 377–404.

Manian, Maya. "Immigration Detention and Coerced Sterilization History Tragically Repeats Itself." ACLU, September 29, 2020. https://www.aclu.org/news/immigrants-rights/immigration-detention-and-coerced-sterilization-history-tragically-repeats-itself.

Marans, Robert W., and Mary Ellen Colten. *A Report on Measuring Restrictive Rental Practices Affecting Families with Children: A National Survey*. The Office of Policy Development and Research. 1980.

Marchevsky, Alejandra, and Jeanne Theoharis. "Welfare Reform, Globalization, and the Racialization of Entitlement." *American Studies* 41, no. 2/3 (2000): 235–65.

Marcuse, Peter. "To Control Gentrification: Anti-Displacement Zoning and Planning for Stable Residential Districts." *NYU Review of Law and Social Change* 13 (1984): 931–52.

Markley, Scott. "Suburban Gentrification? Examining the Geographies of New Urbanism in Atlanta's Inner Suburbs." *Urban Geography* 39, no. 4 (2018): 606–30.

Mavelli, Luca. "Citizenship for Sale and the Neoliberal Political Economy of Belonging." *International Studies Quarterly* 62, no. 3 (2018): 482–93.

Mayer, Margit. "The 'Right to the City' in the Context of Shifting Mottos of Urban Social Movements." *City* 13, no. 2–3 (2009): 362–74.

Mayhood, Parris. "A Threatened Species of Homeowner: Mobile Home Owner-Tenants and Their Shocking Lack of Legal Safeguards." *UMKC Law Review* 90 (2021): 481–92.

McClain, Charles J. *In Search of Equality: The Chinese Struggle against Discrimination in Nineteenth-Century America.* Oakland: University of California Press, 1994.

McNee, Georgina, and Dorina Pojani. "NIMBYism as a Barrier to Housing and Social Mix in San Francisco." *Journal of Housing and the Built Environment* 37, no. 1 (2022): 553–73.

Menel, Richard. *Why Youth Incarceration Fails: An Updated Review of the Evidence.* The Sentencing Project, March 1, 2023. https://www.sentencingproject.org/reports/why-youth-incarceration-fails-an-updated-review-of-the-evidence/.

Menjívar, Cecilia. "Liminal Legality: Salvadoran and Guatemalan Immigrants' Lives in the United States." *American Journal of Sociology* 111, no. 4 (2006): 999–1037.

Menjívar, Cecilia, Andrea Gómez Cervantes, and Daniel Alvord. "The Expansion of 'Crimmigration,' Mass Detention, and Deportation." *Sociology Compass* 12, no. 4 (2018): 12573.

Michelson, Sarah. "Hillside Villa Tenants Win Eminent Domain." *KnockLA*, June 8, 2022. https://knock-la.com/hillside-villa-tenants-win-eminent-domain/.

Miller, Nancy K. *What They Saved: Pieces of a Jewish Past.* Lincoln: University of Nebraska Press, 2011.

Millet, Evin. "A Demographic Profile of Undocumented Immigrants from Asia and the Pacific Islands." Center for Migration Studies, June 14, 2022.

Min, Pyong Gap. "The Advantages of Suburban Enclaves over Urban Enclaves for Community Empowerment: Korean Immigrants in Greater New York." *Ethnic and Racial Studies* 46, no. 7 (2023): 1357–77.

———. *Ethnic Solidarity for Economic Survival: Korean Greengrocers in New York City.* New York: Russell Sage Foundation, 2008.

Min, Pyong Gap, and Mehdi Bozorgmehr. "Immigrant Entrepreneurship and Business Patterns: A Comparison of Koreans and Iranians in Los Angeles." *International Migration Review* 34, no. 3 (2000): 707–38.

Mobile Home Park Owners Allegiance. "California MHP Rent Stabilization Ordinances (RSO aka SRSO)." Accessed August 16, 2023. https://mhphoa.com/ca/rso/.

Mobile Home Park Owners Allegiance. "California Mobile Home Park Statistics." Last modified June 1, 2023. https://mhphoa.com/ca/mhp/statistics.

Molinsky, Jennifer. "Older Adults Increasingly Face Housing Affordability Challenges." Housing Perspectives, Joint Center for Housing Studies of Harvard University, September 21, 2018. https://www.jchs.harvard.edu/blog/older-adults -increasingly-face-housing-affordability-challenges.

Molz, Jennie Germann. *Travel Connections: Tourism, Technology and Togetherness in a Mobile World*. New York: Routledge, 2012.

Morawetz, Nancy. "Understanding the Impact of the 1996 Deportation Laws and the Limited Scope of Proposed Reforms." *In Defense of the Alien* 23 (2000): 1–30.

Najmabadi, Afsaneh. *Familial Undercurrents: Untold Stories of Love and Marriage in Modern Iran*. Durham, NC: Duke University Press, 2022.

Naser, Rebecca L., and Nancy G. La Vigne. "Family Support in the Prisoner Reentry Process: Expectations and Realities." *Journal of Offender Rehabilitation* 43, no. 1 (2006): 93–106.

National Low Income Housing Coalition. "Out of Reach: How Much Do You Need to Earn to Afford a Modest Apartment in Your State?" Accessed December 20, 2023. https://nlihc.org/oor.

Nee, Victor, and Jimy Sanders. "The Road to Parity: Determinants of the Socioeconomic Achievements of Asian Americans." In *Asian American Issues Relating to Labor, Economics, and Socioeconomic Status*, edited by Franklin Ng, 157–75. New York: Routledge, 2014.

Nguyễn, An Tuan. "More than Just Refugees—A Historical Overview of Vietnamese Professional Immigration to the United States." *Journal of Vietnamese Studies* 10, no. 3 (2015): 87–125.

Nguyễn, Andy. "Andy Nguyễn: Creating the World's First NFT Restaurant Set to Change the Industry Forever." Well Versed with Jazzy. Interview by Jazzy Cho on June 15, 2022. YouTube video. https://www.youtube.com/watch?v= Gjrm_HKuAT0.

Nguyễn, Phương Trần. *Becoming Refugee American*. Champaign: University of Illinois Press, 2017.

Nguyễn, Việt Thanh, ed. *The Displaced: Refugee Writers on Refugee Lives*. New York: Abrams, 2018.

———. *The Sympathizer*. New York: Grove Atlantic, 2015.

Nguyễn, Vinh. *Lived Refuge: Gratitude, Resentment, Resilience*. Oakland: University of California Press, 2023.

Niedt, Christopher, ed. *Social Justice in Diverse Suburbs: History, Politics, and Prospects*. Philadelphia, PA: Temple University Press, 2013.

Noguchi, Yuki. "Unequal Outcomes: Most ICE Detainees Held in Rural Areas Where Deportation Risks Soar." NPR, August 15, 2019. https://www.npr .org/2019/08/15/748764322/unequal-outcomes-most-ice-detainees-held-in-rural -areas-where-deportation-risks.

O'Brien, Kean, Leonardo Vilchis, and Corina Maritescu. "Boyle Heights and the Fight against Gentrification as State Violence." *American Quarterly* 71, no. 2 (2019): 389–96.

Oh, Sookhee, and Angie Chung. "A Study on the Sociospatial Context of Ethnic Politics and Entrepreneurial Growth in Koreatown and Monterey Park." *Geo-Journal* 79 (2014): 59–71.

Oh, Angela E., and Karen Umemoto. "Asian Americans and Pacific Islanders: From Incarceration to Re-Entry." *Amerasia Journal* 31, no. 3 (2005): 43–59.

Oguztimur, Senay, and Ulun Akturan. "Synthesis of City Branding Literature (1988–2014) as a Research Domain." *International Journal of Tourism Research* 18, no. 4 (2016): 357–72.

Oleschuk, Merin. "Foodies of Color: Authenticity and Exoticism in Omnivorous Food Culture." *Cultural Sociology* 11, no. 2 (2017): 217–33.

Ong, Paul, Chhandara Pech, Melany De-La Cruz Viesca, and Caroline Calderon. *Crisis to Impact: Reflecting on a Decade of Housing Counseling Services in Asian American and Pacific Islander Communities.* UCLA Asian American Studies Center. 2021.

Othering and Belonging Institute, University of California, Berkeley. "Greater LA Region Zoning Maps." Accessed December 20, 2023. https://belonging.berkeley .edu/greater-la-region-zoning-maps.

Pader, Ellen. "Housing Occupancy Standards: Inscribing Ethnicity and Family Relations on the Land." *Journal of Architectural and Planning Research* 19, no. 4 (2002): 300–18.

Paragan, Michelle. "Sonny Nguyễn, Co-Founder of 7 Leaves Café, on the Company's Rapid Growth." *Orange Coast Magazine*, April 8, 2019.

Park, Lisa Sun-Hee. *Consuming Citizenship: Children of Asian Immigrant Entrepreneurs.* Redwood City, CA: Stanford University Press, 2005.

Passel, Jeffrey, and D'Vera Cohn. "20 Metro Areas Are Home to Six-in-Ten Unauthorized Immigrants in US." PEW Research Center, June 12, 2019. https://www .pewresearch.org. https://www.pewresearch.org/short-reads/2019/03/11/us -metro-areas-unauthorized-immigrants/.

Persaud, Justin G. "New Markets Tax Credits and EB-5: Combining Two Programs for One Goal." *Journal of Affordable Housing & Community Development Law* (2012): 249–64.

Phan, Hiếu Trân. "Subletting Is Dream Down Payment." *Orange County Register*, May 31, 2001.

Pierce, Sarah, and Andrew Selee. *Immigration under Trump: A Review of Policy Shifts in the Year since the Election.* Washington, DC: Migration Policy Institute, 2017.

Ponsi, Lou. "Rent Increases Will Be Limited at One OC Mobile Home Park." *Orange County Register*, October 29, 2021. https://www.ocregister.com/2021/10/29 /in-january-one-oc-mobile-home-park-will-have-limits-on-rent-increases/.

Portes, Alejandro, and Ariel C. Armony. *The Global Edge: Miami in the Twenty-First Century.* Oakland: University of California Press, 2018.

Portes, Alejandro, and Brandon P. Martinez. "They Are Not All the Same: Immigrant Enterprises, Transnationalism, and Development." *Journal of Ethnic and Migration Studies* 46, no. 10 (2020): 1991–2007.

Portes, Alejandro, and Jessica Yiu. "Entrepreneurship, Transnationalism, and Development." *Migration Studies* 1, no. 1 (2013): 75–95.

Portes, Alejandro, and Min Zhou. "Self-Employment and the Earnings of Immigrants." *American Sociological Review* (1996): 219–30.

Pratt, Alexa. "Orange County Housing Authority Opens Their Waiting List for the Housing Choice Voucher Program." Orange County Government, September 29, 2023. https://www.ocgov.com/press/oc-housing-authority-opens-housing-choice-voucher-program-waiting-list.

Quigley, John M., and Steven Raphael. "Is Housing Unaffordable? Why Isn't It More Affordable?" *Journal of Economic Perspectives* 18, no. 1 (2004): 191–214.

Ramakrishnan, Kriti, Elizabeth Champion, Megan Gallagher, and Keith Fudge. *Why Housing Matters for Upward Mobility: Evidence and Indicators for Practitioners and Policymakers*. Washington, DC: Urban Institute, 2021. https://www.urban.org/research/publication/why-housing-matters-upward-mobility-evidence-and-indicators-practitioners-and-policymakers.

Ramakrishnan, Karthick, and Sono Shah. "One Out of Every 7 Asian Immigrants Is Undocumented." AAPI Data. September 8, 2017. http://aapidata.com/blog/asian-undoc-1in7/.

Ramiller, Alex. "Displacement through Development? Property Turnover and Eviction Risk in Seattle." *Urban Studies* 59, no. 6 (2021).

Rangaswamy, Padma. "South Asians in Dunkin' Donuts: Niche Development in the Franchise Industry." *Journal of Ethnic and Migration Studies* 33, no. 4 (2007): 671–86.

Rankin, Katharine N., and Heather McLean. "Governing the City's Commercial Streets: New Terrains of Disinvestment and Gentrification in Toronto's Inner Suburbs." *Antipode* 47, no. 1 (2015): 216–39.

Reagor, Catherine, Juliette Rihl, and Kunle Falayi. "'We Are Going to Be Homeless': How Mobile Homeowners Are Being Forced Out in Metro Phoenix." *Arizona Republic*, October 22, 2022.

Reyes, David. "250,000 Expected for Little Saigon's 3 Day Tet Festival." *Los Angeles Times*, January 29, 1989. https://www.latimes.com/archives/la-xpm-1989-01-29-me-2037-story.html.

Rhee, Isabella. "Santa Ana's Mobile Home Communities Deserve Rent Control." *Voice of OC*, January 12, 2022. https://voiceofoc.org/2022/01/rhee-santa-anas-mobile-home-communities-deserve-rent-control/?amp=.

Richardson, Ian. "Iowa Mobile Home Owners Get Extra 30 Days Before Steep Rent Increases Begin." *Des Moines Register*, April 18, 2019.

Right to the City. "Our Story." Accessed October 22, 2022. https://www.righttothecity.org/our-story.

Rigoni, Brandon, and Amy Adkins. "What Millennials Want from a New Job." *Harvard Business Review* 11 (2016).

Rolfe, Frank. "Why Invest in Mobile Home Parks." Mobile Home University. Accessed August 17, 2023. https://www.mobilehomeuniversity.com.

Rolnik, Raquel. *Special Rapporteur on Adequate Housing as a Component of the Right to an Adequate Standard of Living and on the Right to Nondiscrimination in this Context*. General Assembly, Sixty-Seventh Session/286. New York: United Nations Human Rights Council, 2012.

Roman, Gabriel San. "Santa Ana Prepares Formal Apology for 1906 Chinatown Burning, Past Anti-Chinese Racism." *Los Angeles Times*, May 4, 2022.

Rose, Geoff, and Richard Harris. "The Three Tenures: A Case of Property Maintenance." *Urban Studies* 59, no. 9 (2022): 1926–43.

Rosen, Eva. *The Voucher Promise: "Section 8" and the Fate of an American Neighborhood*. Princeton, NJ: Princeton University Press, 2020.

Rosenthal, Tracy Jeanne. "101 Notes on the LA Tenants Union (You Can't Do Politics Alone)." *Housing Justice in Unequal Cities* (2019): 51–59.

Ross, Andrew. *Sunbelt Blues: The Failure of American Housing*. New York: Metropolitan Books, 2021.

Rothstein, Richard. *The Color of Law: A Forgotten History of How Our Government Segregated America*. New York: Liveright Publishing Corporation, 2017.

Roy, Ananya. "Dis/possessive Collectivism: Property and Personhood at City's End." *Geoforum* 80 (2017): 1–11.

———. "Housing Justice towards a Field of Inquiry." In *Housing Justice in Unequal Cities*, edited by Ananya Roy and Hilary Malson, 14–19. Los Angeles: UCLA Institute on Inequality and Democracy, 2019. https://challengeinequality.luskin.ucla.edu/wp-content/uploads/sites/16/2019/10/Housing-Justice-in-Unequal-Cities.pdf.

———. "Racial Banishment." In *Keywords in Radical Geography: Antipode at 50*, edited by Tariq Jazeel et al., 227–30. Hoboken, NJ: John Wiley and Sons, Inc, 2019.

Roy, Ananya, Gary Blasi, Jonny Coleman, and Elana Eden. *Hotel California: Housing the Crisis*. Los Angeles: UCLA Institute on Inequality and Democracy, 2020.

Roy, Ananya, and Emma Shaw Crane, eds. *Territories of Poverty: Rethinking North and South*. Athens: University of Georgia Press, 2015.

Roy, Ananya, and Hilary Malson, eds. *Housing Justice in Unequal Cities*. Los Angeles: UCLA Institute on Inequality and Democracy, 2019.

Rummel, RJ. *Statistics of Democide: Genocide and Mass Murder Since 1900*. Munster, Germany: LIT Verlag, 1998.

Saito, Leland. "From Whiteness to Colorblindness in Public Policies: Racial Formation and Urban Development." *Sociology of Race and Ethnicity* 1, no. 1 (2015): 37–51.

Salamon, Sonya, and Katherine MacTavish. "Quasi-Homelessness among Rural Trailer-Park Households in the United States." In *International Perspectives on Rural Homelessness*, edited by Paul Cloke and Paul Milbourne, 45–62. London: Routledge, 2006.

Sánchez, George J. *Boyle Heights: How a Los Angeles Neighborhood Became the Future of American Democracy*. Oakland: University of California Press, 2021.

Scally, Corianne, and Dulce Gonzalez. *Homeowner and Renter Experiences of Material Hardship*. Washington, DC: Urban Institute, 2018.

Scally, Corianne Payton, and J. Rosie Tighe. "Democracy in Action? NIMBY as Impediment to Equitable Affordable Housing Siting: Housing Studies, 2015." In *The Affordable Housing Reader*, edited by Elizabeth Mueller and J. Rosie Tighe, 337–54. New York: Routledge, 2022.

Shachar, Ayelet. "Unequal Access: Wealth as Barrier and Accelerator to Citizenship." *Citizenship Studies* 25, no. 4 (2021): 543–63.

Schafran, Alex. *The Road to Resegregation: Northern California and the Failure of Politics*. Oakland: University of California Press, 2018.

Schleicher, David. "Stuck! The Law and Economics of Residential Stagnation." *Yale Law Journal* (2017): 78–154.

Schuetz, Jenny. *Fixer-Upper: How to Repair America's Broken Housing Systems*. Washington, DC: Brookings Institution, 2022.

Sezgin, Erkan, and Beyza Uyanik. "Priorities of Consumers for Restaurant Preferences: A Conjoint Analysis Study on Generation Z." *Journal of Tourism Leisure and Hospitality* 4, no. 2 (2021): 141–48.

Shin, HaeRan. *The Cultural Politics of Urban Development in South Korea: Art, Memory and Urban Boosterism in Gwangju*. New York: Routledge, 2020.

Shroyer, Aaron. "How Manufactured Housing Can Fill Affordable Housing Gaps." Housing Matters, Urban Institute, July 8, 2020. https://housingmatters.urban .org/articles/how-manufactured-housing-can-fill-affordable-housing-gaps.

Silva, Gina. "Paramount Families Fear Homelessness after New Owners Raise Rent." FOX 11 News Los Angeles, June 12, 2023. https://www.foxla.com/news /paramount-homeless-fear-higher-rent.

Simons, Robert A., Jing Wu, Jie Xu, and Yu Fei. "Chinese Investment in US Real Estate Markets Using the EB-5 Program." *Economic Development Quarterly* 30, no. 1 (2016): 75–87.

Singer, Audrey, and Camille Galdes. *Improving the EB-5 Investor Visa Program*. Washington, DC: Brookings Institution, 2014.

Singer, Audrey, Susan Hardwick, and Caroline Brettell. "Twenty-First Century Gateways: Immigrants in Suburban America." Migration Policy Institute, April 30, 2008. https://www.migrationpolicy.org/article/twenty-first-century-gateways -immigrants-suburban-america.

Siu, Lok. "Chino Latino Restaurants: Converging Communities, Identities, and Cultures." *Afro-Hispanic Review* 27, no. 1 (2008): 161–71.

———. "Twenty-First-Century Food Trucks: Mobility, Social Media, and Urban Hipness." *Eating Asian America: A Food Studies Reader* (2013): 231–44.

Slack, Jeremy. *Deported to Death: How Drug Violence Is Changing Migration on the US–Mexico Border*. Oakland: University of California Press, 2019.

Slater, Tom. "The Eviction of Critical Perspectives from Gentrification Research." *Journal of Urban and Regional Research* 30, no. 4 (2006): 737–57.

Smith, Edward S. "Revitalizing Urban America through the EB-5 Immigrant Investor Program." *Immigrant Entrepreneurship in Cities: Global Perspectives* (2021): 265–77.

Smith, Merill, ed. *Warehousing Refugees: A Denial of Rights, a Waste of Humanity*. Arlington, VA: US Committee for Refugees and Immigrants, 2005.

Smith, Neil. *The New Urban Frontier: Gentrification and the Revanchist City*. New York: Routledge, 2005.

Smith, William, and Michael Teitz. *Rent Control in North America and Four European Countries: Regulation and the Rental Housing Market*. New York: Routledge, 2020.

Southeast Asia Resource Action Center. "The Devastating Impact of Deportation on Southeast Asian Americans." SEARAC Fact Sheet. https://www.searac.org/wp-content/uploads/2018/04/The-Devastating-Impact-of-Deportation-on-Southeast-Asian-Americans-1.pdf.

Southeast Asia Resource Action Center. "SEADRA 118th Reintroduction Press Conference." Facebook, https://fb.watch/tS5ghpuqEm/, August 22, 2013.

Stout, Noelle. *Dispossessed: How Predatory Bureaucracy Foreclosed on the American Middle Class*. Oakland: University of California Press, 2019.

Sullivan, Esther. "Becoming Visible in the Public Sphere: Mobile Home Park Residents' Political Engagement in City Council Hearings." *Qualitative Sociology* 44, no. 3 (2021): 349–66.

———. "Displaced in Place: Manufactured Housing, Mass Eviction, and the Paradox of State Intervention." *American Sociological Review* 82, no. 2 (2017): 243–69.

———. *Manufactured Insecurity: Mobile Home Parks and Americans' Tenuous Right to Place*. Oakland: University of California Press, 2018.

———. "Moving Out: Mapping Mobile Home Park Closures to Analyze Spatial Patterns of Low–Income Residential Displacement." *City & Community* 16, no. 3 (2017): 304–29.

———. "Personal, Not Real: Manufactured Housing Insecurity, Real Property, and the Law." *Annual Review of Law and Social Science* 18 (2022): 119–38.

Surak, Kristin. *The Golden Passport: Global Mobility for Millionaires*. Cambridge, MA: Harvard University Press, 2023.

Suro, Roberto, Jill H. Wilson, and Audrey Singer. *Immigration and Poverty in America's Suburbs*. Washington, DC: Brookings Institution, 2011.

Sutton, Stacey. "What We Don't Understand about Gentrification." Filmed January 15, 2015 in New York, NY. TEDx Talks. https://noureanthology.wordpress.com/2015/04/24/what-we-dont-understand-about-gentrification/.

Taylor, Keeanga-Yamahtta. *Race for Profit: How Banks and the Real Estate Industry Undermined Black Homeownership*. Chapel Hill: University of North Carolina Press, 2019.

Teresa, Benjamin F. "New Dynamics of Rent Gap Formation in New York City Rent-Regulated Housing: Privatization, Financialization, and Uneven Development." *Urban Geography* 40, no. 10 (2019): 1399–1421.

Theodos, Brett, Eric Hangen, Brady Meixell, and Prasanna Rajasekaran. *Neighborhood Disparities in Investment Flows in Chicago*. Washington, DC: Urban Institute, 2019.

Tienda, Marta, and Rebeca Raijman. "Promoting Hispanic Immigrant Entrepreneurship in Chicago." *Journal of Developmental Entrepreneurship* 9, no. 1 (2004): 1–22.

Tobias, Manuela. "Are Immigrants Getting Left Out of California's Rent Relief?" Cal Matters, October 13, 2021. https://calmatters.org/housing/2021/10/california-rent-relief-immigrants-barriers/.

Tobias, Manuela, and Jackie Botts. "Lawmakers Tackle a Severe Housing Shortage for Renters Who Have Federal Vouchers." CalMatters, August 28, 2019. https://calmatters.org/california-divide/2019/08/section-8-voucher-discrimination-california-housing-crisis/

———. "California's Section 8 Renters Face a Severe Housing Shortage. Can Lawmakers Help?" KQED News, August 30, 2019. https://www.kqed.org/news/11771019/californias-section-8-renters-face-a-severe-housin.

Tötösy de Zepetnek, Steven, and I-Chun Wang, eds. *Mapping the World, Culture, and Border-Crossing*. Kaohsiung, Taiwan: National Sun Yat-Sen University Press, 2010.

Trần, Ly Thi Hai. "Outsiders No More?: The Discourse of Political Incorporation of Vietnamese Refugees in the United States (1975–2020)." *Journal of Asian American Studies* 23, no. 2 (2020): 229–64.

Travis, Adam. "The Organization of Neglect: Limited Liability Companies and Housing Disinvestment." *American Sociological Review* 84, no. 1 (2019): 142–70.

Trường, Trinh. "Trinh v. Homan: The Indefinite Detention of Vietnamese Refugees in the 21st Century." *Southern California Review of Law and Social Justice* 30 (2021): 415–47.

Turner, Anthony. "Generation Z: Technology and Social Interest." *Journal of Individual Psychology* 71, no. 2 (2015): 103–13.

Turner, Graeme. "The Cosmopolitan City and Its Other: The Ethnicizing of the Australian Suburb." *Inter-Asia Cultural Studies* 9, no. 4 (2008): 568–82.

Tuttle, Steven. "Place Attachment and Alienation from Place: Cultural Displacement in Gentrifying Ethnic Enclaves." *Critical Sociology* 48, no. 3 (2022): 517–31.

Tuttle, Steven, and Alfredo Huante. "Taking Race Seriously in Gentrification Research." In *A Research Agenda for Gentrification*, edited by Winifred Curran and Leslie Kern. Northampton, MA: Edward Elgar Publishing, 2023.

United Nations High Commissioner for Refugees. "Protracted Refugee Situations Explained." Accessed January 28, 2020. https://www.unrefugees.org/news/protracted-refugee-situations-explained/.

Urban Displacement Project, University of California, Berkeley. "What Are Gentrification and Displacement?" Last updated 2021. https://www.urbandisplacement.org/about/what-are-gentrification-and-displacement/.

US Citizenship and Immigration Services. "Humanitarian Parole." Accessed November 2, 2023. https://www.dhs.gov/allieswelcome.

Uyeda, Cody. "Addressing Gendered Trauma, Identity, and the Crime-to-Deportation Pipeline among Southeast Asian Men." *UCLA Asian Pacific American Law Journal* 25, no. 1 (2021): 161–94.

Valverde, Kiều Linh Caroline. *Transnationalizing Viet Nam: Community, Culture, and Politics in the Diaspora*. Philadelphia, PA: Temple University Press, 2012.

Vásquez, Hugo, Laia Palència, Ingrid Magna, Carlos Mena, Jaime Neira, and Carme Borrell. "The Threat of Home Eviction and Its Effects on Health through the Equity Lens: A Systematic Review." *Social Science & Medicine* 175 (2017): 199–208.

Veblen, Thorstein, and C. Wright Mills. *The Theory of the Leisure Class*. New York: Routledge, 2017.

Võ, Linda Trinh. "Constructing a Vietnamese American Community: Economic and Political Transformation in Little Saigon, Orange County." *Amerasia Journal* 34, no. 3 (2008): 85–109.

———. *Mobilizing an Asian American Community*. Philadelphia, PA: Temple University Press, 2004.

Võ, Linda Trinh, and Mary Yu Danico. "The Formation of Post-Suburban Communities: Koreatown and Little Saigon, Orange County." *International Journal of Sociology and Social Policy* 24, no. 7/8 (2004): 15–45.

Võ, Thy. "Anaheim's New Oversized Vehicle Parking Ban Leaves Dwellers Wondering Where to Live." *Voice of Orange County News*, December 8, 2020. https:// voiceofoc.org/2018/06/anaheims-new-oversized-vehicle-parking-ban-leaves-rv -dwellers-wondering-where-to-live/.

———. "Evicted Garden Grove RV Park Residents Sue State." *Voice of OC*, December 29, 2014. https://voiceofoc.org/2014/12/evicted-garden-grove-rv-park-residents -sue-state/.

———. "Seniors, Refugees Protest Closure of Westminster Mobile Home Park." *Voice of OC*, March 7, 2018. https://voiceofoc.org/2018/03/seniors-refugees -protest-closure-of-westminster-mobile-home-park/.

Vương, Ocean. *On Earth We're Briefly Gorgeous: A Novel*. New York: Penguin, 2021.

Wakin, Michele. "Not Sheltered, Not Homeless: RVs as Makeshifts." *American Behavioral Scientist* 48, no. 8 (2005): 1013–32.

———. "The Regulation-Resistance Dynamic: An Ethnographic Study of RV Living in Santa Barbara, California." PhD diss., University of California Santa Barbara, 2005.

Walker, Fay, and Eleanor Noble. "Ensuring Safe and Affordable Housing Starts with Understanding Who Owns Rental Units." Urban Institute, September 6, 2022. https://www.urban.org/urban-wire/ensuring-safe-and-affordable-housing -stock-starts-understanding-who-owns-rental-units

Walker, Theresa. "Nonprofits Join Forces in Experimental Program to Help OC Homeless." *Orange County Register*, August 28, 2020. https://www.ocregister .com/2020/08/28/nonprofits-join-forces-in-experimental-program-to-help -o-c-homeless/.

Walters, Dan. *High Living Costs Solidify California's Two-Tier Economy*. Sacramento, CA: CALMatters, 2023.

Warner, Karen A. *City of Yorba Linda 2021–2029 Housing Element Draft*. Yorba Linda, CA: City of Yorba Linda Community Development Department, 2021.

Wiese, Andrew. *Places of Their Own*. Chicago, IL: University of Chicago Press, 2009.

Williams, Michael Wayne. "From Orange Groves to High-Tech in San Fernando Valley: Boosterism, Rezoning, and the Emergence of a R&D Regional Economy." *Southern California Quarterly* 80, no. 3 (1998): 315–48.

Williams, Stockton. *Preserving Multifamily Workforce and Affordable Housing: New Approaches for Investing in a Vital National Asset*. Washington DC: Urban Land Institute, 2015.

Woetzel, Jonathon, Jan Mischke, Shannon Peloquin, and Daniel Weisfield. *Closing California's Housing Gap*. New York: McKinsey Global Institute, 2016.

Woo, Angela. "Understanding the Research on Millennial Shopping Behaviors." *Forbes*, June 4, 2018. https://www.forbes.com/sites/forbesagencycouncil/2018/06/04/understanding-the-research-on-millennial-shopping-behaviors/.

Woolsey, Brittany. "An Update on the Vietnamese Dining Experience." *Los Angeles Times*, December 11, 2015. https://www.latimes.com/socal/daily-pilot/tn-wknd-et-1213-nudo-nudo-20151211-story.html.

Yamane, Linus. "Labor Market Discrimination: Vietnamese Immigrants." *Journal of Southeast Asian American Education and Advancement* 7, no. 1 (2012): 1–27.

Yusuf, Ahmed Ismail. *Somalis in Minnesota*. St. Paul, MN: Minnesota Historical Society Press, 2012.

Zeimer, Sara. "Exclusionary Zoning, School Segregation, and Housing Segregation: An Investigation into a Modern Desegregation Case and Solutions to Housing Segregation." *Hastings Constitutional Law Quarterly* 48 (2020): 205–30.

Zhou, Min. "Revisiting Ethnic Entrepreneurship: Convergencies, Controversies, and Conceptual Advancements 1." *International Migration Review* 38, no. 3 (2004): 1040–74.

Zimmerman, Tom. "Paradise Promoted: Boosterism and the Los Angeles Chamber of Commerce." *California History* 64, no. 1 (1985): 22–33.

Zukin, Sharon. "Urban Lifestyles: Diversity and Standardization in Spaces of Consumption." *Urban Studies* 35, no. 5–6 (1998): 825–39.

Zukin, Sharon, Valerie Trujillo, Peter Frase, Danielle Jackson, Time Recuber, Abraham Walker. "New Retail Capital and Neighborhood Change: Boutiques and Gentrification in New York City." *City & Community* 8, no. 1 (2009): 47–64

INDEX

Dominican Republic deportees, 141
Duffy, Brook Erin, 39

entrepreneurs and entrepreneurship: creative, 28–30; displacement and, 47;
expressive, 28, 30, 41, 43, 172n39; first
and second generation, 39–43; food, 25;
gentrification and, 24; immigrant, 26;
intergenerational, 44–47; mobility and,
39–43; neoliberal aspects of, 43; reimagining, 39; structural incentives for,
28–29, 52; transnational, 46–47; urban
entrepreneuralism, 48; women, 153. *See
also* Nguyễn, Andy (entrepreneur)
Espiritu, Yến Lê, 5, 10
ethnic gentrifiers: agency of, 32; characteristics of, 26–28; displacement and, 30;
food adventuring and, 32–33; Latinx,
30; marketing and hype of, 36–38;
process of, 172n28; significance of, 54.
See also gentrification
eviction, 75–76, 95–98, 114, 147. *See also*
Green Lantern Village mobile home
park
exclusionary policies and practices, 59–60,
70–73, 150, 189n111
expressive entrepreneurship, 28–30

Fair Housing Act (FHA), 62, 74
family and occupancy standards, 71–73
family separation, 135–37
Federal Housing Administration, 181n18
Fernández-Kelly, Patricia, 43, 172n39
financial crisis of 2007, 29, 30, 57
financialization of housing, 96, 149
financialization of mobile home parks,
93–94
financialized gentrification, 93, 114
financialized landlords, 74, 93, 116, 149
food adventuring, 32–36, 41. *See also*
restaurants
food gentrification, 6, 23, 52
Fountain Valley, California, 4, 14*fig.*, 50
fusion food, 33–36, 53

gangs, youth, 125–27, 132
Gang Violence and Juvenile Crime Prevention Act (Proposition 21), 126

García, Angela, 130
Garden Grove, California: ADUs in,
184n56; density of Vietnamese, 14*fig.*;
development in, 13; Main and
Brookhurst Streets, 49*fig.*; occupancy
standards in, 72; single-family zoning
in, 59; Tết festival and parade, 50
Gen A, 174n76
gente-fication, 26–27, 146, 172n28
gentrification: definition of, 190n15; entrepreneurship and, 24; financialized, 93;
food, 6, 23, 26; gente-fication, 26; home-
grown, 53; impact of, 23–24; in Little
Havana, Miami, 54; process of, 171n26;
race and ethnic aspects of, 147, 172n33;
resistance to, 94; suburban, 190n16. *See
also* ethnic gentrifiers
Gen Z, 41, 174n76
Global trade organizations, 12
Golash-Boza, Tanya, 136, 141
Golden State Manufactured-Home Owners League, 107
Goodman, Adam, 143
Graham, Lili Võ (attorney), 99–100, 118
Great Recession, 29, 30
green card holders, 122, 132
Green Lantern Village mobile home park:
closure and conversion of, 97–100;
demoviction and, 95–96; future of, 119;
nature and significance of, 94–95;
owners of, 97, 108, 116; photo of, 92*fig.*;
rent control and, 110–11; sale of, 108. *See
also* Green Lantern Village residents;
mobile homes and mobile home parks
Green Lantern Village residents: at City
Hall, 98–102; Green Lantern Village
Residents Association, 103–4; protracted displacement of, 120; resistance
of, 97–98, 114, 115, 119–20. *See also* rent
control fight in Santa Ana
Groth, Paul, 64

Hà, Vũ, 133, 134
Hạnh (landlord), 68–69
Harmony Bridge proposal, 51–52
Harvey, David, 39, 48
Hausman, David, 133–34
Hiếu Phan (journalist), 70

high opportunity neighborhoods, 201n23
Hoàng Trinh, 133, 134, 135
Hoa Phàt Money Transfer, 46
home equity loans, 56
home-grown gentrification, 53
homeowners, support for, 63
hourglass economy, 39
housing: cost burden, 58, 70, 149; finan-
    cialization of, 9, 10, 96, 117, 149; housing
    insecurity, 54–55, 61, 64, 149–50; hous-
    ing justice, 6, 16, 156–57; housing rights
    rally, 1; rental market, 23; right to, 19;
    RV living, 61–62; shortage of, 39–40;
    Social Housing Development Author-
    ity, 148–49; social mobility linked to,
    67; subsidized, 62–63, 182n40; values in
    Orange County, 5–6; zoning practices
    and, 59–60. See also affordable housing;
    rent control; rent control fight in Santa
    Ana
Huante, Alfredo, 30
Humanitarian Operation program, 105,
    117, 166n8
Huntington Beach, California, 49*fig.*

Illegal Immigration Reform and Immi-
    grant Responsibility Act (IIRIRA), 132
immigrants and immigration: Chinese, 13,
    60; criminalization of, 132–33, 148;
    deportation of, 121; detention of, 131;
    entrepreneurship and, 26; ICE, 122,
    131–32, 133, 135, 140; Illegal Immigration
    Reform and Immigrant Responsibility
    Act, 132; Illegal Immigration Reform
    and Immigrant Responsibility Act
    (IIRIRA), 132; legal passing and, 130;
    mixed-status families, 136; neoliberal
    policies, 124; suburban, 7–8; undocu-
    mented, 14–15, 20, 122; US-Vietnam
    MOU, 128; zoning practices and, 60.
    See also deportations, refugee
inclusionary policies and practices, 148–49
inequality, suburban: Allard on, 146–47;
    causes, 23; nature and significance of,
    2–3; researching, 16; solutions to, 148–
    49; understanding, 145
intergenerational organizing and leader-
    ship, 83–86, 87

Jao, Frank, 51–52
Japanese in Orange County, 13
Jiménez, Tomás, 163
job growth and housing, 39–40
Jossart-Marcelli, Pascale, 35
Just Cause evictions, 75, 78

Kerner Commission, 74
Kibria, Nazli, 69, 154
Krueger, Alan, 29

La, Tracy (organizer), 15, 81–83
labor, entrepreneurial, 39
labor market constraints, 26, 28–29,
    43, 44
landlords, financialized, 93, 94, 114, 116,
    149
landlord-tenant relations, 66–70, 73–75
land-use laws, 59
Lan Lý (organizer and community leader),
    136–37
Latin-Asian fusion food, 33
Latinx business owners, 30
Latinx organizations, 79–81
Latinx population, suburban, 7
Lê, Cát Bao (organizer), 137–39
Lê, Tammy (foodie), 28–29
leases, non-traditional, 73–75
Lees, Loretta, 190n15
Legal Aid Society of Orange County, 99,
    104
legal passing, 130
Li, Wei, 7
liminality, 134–35, 143, 144
Lincoln Institute, 93
Linda Tang (organizer), 98, 118
Little Saigon: Ad Hoc Committee to
    Safeguard Little Saigon, 51; architec-
    ture, 51–52; boosterism and branding
    for, 47–52; as food mecca, 25, 32; future
    of, 153; geographic aspects of, 4; *Little
    Saigon Blueprint for Investment*, 23–24,
    49*fig.*; nature and significance of, 3–6;
    origin of, 13–14; population density,
    14*fig.*; rally in, 8*fig.* See also Orange
    County, California; placemaking,
    refugee; Santa Ana, California; West-
    minster, California

9–10; Orange County Mobile Home Resident Coalition, 91, 105–7; organizing playbook, 156–58; significance of, 18; tenant advocacy organizations, 75; Tenants United, 16, 79–81, 86, 87. *See also* Green Lantern Village residents; rent control fight in Santa Ana; Sơn Do (activist)

restaurants, 36, 40–42. *See also* food adventuring; food gentrification; *specific restaurant names*

Right to the City, 8, 168n33

ROC USA, 119

Rodeo 39 Public Market, 19, 21–23, 22*fig.*, 25, 32–33

room rentals, suburban, 64–70, 74

Roy, Ananya, 147

RV living, 61–62

Sánchez, George, 53, 146

San Francisco, California, 65, 146

San Gabriel Valley, 7

Santa Ana, California: Chinese in, 13; density of Vietnamese, 14*fig.*; downtown, 49*fig.*; Newport Beach juxtaposed to, 17; occupancy standards in, 72; rent control in, 16, 76–88, 89; significance of, 19; single-family zoning in, 59; SROs in, 65. *See also* Orange County, California

Schafran, Alex, 146

Schuetz, Jenny, 149

Section 8 vouchers, 62–63, 182n40

self-gentrification, 53

7 Leaves Cafe, 27, 31–32, 37*fig.*

single-family zoning, 59–60, 75

Siu, Lok, 34

$16 Taco, The (Joassart-Marcelli), 35

Smith, Charles, 52

Smith, Neil, 95–96

Social Housing Development Authority, 148–49

social mobility, 26, 44–47, 67

Somali refugees, 134

Sơn Do (activist): AB 2782 and, 2; activism of, 105–7; Caritas, 115–16; on eviction fight, 115; on mobile homes, 95; on rents and incomes, 117; significance of, 1, 3;

testimony of, 91. *See also* Green Lantern Village mobile home park; Green Lantern Village residents

Southeast Asian Archive, 15

Southeast Asian Coalition (SEAC), 16, 137–39, 198n70

Southeast Asian Deportation Relief Act, 136

SROs (single room occupancies), 64–65, 183n51

state violence: banishment in relation to, 147, 148; under Biden, 134; policies in relation to, 132; refugee warehousing in relation to, 143, 144

Stewart Detention Center, 140

structural forces: affordable housing, 59; discrimination, 42; of displacement, 18; in entrepreneurship, 39; governmental, 53; labor market constraints, 26, 28–29; researching, 16; significance of, 6, 52–53; Tammy Lê on, 28; zoning practices, 59–60, 62, 70–73, 150

students, incarcerated, 135–36

subletting rooms, 66–68, 70–71

subsidized housing, 62–63, 182n40

suburbs: cosmopolitan aspects, 38; displacement in, 6–7, 19–20; diversity of, 7–8, 150; electoral politics in, 102–3; immigrants in, 3; immigration to, 18; inequality in the, 2–3, 23, 145–49; mobile homes in, 91–92; room rentals in, 64–70, 74; suburban city planning, 6; suburban organizing playbook, 147; zoning in, 59–60, 64–66, 70–73, 150; zoning in the, 64–66. *See also* Little Saigon; placemaking, refugee; resistance, suburban

Sullivan, Esther, 97, 111

Tạ, Trí (politician), 99

Tâm Nguyễn (Advanced Beauty College), 44–45, 47

Tang, Linda (organizer), 98, 118

tenant advocacy organizations, 75

tenant-landlord relations, 66–70, 73–75

Tenants United, 16, 79–81, 86, 87

Tết festival and parade, 50–51

Theory of the Leisure Class, The (Veblen), 37

three-strikes law (Proposition 184), 126
Tín Nguyễn (organizer), 135–36, 137
Toronto suburbs, 146
tourists and tourism, 48, 50, 52
Trinh, Hoàng, 133, 134, 135
Trump administration, 128, 131–32, 140, 145
Trương, Lynn (Green Lantern Village resident), 103

undocumented Asians, 14–15, 122, 131
United Nations Convention for the Protection of Refugees, 137
United Nations on refugees, 123–24, 155
University of California, Irvine, 15, 160
University of California, Los Angeles, 156–57
University of Southern California, 121
"Update on the Vietnamese Dining Experience, An" (Woolsey), 25
upward mobility, 18
urban entrepreneurialism, 48
Urban Institute, 78, 97
urban planning laws, 59

Veblen, Thorstein, 37
Venezuelans refugees, 134
VietCARE, 16
Vietnam, deportees in, 137–44
Vietnamese American Chamber of Commerce, 4, 44

Vietnamese resettlement. *See* resettlement, refugee
Vietnam War, 5, 10
VietRISE: intergenerational organizing in the, 83–86; origin and nature of, 81; purpose of, 88; rally, 2*fig.*; significance of, 16; Tracy and, 15, 81–83, 87
VISION Act (AB 937), 82, 145, 148
Võ, Linda, 13
Vũ, Indigo (organizer), 81
Vũ Hà, 133, 134

Westminster, California: ADUs in, 184n56; blueprint for investment, 48–49; Bolsa Row, 4*fig.*; City Council, 98–99, 192n29; density of Vietnamese, 14*fig.*; development in, 13–14; displacement in, 19–20; historical aspects of, 11; Hò Phàt Money Transfer in, 46; *Little Saigon Blueprint for Investment*, 23–24; occupancy standards in, 72; rally in, 2*fig.*; rent burdens in, 58; Section 8 vouchers in, 63; Charles Smith and, 52; Tết festival and parade, 50; zoning practices in, 59, 60. *See also* Little Saigon; Orange County, California
Wong, Janelle, 192n40

zoning codes, exclusionary, 59–60, 64–66, 70–73, 150

Founded in 1893,
UNIVERSITY OF CALIFORNIA PRESS
publishes bold, progressive books and journals
on topics in the arts, humanities, social sciences,
and natural sciences—with a focus on social
justice issues—that inspire thought and action
among readers worldwide.

The UC PRESS FOUNDATION
raises funds to uphold the press's vital role
as an independent, nonprofit publisher, and
receives philanthropic support from a wide
range of individuals and institutions—and from
committed readers like you. To learn more, visit
ucpress.edu/supportus.

www.ingramcontent.com/pod-product-compliance
Lightning Source LLC
Chambersburg PA
CBHW020855270326
41928CB00006B/719